• BANTAM AIR & SPACE SERIES •

7

To contemporary artist William S. Phillips,
power, speed, and beauty are synonymous
with flight. He has done much flying himself,
has participated in the Air Force, NASA,
and Navy Art Programs, and receives many private
commissions for his work.

"Bill Phillips is one of the very few
aviation artists in whose work you can 'see
the air' and feel the exhilaration of flight."
—Donald S. Lopez, National Air & Space Museum

The detail from the above painting that
appears on the cover of this book
is used by courtesy of
The Greenwich Workshop.

Contents

Preface

Test flying aircraft of the experimental type is probably not the safest profession in the world. Down through the years the record will show that a test pilot generally doesn't reach a ripe old age. As the saying goes, there are bold pilots and there are old pilots, but there are no old bold pilots.

This may be true to some extent, but if you were not a little bold, as the term is used, you probably wouldn't have any place in the test-flying business. I have found that if you quit when things get a little bit on the rough side the work would never get done.

I am not going to try and scare the reader, nor do I wish to paint a picture of myself as some sort of superman. This book is my life history as told by myself as accurately as it can possibly be presented. It is my life and the story of my flying career. I suppose there are many men who have had more thrilling experiences, but I think you will agree when you finish reading it that our good Lord has favored me on many occasions.

I myself like to think that I am an average sort of fellow. I have a home, a lovely wife and two young daughters. There are times when I become provoked and yell at my kids and there have been some heated arguments with my wife. Aside from that I am a peaceful sort of fellow.

My wife is forever asking me what I did at work today and I usually give her a quick brushoff that not much happened. She knows very little about my work, except that I am a test pilot. I never tell her what I am doing as far as my testing is concerned because she would just worry.

As far as my neighbors are concerned, there are many kids in the neighborhood, and they think that I am flying every airplane that flies over. Even when airplanes fly dangerously low in what is referred to as a buzz job, I am often blamed for that. I must confess, however, that I did my share in earlier years. The records will show that I have been grounded for one reason or another at least five times in my long flying career. I am not particularly proud of that, yet I think I learned my lessons from being grounded.

I don't suppose there is a test pilot who has ever flown, and I am no exception, who hasn't been called crazy. There is an old saying that you don't have to be crazy to be a test pilot but it helps. However, I won't go along with that, as I don't think that flying and testing airplanes has any place for a crazy man.

Through the years that I have been flying and testing I have always tried to stay one jump ahead of the airplane. On the many occasions when I failed to do so, I have sometimes ended up in near-accidents or crashes. However, each and every one left its mark in the way of experience, and I think this experience or seasoning is probably the most important thing in flying.

As far as flying airplanes is concerned, I have always been willing to try anything once if it looked like there was a reasonable possibility of success. I figured my chances pretty close and acted accordingly. If I've had my share of luck it was the Lord watching over me.

TONY LEVIER

La Canada, California
October 22, 1953

Through The Sound Barrier

It was early one morning in April, 1950, that I first flew faster than sound. I was at forty thousand feet over the great Mojave Desert in southern California on a test flight in a new swept-wing fighter plane, the Lockheed F-90, which was one of the first planes built to penetrate the sound barrier. For nearly a year we had been testing this new airplane, since the first time I took it off the ground, and now the time had come to find out how fast it would fly. That was my assignment this morning.

I gave my instruments a final check, tightened my shoulder harness again for the last time and turned west. Above me the desert sky was a bowl of dark blue, and before me the California mountains stretched hundreds of miles north and south. Fifty miles ahead and below I could see Edwards Air Force Base, the U. S. Air Force's great test center on the edge of the famous Muroc Dry Lake, where I had flown so many times in other new jets.

Waiting and listening for me down there on the ground was a group of Lockheed men, most of whom I had known and worked with almost daily for nearly ten years—Kelly Johnson, our chief research engineer, who was responsible for the design of this airplane; Dorsey Kammerer, foreman of the jet division of our experimental shop, in charge of its maintenance; and Jim White, my old running mate and a test pilot

1

like myself. Knowing Kelly was there always made me feel good, especially at a time like this, because of his personal interest in the safety of the pilot. Often he flew with me in our new planes. This was a single-place airplane and I was alone today, but not in the true sense, because they were down there rooting for me and hoping for my success. I knew that many of them had their fingers crossed and were probably saying a little silent prayer.

I was too. Up to now not many men—or airplanes—had broken through the sound barrier. The 90 was a big plane for one man, weighing over twenty-six thousand pounds, and it had two jet engines to enable it to climb very high and fly very fast. It was designed for supersonic speeds and today we wanted to find out if it would stand up to the test. The only way to do that was to dive it through the sound barrier.

The plane was thoroughly instrumented. Up in front was an automatic observer, a motion picture camera of special design which continually photographed an instrument panel in the nose of the plane. I also carried an oscillograph, an instrument connected to the various critical points of the air frame to record the stresses on the structure. In addition, I had an audograph to record my comments and an open microphone to the ground. We were taking no chance on missing anything that happened, as many thousands of dollars had been spent in preparation for this flight, and to miss the smallest incident could not only cost a great deal of money but possibly my life on some future flight.

On preliminary dives earlier in our test program, I had encountered a severe and alarming control problem on the 90, caused by the elevators seizing up and making it virtually impossible to move the stick and change the flight path of the airplane. At high speeds the air pressure on the elevators was ten to twenty times greater than normal. We overcame this condition by installing a hydraulic power boost for the controls, to aid in maneuvering the airplane during high-speed flight.

I had also been bothered by the adjustable stabilizer which was used on the 90 to trim the airplane in flight. Unlike the elevators, it was too sensitive and caused overcontrolling,

F-90

making the plane pitch up and down quite sharply, much like a roller coaster only more abrupt. I had also run into compressibility, the sudden change in air pressures at high speeds that can transform a normal airplane into a beast. But the 90 was not a beast, and compressibility never bothered this plane unduly, although it affects all planes and the problem certainly was there.

The new hydraulic boost and the adjustable stabilizer had been tested on previous flights and everything should have been satisfactory. I was all squared off now, pulling top rpm in my engines with both afterburners going, and was rapidly approaching maximum level flight speed, which at forty thousand feet was around six hundred miles an hour. I was in constant radio communication with the engineers on the ground, giving them my position, and east of North Base at Muroc I told them to stand by for my dive.

The method I always used in dive testing was to push

forward on the stick and drop the nose without rolling the airplane. I arrived at the conclusion over years of testing that this method is probably the best from the standpoint of reaching the greatest speed. However, pushing over is an extremely uncomfortable maneuver, and one must be buckled in his seat very firmly and have his shoulder harness pulled tight to the point where it hurts.

I pushed over at zero G, where my body was weightless and also the airplane, a maneuver considered to be the best for getting into a steep angle for a dive because it creates the least amount of drag. I was attempting to reach a sixty-degree angle within a space of two or three thousand feet. Normally flying through the air at constant altitude the plane and the pilot are pressing downward at one G, or equivalent to their own weight. By suddenly changing the path of the airplane downward equal to one G, or the pull of gravity, weight vanishes.

Watching my contrails high in the desert sky, the group on the ground at Muroc could see me coming from the east. At great altitudes there is almost always a small amount of moisture present in the atmosphere, even in clear air, and when stirred up it freezes into small ice crystals, leaving a trail of white in the wake of the plane. When the ground crew saw my contrails approach and suddenly bend downward and the reflection of the sun on my silver wings they knew I had entered my dive.

Up in the cockpit everything appeared to be normal. All instruments checked okay. I trimmed my stabilizer for a nose-down condition and also to hold my dive at a very steep angle. As I got closer and closer to the magic number of Mach 1 I experienced all the little peculiar characteristics that take place in the transonic zone. I noticed the tendency of the wing to drop, the sudden tucking and pitching, and the sudden action of the rudder as it trembled and kicked over several degrees. All this I was experiencing and talking off over my hot mike, explaining these behaviors of the aircraft and telling our ground crew my sensations as I rushed down faster and steeper.

As I approached the sound barrier it seemed a thousand hands were pulling back on the airplane, as if it were reaching a wall that was impenetrable. Then suddenly something released and the airplane shot ahead. It is true, there is a wall there—a wall of tremendous drag—but once you have reached the speed of sound and the compressibility effects are stabilized, drag suddenly changes, and the airplane slips on ahead as though it were on a greased platter. The sound level even changes. The air rushing over the airplane and the roar of the engines behind you all add up to make noise, but as the speed of sound is exceeded this noise no longer can reach you, and you are ahead of this noise, traveling faster than sound. This sudden change in the sound level was one way I knew I had gone through the barrier.

As I passed it my mach indicator stood at 1, and I said over the radio, "There she is." My speed was near eight hundred miles an hour and altitude about twenty-seven thousand feet. Now it was time to pull out of the dive.

From force of habit I pulled back on the stick but to no avail; it might just as well have been anchored in concrete. I immediately actuated the stabilizer switch on top of the pilot's stick grip to raise the nose of the airplane and effect recovery from the dive. Ordinarily the stabilizer would react almost instantly and the nose start rising, but this time nothing happened.

For several moments of bewilderment I sat motionless in the cockpit, with no apparent movement or change in the plane's attitude, watching the ground rush up to meet me at a thousand feet a second. I could see North Base, the large expanse of dry lake bed where I had taken off only minutes before. The hangars along the edge of the lake and the ramp with other experimental aircraft ready for testing were in plain view. Startled and frightened, I had even stopped talking, and the engineers sitting in the radio room heard nothing but the sound of my heavy and rapid breathing over the radio.

I was about to resort to the emergency stabilizer actuator and dive recovery flaps when I noticed the nose, ever so slightly, begin to rise. Then with the same abruptness with which it had burst beyond the sonic barrier, the airplane came back through again. All the same weird characteristics were evident once more, but now the mach number was dropping so rapidly they appeared as sharp jolts, such as are experienced when flying through extremely turbulent air.

By this time I was only twenty thousand feet from the ground, and now the 90 was being subjected to air loads four times greater than at the beginning of the dive, where the air was much thinner. My indicated air speed was well over five hundred miles an hour, which produces an impact pressure of about 650 pounds per square foot. It was this combination of tremendous forces and the high G's reacting on the 90 in its dive recovery that would have caused most airplanes to disintegrate. Now it was being put to its crucial test. Bucking like an untamed bronco it plunged earthward, and then suddenly it was in level flight and still in one piece.

As I flashed down toward the ground I entered a haze level around twenty thousand feet and the crew on the ground lost me from view. After what seemed a matter of seconds they heard two tremendous explosions in rapid succession, and off in the distance across the dry lake bed there rose a large cloud of dust from the desert floor. Jim White exclaimed, "My God, he dove in!" Nobody else said anything. Kelly Johnson almost went to his knees and turned and ran into the hangar.

It was quite obvious to them I had crashed. Two explosions and a cloud of dust—what else could it be? But by the time they had gotten into the radio shack I was out of my dive and back on the radio. I reported pullout had just been made and everything was okay.

The explosions they heard were sonic explosions—the first time this phenomenon had ever occurred in the West. No one at Muroc that day had ever heard it before. It had been predicted years earlier, but no one gave it a second thought. Today, when supersonic dives are fairly common, this sonic boom is familiar to many people. Especially in southern California, where modern high-speed planes are produced and test flown, civilians living in a number of populated areas have experienced this noise. But it is a sound that no one will ever get used to, it is too tremendous and jolting.

It is caused by the noise of the airplane and its jet engine piling up behind the plane as it exceeds the speed of sound and building up a pocket of noise. Then as the plane slows up and starts to pull out of its dive it creates a new pocket of noise. That is why a sonic dive usually produces a double explosion when these noise pockets hit the ground—the first explosion being the last noise pocket the plane made, and the second explosion being the first noise pocket, which follows behind the plane and reaches the ground last.

The cloud of dust the ground crew saw when they heard my "booms" was one of those freak coincidences that had nothing to do with me. That same morning the Air Force was conducting practice bombing at a nearby bombing range. Apparently a bomber dropped a dummy bomb at the same time I made my dive. It hit six or seven miles from the ground crew, and it raised a dust cloud that could easily be thrown up by an airplane crashing at high speed into the desert floor.

We also learned later why I had trouble pulling out of my dive. The stabilizer turned out to be responding only 10 per cent as fast as normal. In correcting the sensitivity I had complained of earlier, the engineers had rewound the armature in the electric motor to reduce its speed, which of course reduced its power. These are some of the little mistakes that can catch up with you and sometimes cause you trouble.

Since that time I have flown faster than sound many times, not only in the F-90 but also in other planes, such as the North American F-86 and the Lockheed F-94C Starfire, a new jet plane which is used by the Air Force as an all-weather interceptor. Except for experimental research aircraft, it was the first straight-wing airplane to exceed the speed of sound. Both swept wings and straight wings have their advantages and disadvantages, but both can go equally fast, assuming that the wing is built for high speeds and they have the necessary power.

The limiting factor on the speed of any airplane, given adequate power, is its limit dive speed, or the maximum speed at which it can dive and still not break up. All planes are designed for certain air speeds, some faster than others,

F-94C "Starfire"

and are built accordingly. It is then the job of the test pilot to take them up and see if they will do what they are built for.

In the case of the F-90, the requirements were established by the Air Force, and called for a penetration fighter that was fast enough to protect itself against enemy fighters and still strong enough to withstand anti-aircraft fire in low-level ground support. With this philosophy in mind we designed probably the strongest fighter plane ever built. Kelly Johnson and his engineers were taking calculated risks when they made it big and heavy, but at least they knew it was put together properly and was strong enough for the job assigned to it.

My job as a test pilot is to be the final inspector on a new airplane—to warn our engineers of its troubles and its limits. I feel I am part of the plane I am flying. There are still some things you can't test for in a wind tunnel, and no airplane can be instrumented to the point of perfection. Up to 90 per cent of any new plane can be proved out before it flies, if you want to spend the money to do it, but it is the test pilot who has to find out the remaining 10 per cent.

I don't worry much about my job, if at all. Maybe I am lucky in many ways to have a certain feeling of security and not a tendency toward worrying and fretting about some dangerous test flight. I look back many years when I was just a boy and danger has always been more or less a part of me. I guess what may seem dangerous to others is different to me because flying is my business.

Not long ago I saw a boyhood friend, whom in my younger days I had roamed with and done many exciting things. I will never forget one of the first things he said: "You know, Tony, it's amazing you are still alive. When we were kids you were always doing something for a thrill."

I thought for a moment, "Is that really true?" All through the years apparently I have given people that opinion and left that impression on them. Yet I don't think truly that I do things recklessly. Surely I couldn't have stayed alive as a "reckless" type.

No, a long time ago I put a sort of calculated risk on most things dealing with danger. I mean by that, I don't deliberately take a chance, I simply calculate the best I know how the risk involved, and more or less act accordingly. I think probably most people do the same thing. I am sure Kelly Johnson has taken many calculated risks; that is his job, to make the right decision based on calculations.

Although I am still a young man, I have been flying more than twenty-five years. I took my first flying lesson when I was only fifteen and aviation has been my sole interest ever since. It doesn't seem long, looking back on it, but I have been a pilot more than a quarter of a century, and in that period of time aviation has been transformed. I have seen it change from a sport to a science. And as airplanes became more sophisticated, pilots had to change too. In order to tell the engineers how their planes flew, we had to know what we were talking about; as a result, the test pilot became a flying scientist. He is also a translator. After the engineers analyze his flight reports, he can describe the engineering problems to other pilots in language they understand.

I have been testing new airplanes for Lockheed Aircraft Corporation since 1941, and since 1945 I have been my company's chief engineering test pilot. In my Lockheed job I have been flying jets longer than anybody in the country. The F-80 Shooting Star which we built was America's first jet airplane in production and I began flying it in 1944. Since then I have flown all of Lockheed's newer jets. I have also flown bombers and transport planes, but I like to fly fast, and for that reason I prefer fighters. Since the war I have specialized almost exclusively in jets. As Lockheed is America's oldest and largest manufacturer of jet airplanes, I have had ample opportunity to indulge my passion for speed.

But test flying today also calls for teamwork, in the air and on the ground, and I am only part of a large and highly-skilled team of other pilots and engineers who fly, ride and work with me. We are members of the flight test division of the engineering department, and we have a common goal—better and faster airplanes. Because the bulk of Lockheed's planes today are military, we work mostly with tactical aircraft, but the things we are learning about high-speed flight for the Air Force and Navy can be applied equally well to transport planes for civilian passengers when the airlines are ready to put jets into commercial service.

My job on the team is flying new planes and planes that have never flown before. In the past few years, in addition to the F-90, these have included the T-33, America's first jet training plane, and the various models of the F-94, the nation's first all-weather jet interceptor. Nine other pilots help me on the test programs required on new airplanes. They usually specialize on one type of plane, some flying jets while others handle transports or bombers, but generally speaking they can fly anything.

We make the first flights on prototype models and engineering test flights on prototype and production planes. If there are any major problems in an airplane, such as duct rumble and aileron buzz on the F-80, they become known after the first few flights. When they are corrected we then go into our basic flight tests to collect operating data on the plane. After proving it as a flying machine we next prove engine performance. When the bugs are out we demonstrate the plane to the customers—to help sell it if it is new, or to familiarize them with it if it is already on order.

Except for the F-80 and the F-90, all of Lockheed's post-war planes have been multiseat aicraft, including the jet trainer and the all-weather fighter. Because this has made it possible to carry passengers even in our jets, we have been able to take our flight test engineers up with us, and they fly at all times except on first flights and extra-hazardous tests such as spins and dives, in which event they thoroughly instrument the airplane to be tested. We carry up to forty instruments in fighters, as high as 300 in bigger planes. Each engineer sets up the test program for his airplane, collects and summarizes the data, and turns it over to our data reduction people for analysis.

They consider the human brain just a computing machine, and to them a good test pilot is one who can speed up the rate at which his brain functions. There are still unknowns like controllability and dynamic phenomena in flying, so they must depend on the pilot's senses to warn them of the limits of the airplane. They have not yet learned how to measure what he feels, but they need the information, so until they develop instruments that will do so, they still need test pilots to build new airplanes.

They will be built, of course. Looking back over the distance we have come, it is easy to see that we have just begun to fly. Getting through the sound barrier was the first big step. Until a few years ago it was virtually impossible to get even near it. The effects on approaching it were so violent that in most cases the airplane became uncontrollable and in many instances disintegrated in midair from the violent forces reacting on the aircraft. Now that we have learned how to design planes to meet and overcome these forces, the next big step is developing engines with enough power to penetrate the sound barrier in level flight. Jet engines can do it now, but only with help from an afterburner.

In supersonic flight the real trouble occurs before you reach the speed of sound, when the true speed of the airplane is constant but the air through which it is passing is accelerating faster over the thicker parts of the plane. As these velocities reach a sonic speed they set up disturbances in the form of shock waves that exert uneven pressures on the airframe, putting severe loads on the structure and causing shock stalls that affect its ability to maintain steady flight. An increase of two or three miles an hour in speed in the transonic zone, and an increment or two in the mach range, can change the air pressure so greatly that the airplane may become virtually uncontrollable.

As soon as the entire airplane reaches the speed of sound, the air flow becomes stabilized and these disturbances greatly diminish. The whole thing is a function of pressure, and the ability of pressure to send out signals in the proper direction. When an airplane is flying at the speed of sound, the pressure waves cannot propagate upstream to forewarn the air out in front that it is about to be approached. In other words, supersonic air flow is stable because the air in front has no way of knowing the plane is coming.

I am often asked how fast we can fly. Theoretically there is no limit. Since these disturbances don't exist beyond the speed of sound, theoretically any airplane that can go that fast can fly at any speed, assuming it has enough power. Actually, it's not that simple. Heat created at high speeds is one of the next things that is going to trouble us. Heat rise due to compression and friction will be so great the structure of the airplane will lose its strength and come apart. Nor is it easy to design a supersonic airplane that is also slow enough to take off and land on present-day airports. To build a plane that will have good stability and control over a wide speed range— there is the problem.

With so much still to be done, it sometimes seems wrong for me to take time out to write this book about what has gone before. But here at the sound barrier may be the place to pause and reflect, while we are still close enough to the past to remember it. Men who have pushed the speed of flight from one hundred to sixteen hundred miles an hour in twenty-five years may soon be going too fast to look back.

Yet without the trials and errors of the last quarter-century we would not be here now, for today's achievements are built on the experience of men who learned the hard way. For my part I know that every minute counted; the road from that first dirt airport to the speed of sound was a long one, but it was the only way I could get here.

2

Early Days

Weak eyes kept me out of the Air Force and I couldn't be an airline pilot because of a bad heart, so I took the only flying job left open to me and became a test pilot.

I was born in 1913 at Duluth, Minnesota, the younger of two children. My father was Anthony Puck, a Duluth architect, who came to this country from Norway as a boy. My mother was Aloysia Evans of Wilson, New York, the daughter of a ship engineer on the Great Lakes. From her I got the encouragement and inspiration to follow my ambition to be a pilot.

My father passed on to me an athlete's reflexes and a love for sports. He was commodore of the Duluth Boat Club and one of its best oarsmen, a singles sculler and stroke of the racing eight. He was also a good swimmer and was in the water most of the year, often breaking the ice in Lake Superior to start spring training. When I was old enough he took me with him, carrying me on his back or on his stomach while he was floating.

When the war started in 1917 he joined the Minnesota Home Guard, and I often saw him don his uniform and the campaign hat of that day and take off for drilling and training. It was the first winter of the war, at the guard armory in St. Paul, that he caught cold sleeping on the floor. The cold developed into pneumonia and then into tuberculosis from which he never recovered.

I knew my dad was sick but I didn't really know what was the matter. However, my mother became extremely concerned for the health of the whole family, and she was always hauling my sister and me down to the doctor for X-rays and other examinations for fear we would get the same disease. When we both came down with whooping cough she decided to get the family out of that climate. She thought it was too severe for us, especially for my father; he planned to close out his business in Duluth and we would just pack up lock, stock and barrel and migrate to California.

My mother had southern California picked out because the advertising about the climate in those days was really something. My father decided the best thing to do was to send mother and us kids on out and he would follow us. In 1919 we came to Los Angeles without him, and then he got too sick to join us.

I believe, as I would like to, that my father was one really fine guy; by that I mean his moral standards and everything were very high. Shortly before he died he took me aside and talked to me. He apparently knew he wouldn't get well and he wanted to instill in my mind a few things to carry on from him. I've never forgotten what he told me: never steal, never tell a lie, and be good to your mother.

He didn't leave us much money. Most of it had gone in doctor bills, and Mother went to work to support us until we could take care of ourselves. One of the first jobs she got was playing bit parts in the movies around 1920. Of course she didn't have acting experience, but she was small and very young-looking, and she often was cast as a high school or college girl in mob scenes, as they called them.

Our first home in California was in Ocean Park, near Los Angeles. I went to school right away and the kids made fun of me because of my clothing. I came from a different part of the country, where it was cold and the dress was different. I remember my shoes were different and they made fun of them—just kid stuff, but it had an impact on me. Naturally my mother didn't have much money to suddenly make a quick change and buy us brand-new wardrobes. After all, we were practical about things like that, and our clothes had to be worn out before we got new ones.

I didn't like school because I was afraid of it. It was too confining. I thought that what it stood for was all against me. I didn't dislike the teachers but there was something about them that frightened me. I just didn't want to be around them. I didn't want to sit at a desk and I am that way now.

In about six months we moved to U. S. Island in Venice, California, and my Aunt Georgia Evans came out from Duluth to live with us. I was about seven years old at the time. It was here I made my first acquaintance with aiplanes. Clarence Prest, a movie stunt flyer, lived next door to us, and through family friendship I was often taken to the old Crawford Airport, located at that time at Washington Boulevard and the Venice Shortline. This was only a few blocks from home, and before long I started going over alone and spending a lot of time just wandering around the airport.

The old Curtiss JN4-D, the primary training plane of World War I and better known as the Jenny, was the most common type of plane at the field. After the war it was the cheapest plane of its day, and almost every aviator had one who could afford it. A low, squat biplane with a long upper wing, it was a slow airplane, with a top speed of sixty-five or seventy miles an hour. Like the standard biplane of that era, it had an open two-place cockpit. Except for aluminum in the cockpit and engine cowling it was made of wood, covered with cotton muslin fabric which was treated with airplane dope. This was a liquid preparation that soaked into the cloth and dried, contracting and making the fabric tight and air-resistant.

The Jenny was powered by the famous Curtiss OX-5 engine, the largest mass-produced aircraft power plant of the first war. It was an eight-cylinder, V-type water-cooled engine, with the propeller shaft running through a hole in the radiator. Certain parts of this engine were poorly-designed and difficult to maintain, the exposed rocker arm assembly being the most troublesome. Even after constant adjustment and lubrication it was not uncommon for parts of the overhead to come apart in the air and fly back in the pilot's face. Another shortcoming of the OX-5 engine was its single ignition system. In heavy rain the magneto would often short out, and the water pump leaking into the carburetor caused many forced landings.

Most planes of the 1920's were built of wood. Spruce was the wood used most often in the wings, with basswood for the ribs and strong woods like Oregon pine and Douglas fir for the struts. The fuselage was generally made of hard woods like ash and oak. All the early planes had a strong smell of oil-soaked wood, mixed with the paint and varnish and the smell of dope on the fabric. The fabric would stand about a year of weather and when it broke it would snap like a drum.

Even the landing gear was made of wood, reinforced with steel fittings. Wheels were fairly close together. As airports were dirt fields without runways and full of bumps and holes, airplanes were always pitching to one side or the other when running on the ground. To protect the wings they had skids on the wing tips, made of heavy reed bent in a half loop, and wing walkers would hang by their knees from these loops when putting on their stunts in the early air shows. They were all open-cockpit planes and used mostly liquid-cooled engines.

From U. S. Island we moved to Los Angeles to a house on Dean Avenue, where mother went into real estate. We lived near another airport in Los Angeles, the old Rogers field at Wilshire Boulevard and Fairfax Avenue, and I spent a great deal of time there, especially on weekends. I also spent a lot of time at the old swimming hole at the end of the Pico Street car line. It was a typical swimming hole and the place where I learned to swim. I was thrown in by my friends, and as the water was over my head, it was sink or swim.

I guess every boy sells newspapers sometime or other, and I was no exception. I had an *Evening Herald* paper route and also a newsstand at the end of the car line. I put the money I made from selling papers into my clothes. Sometimes in a generous mood I would open my bank, take out the money I had saved and stand treat for the neighborhood. Every time I did, though, my mother would give me a lecture about thrift. She said I could do what I wanted with my own money, but she was trying to get me to understand that I should use it for something more practical than buying trinkets for the kids.

These were things that can happen in any boy's life, but for some reason airplanes kept getting into mine. I built my first airplane before I was ten, planning to get a motorcycle engine to make it fly. I had my mind set on a Harley-Davidson. In my imagination I had already flown. A family friend asked me what I was doing and I told him I was building an airplane. "Have you flown it yet?" he asked, and I said yes. "How high have you gone?" he then asked me, and I replied,"About as high as the telephone pole."

One day coming home from school I saw a crowd running down the street, and feeling something was wrong, I turned and followed them. A couple of blocks away, in the middle of the street, I saw an airplane. It had crashed and there was nothing left but a pile of junk. It made my eyes stand out like sticks. I'll never forget the smell of busted-up wood and fabric and the peculiar odor of the oil-soaked wreckage. To this day an airplane smells the same way to me when it cracks up.

When I was ten years old we moved from Los Angeles to the nearby town of Whittier, where I learned to fly and spent the years that made me a pilot. It was a good place for a boy to grow up—a small town of about ten thousand people, set in a cove on the west slope of the Whittier hills, with lots of room and sun and fresh air. Thirty years ago there was open country most of the way to Los Angeles, and that's where I found the little dirt airports and the kindly, generous men who taught me to fly.

Whittier was old as towns go in southern California, dating back to about 1870, and because it had been settled a long time by hard-working Quakers who saved their money it was a wealthy town too. Being Quaker, it was also very religious. I always thought the Quaker church in Whittier was the biggest in the world. Mother moved to Whittier because she thought it would be a good environment for my sister Nancy and me, and it was. Some of the friends we made in Whittier, like Gene and Reva French and their children, are still our best friends today. Mother and Nancy moved back to Los

Angeles later when Nancy finished school and went to work, but Whittier was home to me in one way or another for nearly twenty years. I strayed, but I always came back.

In 1926, when I was thirteen years old, I began to renew my interest in flying. I wasn't old enough to learn to fly an airplane, and if I had been I didn't have enough money to take lessons, but I wanted to ride in an airplane and I saved up $5 for a flight at the local airport. It was on Whittier Boulevard between Pico and Montebello, west of Whittier, and later on became known as the Los Angeles Eastside Airport. I told various friends I was going to take an aiplane ride the next Sunday, and a good many of them accompanied me to the airport, which was more or less a cow pasture.

There were several planes on the field that day carrying passengers, and surprisingly enough quite a number of people were going up. I looked all the planes over very carefully and picked out one that looked the best; at least it was cleanest and a little neater than the rest. But there was something about it that didn't look exactly airworthy to me, and every time I would get enough nerve to go ahead and buy a ticket I would cool off before I actually got out my $5.

After doing this two or three times during the day I finally decided I just didn't want to go up. It unquestionably was due to the fact that I just didn't trust the machines at the airport. I don't know why. However, there was no govermnent control of aircraft at that time, and people could fly any kind of kite. Needless to say, there were many accidents because of the junk that was flying through the air and some incompetent pilots. Maybe that is what bothered me. Be that as it may, on my first venture in aviation I was too scared to fly, and I didn't try again for another year.

Along about this time my mother met a man by the name of Oscar LeVier, who had a radio repair and sales shop just across the alley from the gift shop she had opened in the new William Penn Hotel. They became good friends and it wasn't long before they were married. My new dad—and I did call him Dad—was very mechanical. He had been in the automobile business around Wheeling, West Virginia, back in the early twenties, and then came out west for the same reason my mother did, more or less to get into new territory. He was still interested in automobiles and was always horse-trading, and besides the family car he usually had another sitting around that he had traded or taken in on a bad debt. It was only natural that I became interested in autos too.

When I asked him if I could have a car of my own, he said if I was a good boy and did my chores and was good to my mother, he would buy me an automobile for my fourteenth birthday. Well, I got my car and a license to drive at the same time. I will never forget that morning.

We started out early, visiting all the used-car lots in town and looking over the different automobiles. Those we saw weren't worth the price, in his opinion, so we went to see his uncle on Franklin Avenue. He had a Ford he no longer used and sold it to my dad for $25. It was a 1918 touring car with a magneto ignition, and the lights were powered by a six-volt wet battery fastened to the running board. I had already taught myself to drive on my dad's Ford coupé, so I was ready to take the wheel. Both my sister and I had soloed his Model T unknown to him.

My friend Don Croskrey and I rode all over town that day, and in that open touring car the breeze kept hitting me. It was February and pretty cool, and I was more or less a puny kid at the time anyway; that evening when I came home I started coughing. I'll never forget coughing all night and my mother and father arguing about getting rid of my automobile. Mother said it would be the death of me, but Dad wanted to give me a chance. "We can put wind wings on it to keep the wind out and we can put the top up, but let's not take the car away just yet," he said. Needless to say, my dad won out.

I'm glad he did, because I started using my Ford to make the rounds of several nearby airports, especially on weekends. I looked over the airplanes again, but I still lacked enthusiasm to take the first ride. Then something happened to change my mind. The 1927 air race from New York to Paris was coming up and our newspapers were full of it. Lindbergh's name meant nothing at all to me before the flight, but when he flew alone across the Atlantic and the news got to Whittier, everyone in town was talking about it.

His flight did something to me. I was only in the seventh grade at the time but I just couldn't get flying out of my mind. This fired me up, and now I had to take my first airplane ride. I saved another $5 and the first Sunday I could I went down to the local airport, which now boasted a new and better airplane, a brand-new biplane known as an International.

This time I was determined to go through with it. I was the first customer at the field that morning and I asked the pilot if he would take me up. He replied that he was going up on a test flight and invited me to ride with him in the rear cockpit. I paid my $5 and we took off.

That settled it—flying was for me. It was different than I had expected. First I thought that going up high would be frightening, but it wasn't. There I was, held up by the wings out in space, and there wasn't anything frightening about it at all. Instead of going real fast the plane seemed to be going quite slow. I looked over the side and down at the ground and it seemed I could get out and walk beside the plane.

I enjoyed it. It was exhilarating and gave me a sense of freedom. Here I was flying above everyone on the ground, and it strengthened my desire to fly. There is no question about that. It was just a question of time.

During summer vacation in 1927 Helen Swann, a friend of Mother's from Long Beach, came to visit us. She was opening a new restaurant at Julian, near San Diego, and wanted us to come down and help. Mother couldn't go but I was eager, and with my Ford I guess she thought I might be useful, so I got permission and went.

I did just about everything, cutting wood, running errands and selling candy and cigars. Julian was a mining town in the mountains, and in my spare time I became interested in the local mining activities. I visited many mines in that vicinity, especially one at the bottom of the mountain where I would go when I could get away from my duties at the top.

At this time Julian was also opening up as a resort area, and with more people coming in, the highway system needed improvement, including new roads. It was here I learned the use of dynamite. I became friendly with one of the men doing road work, and he showed me how to make a hole in the dynamite with a nail and put the fuse in. I learned that you must take great caution when you insert the fuse in the open end of the cap, and be sure there isn't any nitroglycerin that might accidentally go off when you crimp the end of the cap over the fuse.

As summer progressed I lost interest in the restaurant, which by now was well established, and I told Mrs. Swann I wanted to go home. She gave me enough money to buy gasoline and I loaded my few belongings in my Ford and left. The mountain roads were still pretty bad, so I went by way of San Diego on the paved highway, reaching Whittier just in time for the annual coaster race. I rode with my friend Don Croskrey and we got second place. The coaster that beat us was better streamlined than ours, and as I look back now I see the importance of streamlining. It was just like a bug, with a completely enclosed cockpit, while we had a streamlined hood but standard open seats.

I wanted to show my friends what I had learned about dynamiting, so one Sunday four of us drove to Savage Canyon in the hills above Whittier, where a local hardware store kept its powder magazines. We planned to break into these magazines and take some dynamite. Farther on in the hills was an abandoned oil derrick, and we thought it would be fun to blow the legs out from under it and watch it fall into the canyon. When we reached the magazines we found the locks broken and the doors standing open, so we just helped ourselves.

We took a case of dynamite with a roll of fuses and some caps and drove on to the derrick. Here we spent most of the morning blasting away at the supports without much success. We didn't have picks and shovels to do the job properly, and since the ground was hard we couldn't dig very deep holes under the derrick to put the sticks.

I did the actual blasting while my friends watched. After several explosions a hiker came running down the hill to investigate the noise, and we decided it was time to pack up our playthings and take off in the Ford, which was stashed away about a mile back in Sycamore Canyon. On the way to the car we disposed of the remaining dynamite by putting half sticks in gopher holes and old pipes and shooting them off.

When we got home I had four sticks left and hid them in our barn. A few days later I put them in a Mason jar after school and carried them to a dry creek bed in the south end of Whittier, where I attached some fuse and buried them in the creek bank. I rolled out the remainder of the fuse, which was about forty feet long, and lighted it. Then I walked four blocks home, made myself a sandwich and sat on the front porch to wait for the explosion. While I was eating my sandwich it went off. It made an awful noise, but the damage done was no more than a slight increase in the width of the creek at that point. There was a police notice around town of an unexplained explosion but the mystery was never solved.

On a nationwide tour in *The Spirit of St. Louis*, his famous Ryan monoplane, Charles Lindbergh visited Los Angeles. He landed at Vail Field, headquarters of the old Western Air Express, and Whittier schools closed so we could go to the airport and see this great man. I was there when he arrived. He was still my idol and inspiration and I had gone to Los Angeles hoping to meet him.

With the thousands of people at the field, I didn't even get near him that day. But he was spending the night in Los Angeles, so I decided to stay all night at the airport on the chance that I would be first in line to meet him the following morning. With a friend I spent the evening waiting for the crowds to leave, and after they were gone we went back to my Ford and tried to aleep.

After a restless night we were up early, and about ten o'clock Lindbergh's plane was towed out of the hangar and parked on the field behind a barricade of poles and chicken wire. The airport was crowded when he arrived about noon, but I squeezed up to the gate and was actually standing within three feet of him. There I was, trying to get up enough nerve to offer him my hand, when a little old lady broke through the police guard in front of me and spoke to him.

Lindbergh escorted her over to see the plane and I never got near him again. To this day I have never had the pleasure of

Spirit of St. Louis

meeting him. A few minutes later he took off and I returned dejectedly to Whittier. After lunch I went back to school, and when I told the teacher where I had been she had me get up in front of the class and talk about it. It was the first speech I ever made.

Visiting airports was my concern from then on. I was fast losing interest in other matters, and my studies were suffering, especially English, which I never liked anyway. My English teacher told me if I didn't improve I would fail to pass, which meant not graduating with my class. I put on a litile extra effort and just got by. The teacher was a very sweet woman, and as I look back now I feel I must have been a lot of trouble to her.

In the summer of 1928 the family decided to go to Balboa

for two weeks with the French family, who had the use of a cottage on Balboa Island and invited us to stay with them. The night we arrived I went to the local movie theater with Jack French. We were both barefooted, and as I walked down the aisle I saw on the floor what appeared to be a dollar bill. Trying to avoid attention, I picked it up with my toes and went on to my seat, where to my great surprise and pleasure it turned out to be $10. The first thing that came to my mind was to use it for a flying lesson.

I took Jack into my confidence, but swore him to secrecy. The next morning bright and early I packed my clothes and left. I told my mother I was going home, but instead I headed for the nearest flying field, the Martin brothers' airport outside of Santa Ana. Thumbing rides to the field, I walked around looking the planes over and trying to get up enough nerve to state my business.

After some hesitation I finally asked who to see regarding a flying lesson, and was promptly asked who and where was the person who wished to take it. When I replied I wanted to take it, they looked at me and said, "Sonny boy, you are too young. You don't even have a student permit." By this time the government was getting a ruling hand on commercial aviation; both airplanes and pilots had to be licensed now, and even to receive instruction you needed a permit to be a student, which cost $10. I couldn't see spending my $10 for a permit at that time, however, as I felt I was more interested in seeing what this flying business was like instead of getting a permit.

Although turned down at Santa Ana I was still determined to take a lesson that day, and I set out to find somebody who might need a little extra cash and would look the other way. I found him at the local airport between Pico and Montebello, where I took my first airplane ride, and he was agreeable to giving me a twenty-minute lesson for $5. I decided to keep the other $5, possibly for another lesson later.

Our plane was a long-wing "Eaglerock," one of the first modern airplanes, with a fuselage built of steel tubing instead of wood, although the wings were wood and the whole airplane was covered with fabric. Unlike other planes of its day, the lower wing was longer than the top, giving it a distinctive appearance which earned it a nickname early in its career. Built in Colorado Springs, it was a fairly popular airplane, especially in mountain country, where its good high-altitude performance made it especially useful getting in and out of small fields. The three-place open cockpit had tandem seats for two passengers in front, with the pilot in the rear. It was powered by the Curtiss OX-5 water-cooled engine and had a top speed of ninety miles an hour.

Twenty minutes went by and I was glad to get down. I must admit I didn't learn much. I remember the pilot yelling at me from time to time to hold it straight and I tried to follow his instructions, but otherwise the whole thing was a big mystery to me. It wasn't much more than just a high-class joy ride, and two more years elapsed before I finally learned to fly.

3

Solo Flight

Since moving to Whittier my health hadn't been up to par. I was underweight and generally puny, and when I didn't improve my mother became alarmed. My father and his brother both died of tuberculosis and mother began to think it was a family weakness. She took me to a clinic in September, and although I got through the examination the doctor advised her to keep me out of school a year. He wanted me to get plenty of rest and sunshine and try to gain some weight. As a result, I stayed out of school that fall and was free to spend all my time at the airport.

One of the first people I met was Jimmy Karnes, a Montebello boy who had learned to fly down at Eddie Martin's airport in Santa Ana. He came from a well-to-do family and also made good money working in his father's grocery store. Before they would solo him at Santa Ana he was asked to put up cash equal to the value of the airplane, in case he crashed, so he just went ahead and bought it and flew it back to our field. I became friendly with him and offered to help gas and wash his plane, a Curtiss Jenny, just to be around it and maybe get a ride. However, Jimmy was more interested in taking up the good-looking girls around town than a young punk kid fifteen years old. But he drove to Whittier several times in his new Chrysler roadster and took me to evening classes in aviation at various Los Angeles high schools, which helped me learn about flying.

In the late afternoons I used to go to a service station in Whittier where I knew a man named Richard Martin, who had learned to fly several years before under the expert tutelage of Ernie Longbreak. Ernie is now a forgotten flyer, but in the 1920's he was considered one of the great pilots in the West. Dick wanted to start flying again, so he bought the Jenny from Jimmy Karnes. I had worked on it for Jimmy and I got the same job with Dick.

A few days later, while flying near Downey, the engine quit and he made a forced landing on a very small strip of soft ground between an orange grove and the highway. The field was too small for him to take off, and as the plane had to be dismantled anyway to get it back to the Whittier airport, we decided this was a good time for a general overhaul. We took the plane to Roy Scott's barn in east Whittier and Ernie Longbreak came over to help us. I was invited to help too, and this is when I really got my first mechanical experience with an airplane.

We worked several months and completely reconditioned the Jenny. I scraped the varnish off the ribs and wing spars and revarnished them, stitched the fabric on the ribs and doped and painted the wings. When the time came for the first test flight after overhaul, Ernie was asked to make it, and he chose to use a field near the Scott ranch known as the McNally olive orchard. There was a very small strip of clear ground on a knoll and I doubt he had more than six hundred or seven hundred feet.

We assembled the airplane, starting in the morning, and taking the best part of the day. It wasn't finally ready until after dark, but Ernie was so anxious to fly it he went ahead and took off anyway. To this day I don't know how he could see to spot that field and land. The plane was found to be satisfactory, so we tied it down for the night and went home. I had to get home for dinner, but the others went out and had a celebration, which was common in those days after the test flight of an airplane, even for an overhaul.

About this time the Stoody Company, a hard metal manufacturer, was located just southwest of Whittier, and Shelley and Bill Stoody who owned the company were air-minded. They bought a Fokker Super-Universal, a six-passenger monoplane, and hired Vernon Dorrell as pilot. He was a roommate of Millard Scott, who owned the service station where Dick Martin worked, and I had met him on his many visits to the station.

I used to visit Vernon Dorrell at the Stoody factory and hung around a lot. On one of my visits I found part of an old wrecked airplane in storage, one wing of a Lincoln-Paige biplane that Shelley Stoody had bought the year before and cracked up. It wasn't being used for anything, so I asked Shelley if I could have it.

"What in the world do you want with that?" he said. "Well," I replied, "I would just like to have anything around pertaining to an airplane. I don't know what I will do with it, but I would like to have it if you don't want it." He said all right, so I got Jack and Bill French and borrowed their dad's truck and they helped me haul it off to my home. I never used it, but it made me feel good to have it around.

Vernon Dorrell was taught to fly by Ernie Longbreak, and there is no doubt in my mind that he was well taught. He actually learned to fly sitting in Ernie's lap in a Thomas-Morse Scout, a single-seat airplane of the first war. The Scout was a cute little biplane, very light, and racy for its day. It had a foreign look about it and was a little bit on the tricky side. The power plant was a French Le Rhone rotary engine, and the plane always smelled of castor oil, which was the lubricant used in aircraft rotary engines.

A friend of Vern's owned another Scout, which he had just overhauled and flown to the Stoody field, and he asked Vern to try it out. Vern was quite an acrobatic flyer in those days, so he took this Scout up and proceeded to put on a show. The grand finale was to be an aileron roll between the hangar and the factory at treetop height. Apparently Vern got into turbulent air as he rolled upside down between the two buildings and the airplane crashed into the ground. We all rushed up, expecting to find poor Vernon dead, but he was only knocked out. They hauled him off to the hospital and in a day or two he was back at work again as good as ever.

Another time while flying the Stoody Fokker Vern hit a chuck hole on landing, breaking a wing tip and washing off the landing gear, and it was through this accident that I got more work on airplanes. Lou Roos from Lincoln airport in Los Angeles was hired to overhaul the Fokker and I spent several weeks at the hangar helping him as a grease monkey. This was my first experience with the famous Pratt & Whitney Wasp engine, which was used on this airplane.

It was at this time that I met Avery Black, a veteran flyer with wide experience in aviation, whose kindness and generosity gave me my start. He had the Whittier Flying Service, flying an OX-5 Waco in partnership with John Newsom, a Whittier businessman, and gave flying lessons in the Waco. Roy and Millard Scott were among the local businessmen enrolled in his school, and it was through the Scott brothers that Roy Patten became interested in flying and decided to buy an airplane.

Roy was a wealthy Whittier man who made his money in Texas oil. I was at the airport the day his Stinson Junior was delivered, and as the field was pretty dusty the plane became messy-looking after several flights. When Avery asked some of us boys who were standing around if we would like to clean up the airplane I just grabbed a pail and said, "I'm ready." There was no mention of pay, but that evening I was at Scott's service station when Roy drove in and he recognized me as the boy who cleaned his airplane. He gave me $1, which I declined at first, but he said I worked and did a good job and he wanted me to take it. It was the first dollar I ever made in aviation.

Before long Roy decided his Stinson didn't have enough performance, and at Avery's suggestion he traded it in on a larger and more modern airplane, the Travelair 6,000 monoplane with a Wright Whirlwind J6-9 engine. By now the local airport was pretty crowded. It was being used by several different flying services, including Avery Black and his Whittier Flying Service, Dean Banks and Dale Strahl from Pasadena, and Wayne Merrill, a young aviator about two years older than myself. To find more room, Avery and Roy Patten moved to a new airport at the lower end of the same field, and it was at this new airport that I really got my foot in the door—or maybe I should say my head.

I went along with Avery and worked on his airplanes. I was always on hand when he needed me, and knowing that I wanted to fly, in return for my help he planned to give me flying lessons. Up to this time I had had only one lesson, mostly because I lacked a student permit, and Avery decided this was the first thing I had to get. When it became known around the field that he planned to get one for me I took a lot of kidding. Believing my friends who said I had to stand on my head for sixty seconds to pass the test, I practiced this position daily until Avery drove me to Long Beach to take my physical examination for a student permit. Much to my surprise and embarrassment, standing on my head was not one of the requirements.

I was now spending all my time at the airport, and family friends and relatives were making snide remarks about wasting my time around airplanes, which were dangerous, and besides anybody who was a pilot probably would never amount to anything. This clatter went on all the time, but my mother and I always won out. Never once did I hear her question whether I should or should not fly. "All I expect of Tony is to be a good boy, and whatever he does to do it well," she said. "As far as I am concerned, if flying is what Tony wants to do, that is what he shall do."

Roy Patten's interest in aviation continued to grow, and it was not long before he took over both airports at Whittier and combined them into one field known as the Los Angeles Eastside Airport, where he organized the Whittier Airways Company to operate charter flights and teach flying. Avery Black was manager of the new company in charge of all flying activity. The company's fleet included Roy's Cabin Travelair, Avery's Waco 10, Shelley Stoody's Avro Avion, and a new Travelair 4,000 with a J6-5 engine for advanced instruction. New hangars were built along Whittier Boulevard, other operators were invited to use the field, and plans were made to establish it as the nation's finest private airport.

Avery Black, Carol Chidlaw and Vernon Dorrell were the pilots. Sid Willey, one of Avery's students, became secretary, with Frank Bolman as chief mechanic, Erwin Morrison as Frank's assistant, and myself as assistant to Erwin. I wasn't actually hired but was just a necessary evil; you have to have a grease monkey and I was included. But it was a real opportunity for me to become an aviation mechanic and I took advantage of it, learning things like welding, woodwork and engine overhaul that were necessary to repair and maintain aircraft in those days.

Almost immediately Avery took me up in the Avion for my first real flying lesson. The Avion was a two-place tandem open-cockpit trainer, built in England, and had a wood-frame fuselage covered with plywood and fabric. The wings had very light wooden spars and ribs, fabric-covered. A very light biplane, the Avion was powered by a small four-cylinder inline air-cooled Sirrius engine and had a top speed under one hundred miles an hour. This time flying made a little more sense to me. I now had been hanging around airports almost two years and had flown several times as a passenger and knew something about airplanes. I believe this lesson could be termed satisfactory.

A few days later John Hinchey, who was the local distributor for the Velie Monocoupe, loaned Vernon Dorrell one of these planes for his private use, and Vernon suggested I clean it up in return for a couple of flying lessons. A small plane of new design, the Monocoupe was the most popular light sports plane of its day. It was a high-wing cabin monoplane seating two persons side-by-side. The power plant was a Velie five-cylinder radial air-cooled engine developing sixty to sixty-five horsepower, giving the plane a top speed around one hundred miles an hour. Because it was extremely maneuverable the Monocoupe was considered a little bit on the tricky side.

I accepted Vernon's offer and he gave me my third flying lesson, one I shall never forget. Possibly on the theory that my lessons came few and far between and each one should count, he put just about the maximum instruction into the time available to us. That day I learned about slips and skids and stalls and spins by actual experience, and when I came down I was so sick and frightened I never wanted to fly again.

We took off easily and climbed to two thousand feet, which was generally considered normal altitude for maneuvers. Sitting in the quiet cabin with Vern beside me, shielded from the engine noise and rush of air in an open cockpit, I felt entirely at ease. Vern was on the left side, flying the airplane, but I had my hand on the stick and my feet on the rudder pedals to follow through with him on the controls.

First he showed me that no controls are needed in level flight if the airplane is properly trimmed and balanced. We took our hands and feet away from the stick and the pedals and sure enough the little plane flew straight ahead unaided.

Next I learned how the center of gravity affected the flight path of the airplane. We leaned forward, shifting the cg, and I saw the plane nose down. Then we leaned back and the nose came up again. That was trim change, due to our weight shifting fore and aft and changing the balance of the airplane.

Next we pushed on the left rudder pedal and the nose of the plane swerved sharply to the left. I slid against the side of the cockpit, an uncomfortable feeling that made me seem detached from the plane in which I was flying. That was a skid, Vern said, and we don't want airplanes to fly like that.

Now he moved the control stick to the left and the plane banked steeply to the left. The feeling was different this time, and I had the sensation of both myself and the airplane falling. That was a side slip—a useful maneuver if you need it, but one that can get you in trouble if not done correctly.

We made a gentle turn to the left and then to the right, moving the stick and rudder almost simultaneously; hardly any perceptible movement of the controls was necessary. We banked a bit more steeply and held the turn longer; the nose dropped a slight amount in the turn and the plane gathered speed. I felt Vern pull the stick back and the nose came up. The sound of the engine changed as the rpm increased in the slight dive, and changed again when the engine slowed up once more.

Now I made a few gentle turns unaided. I felt the control

stick jiggle in my hand as I did so and Vern told me to relax; I was holding the stick too tightly. As I loosened my grip the jiggling stopped and the plane immediately flew better. I rapidly gained confidence as our flight continued and felt I was making real progress.

Next Vern took the controls from me and said we were going to do a stall. He explained that when an airplane is flown too slowly the wing stalls and loses lift, causing the nose to drop and the airplane to fall toward the ground. I had heard about stalls and I became frightened. Then I looked at Vern and he was smiling, and immediately I felt reassured, thinking he wouldn't do anything dangerous.

The engine noise slackened as he retarded the throttle, and as the rush of air about the cabin lessened I had the sensation of slowing up. The control stick moved backward slowly and the nose of the plane rose upward until I could no longer see the horizon ahead of the plane. It was now at a very steep angle and I became restless and uneasy. Suddenly the plane began to shake. Vern pulled the throttle and the stick back together, and then the plane made one last shudder and the nose dropped sharply forward.

The horizon flashed by in front of me and I felt I was about to be thrown headlong from the airplane. My stomach was pressed against my ribs and I gasped for breath. Now the plane was in a dive. I lost complete control of my feelings and no longer noticed the pilot. I felt sick and wanted only to stop. Vern dived the airplane a few seconds longer, and with flying speed regained he pulled back on the stick and leveled out.

I felt myself being forced down in my seat as the pull of gravity seized us and my face felt distorted by the downward force. As suddenly the pull stopped and we were climbing again. I didn't dare look at Vern, certain he would notice my fright. I was afraid lest he stall the plane again, for I didn't think I could take it. Then we were at two thousand feet again, and Vern spoke to me. An airplane that stalls might fall into a spin, and he was going to demonstrate it. I sat dumbfounded, too terrified to speak.

Once more he throttled back and the nose of the plane

came up. It lost speed abruptly, and just as it started to shake and stall out the nose snapped to the left and the left wing dropped. Suddenly earth and sky blended into a whirling mass of nothing. I was looking at the ground and the earth was spinning—the center going slow, but blurred and moving very fast on the outer fringes. My sensation was one of being suspended motionless in space, and only the earth was turning.

Just as suddenly the spinning stopped as the plane snapped to the right. Now we were going into a right spin in the opposite direction. But it looked the same, and the same torturous sensation gripped me. I felt sick and nauseated. If I could just get my feet on the ground I vowed I would never fly again. When I was about to become physically ill in the cockpit we recovered from the spin and spiraled gently down to the airport, where we entered the traffic pattern and landed. I was so completely terrified I just disappeared and headed for home.

At that time I was traveling back and forth to Whittier, a distance of four miles, by thumbing rides. I had to sit on the curb for a while to regain my composure before I felt strong enough to go on home. It seemed the world was collapsing around me. I couldn't conceive how I could possibly learn to fly if it was going to be like that. I had been sick before as a passenger, and now I was sick again as a student, and I was actually debating with myself whether to give it up or keep on. But the next morning I felt fine and was as eager to fly as ever, so I returned to the airport and Vern gave me another lesson. This time he made it a point to give me a smooth ride, doing nothing but air work, and I felt okay.

While I was working around the airport several Whittier boys and girls my age began taking flying lessons. They all came from wealthy families, and of course their lessons took place regularly every day. I knew all of them, and although I wasn't jealous of them I did feel a certain amount of envy, because it was pretty tough to have so much interest in flying and see them sailing past me.

Near the end of the summer of 1929 I went to see the doctor again and he said I was well enough to go back to school in September. Now I was really frightened. I had experienced a year of complete freedom and all I wanted to do was be around airplanes.

I entered high school anyway, about the same time that Mother moved to Los Angeles to open a boarding house. Through friends she took a large old house on Fifth Street and Commonwealth Avenue and it was planned at first that I would go to school in Los Angeles. This met with great disapproval on my part, as Whittier was home to me, and most important, my flying activities were centered there. To please me, Mother arranged to board me out in Whittier. I don't know what the financial arrangements were, but I slept in a tent in the back yard and got my breakfast and supper, taking my lunch or buying it at school.

This was a new adventure and all right for a short time, but living with strangers finally got the best of me, and before long I gave it up and went home. I had acquired another second-hand Ford, and for the next three months I drove from Los Angeles to Whittier every day, stopping off at the airport each afternoon on my, way home.

My ties at the field were already diminishing. Most of my time was spent in school now, and the few hours I could spare after school were not enough to keep up my activities at the airport. I had never really been hired, and now there was no longer room for the so-called grease monkey. My flying lessons became farther and farther apart, until I finally feared my flying career was ending.

Because of this I decided to leave school for good and devote myself to aviation. That was near the end of the year. I thought it over for several weeks, and after Christmas I made up my mind. I left one afternoon and never went back. The next morning I stayed in bed a little longer than usual, and thinking I must be ill, Mother came in my room and asked what was wrong. "Nothing is wrong," I said. "In fact, I am quite happy. I am leaving school."

After some discussion she finally consented to try it for a while and see what happened. She never interfered in any way with my desire to do certain things as long as they were along good lines, and she probably had a closer feeling to the way I thought and my capabilities than anyone else. Whether it was legal for a boy my age to leave school I'm not certain, but I know that through friends in Whittier who had connections with the dean of boys at high school the truant officer was asked to leave me alone.

I went back to the airport every day now, driving over from Los Angeles early in the morning, but my old place was gone and there were only a few people at the field who still had any interest in me. My flying lessons became so infrequent that I despaired of ever making my solo flight. I had left school to learn to fly, and if my lessons continued at the present rate I would end up being a nobody.

The next morning I went into the office of Whittier Airways to see Avery Black, who was talking to Sid Willey, and I asked Avery if I could see him. I told him of my feelings, that I had one ambition in life, and that was to fly airplanes, and nothing else mattered. I said I had been around now for a period of two years, in which time I had only had a very few hours of instruction, and they had been scattered over such a long period that it seemed as though I would never solo an airplane.

Up to this time I had had three or four different instructors fly me a time or two, and I asked him if he wouldn't put me on the books with the rest of the students and put me through until I could solo. It shouldn't take too long, and I would stick around and do anything to pay the debt. He readily accepted without a second thought. I will never forget that incident, as it could very well have changed the destiny of A. W. LeVier.

I was put on the regular student roster and almost every day I received my regular fifteen- to twenty-minute flying lesson. First I took lessons from a new instructor, Harvey Knifong, who left later and went into Washington and Oregon. My next instructor was Harold Brown, a former Army officer who is now an insurance underwriter at Lockheed Air Terminal. My last instructor who soloed me was a well-known pilot named Harold Chapman.

One morning when I least expected it he crawled out of the front cockpit and said, "Well, kid, it's all yours, make the best of it," and walked off. I took a last look at Harold and then looked ahead to see where I would be going, as the Waco 10 had very poor visibility on the ground.

I opened the throttle enough to move the plane and turned it slightly to the right. All was clear. Then I opened the throttle still more and the engine roar increased. My tachometer showed 1,375 rpm's and my oil pressure and water temperature checked okay. These engine checks are the little things that are so important, the little good habits that are a part of safe flying.

As the Waco 10 gathered speed I turned my head constantly left and right, watching the ground fly past me, and then I felt the tail come up. There was a slight wind from my right and the plane tended to turn into it like a weathercock. I pushed the rudder bar with my left foot to straighten it out—not enough at first, then too much. Then I eased off and the plane was straight again.

As I eased the control stick forward the nose started down and the plane felt lighter than usual; I remembered that now I was flying without an instructor. As it attained a level attitude I eased off a little on the stick pressure and now I could see ahead of me over the engine. This was going to be fun! The plane began skipping from bump to bump, and as I eased the stick back and raised the nose slightly it left the ground. Holding slight back pressure on the stick I climbed smoothly into the air on my first solo flight.

I passed over the road at the south end of the field and made a slight turn to the right. Being alone in the air for the first time was a different feeling. I wasn't frightened but I felt lonely. I looked right and left at the ground below me, planning which field I would use if my engine quit and I made a forced landing—an important thing in this airplane, because the OX-5 engine had a habit of conking out without much warning. I checked my instruments again—tachometer reading 1,425 rpm's now, so I eased the throttle back and the rpm settled to 1,400.

My altitude was a little over five hundred feet and I had nearly reached the point where I would start my turn back to the airport. I looked right and left again to see if the way was clear. It's important to always keep a sharp lookout for other aircraft—you have worlds of room in the sky but airplanes can still fly into you. Then I banked to the right and turned into the downwind leg.

Now I was flying over the San Gabriel River, the same way I flew on my first airplane ride three years before. I was still holding slight back pressure on the control stick to keep the nose up, and I readjusted the stabilizer to relieve the pressure. When I released the stick to check my trim it was just right—now the nose held straight and steady. Then suddenly the rudder bar began to shake, and my first thought was something must be wrong with the engine.

I checked the instruments again and they looked okay, so I glanced down at the rudder bar and wondered if it was me shaking or the airplane. I remembered what Vernon Dorrell said about getting tense and strangling the controls; then I relaxed and the shaking stopped. I took hold of myself with conscious effort. If I didn't make a good landing, Avery might put me back for more instruction; that would be great, after all the trouble he had gone to giving me a chance to become a pilot!

I crossed over Whittier Boulevard at 750 feet, just about the right altitude to start my base leg. At this point I throttled the engine back to idle position and cleared myself for a right turn. Seeing no other planes, I entered my base leg, and halfway around I was a little high. I widened out my turn a little to lose altitude, but not so much I might miss lining up with the runway. That was one thing Harold was fussy about—line the plane up early, to avoid getting messed up about the time you should be landing.

I steepened my bank and opened the throttle a little to clear the engine, then closed it again. I was still too high—not used to flying without an instructor, and his weight made the difference. As I banked to the right more steeply and pressed on the left rudder, the plane side-slipped and then straightened out with the runway ahead to the right. A slight turn to the right, then a turn to the left, and I was lined up to land.

My altitude was now one hundred feet, just fifty feet too high. I cleared my engine a second time and crossed over the high-tension wires at the entrance to the airport. With a

3,500-foot runway in front of me I had plenty of room to get down. I started leveling off about forty feet from the ground. I eased back on the stick and raised the nose, and now it was above the horizon again as I settled toward the ground.

The wind was drifting me toward the left, toward a large hole in the ground we used for a dump. It would wreck an airplane. I dropped my right wing to check the drift. Tufts of devil grass flashed past me on both sides and I noticed the crisscross of tail skids on the runway. I could sense the nearness of the ground. Steadily I eased the stick back still further and leveled my wings. The plane settled more rapidly and then the wheels touched. There was a slight tendency for the nose to rise, as I pulled the stick all the way back and my tail skid came down.

Waco 10

As the main shock struts compressed and absorbed the impact, the little Waco sort of squatted down and rolled easily down the field. The left wing was low, and using stick right all the way and left rudder I got it up again. The dump passed safely by on my left and I gunned my engine to turn back to the flight line, where Harold was waving to attract my attention. In the old days they said any landing you walked away from was a good landing, so I guess mine was satisfactory. I took off and landed two more times that day. It was March 28, 1930, and a real turning point in my flying career.

The Waco 10 was a three-place, open-cockpit biplane, wide-braced, and weighed about fifteen hundred pounds. It had wooden wings and steel tubing fuselage and was fabric-covered. The Waco 10 of that day had some characteristics which were considered pretty good, but in general I would say it was shy many things. Like most airplanes of its time, especially the open-cockpit biplanes, the pilot usually flew from the rear cockpit. With the conventional two-wheel landing gear and a tail skid, vision was extremely poor when sitting on the ground. The position of the radiator below the center section, just aft of the leading edge of the upper wing, added to the lack of visibility. I would consider the tail assembly marginal under certain conditions, and it was known as a ground-looping airplane.

4

Pilot

Important as it was in my flying career, my solo flight was still just the first hurdle. In order to equip myself to the point where I could make a living flying airplanes, I now had to accumulate two hundred flying hours to qualify for a transport license, which would permit me to leave the airport on cross-country flights and carry paying passengers. Although I knew how to fly, I was pretty green and had much to learn, and in the meantime I had to work and eat.

As a start on this problem, I got a job at the airport, although it came about by accident. I was ready to leave one evening when Avery Black asked me to wait for the night watchman, who had not yet turned up, although it was after six o'clock. I cleaned up that evening, including the four airplanes and the shop, hangar and office, and when Avery got to work the next morning he offered me the job of night watchman on a permanent basis.

Mother objected when I told her about it, saying that night was the time to sleep and I would have too much work and not enough rest. But I argued it would be another chance to make money for flying time and I wanted to try it, and on the understanding that I would give up the job if it proved too much for me she gave her permission to take it.

In order to get the maximum amount of flying time, I arranged with Avery to take most of my wages out in trade.

The job paid $100 a month, of which I would spend $80 to fly the company's airplanes at a fixed rate, leaving me $20 in cash to live on. The Waco 10 proved to be the best bargain; Avery gave me a price of $10 an hour for solo flying in this airplane, which worked out so that I actually got sixteen minutes in the air per day.

At this time my mother moved from Los Angeles to Balboa, which was too far for me to drive every day, and I was no longer able to live at home. As I could not afford to live by myself on my income, I arranged to sleep at the airport. I got a bedroll and enough clothing to last several days, and many times I stayed at the field as long as a week at a time. There was a restaurant on the premises, and such meals as I had I ate at the airport.

As my work got heavier and I got hungrier, it became increasingly difficult to live on the small amount of money I allowed myself for food. One week I ran short of funds before pay day and didn't eat for two days. Noticing I hadn't left the field and realizing something might be wrong, Avery asked me if I was hungry. I suggested that if he took me to lunch he would find out. Word got around about the way I ate, because when we came back to the hangar I was invited to eat lunch a second time. It was not unusual in those days to miss meals, and one meal a day was not uncommon. Finally, I found it necessary to make frequent visits to the French family in Whittier around dinnertime, just to get enough to eat.

The next step in my flying career was a private license, which would permit me to leave the vicinity of the airport. In those days, ten hours of solo flying and written and flight examinations were the only requirements for a private license, and in about two months I had enough flying time. I passed the written test, but on my flight check I was unable to satisfy the government inspector on my spot landings and was turned down. I was heartbroken, but Avery and the other boys assured me it didn't mean anything and in another few hours of practice I could try again. Two months later I took the test again and this time I was successful.

About the same time I had my first crash in an airplane.

Wayne Merrill, a young aviator operating out of our airport, was testing an experimental sport plane built by the Schmuck Aircraft Company in Los Angeles for a local sportsman. The Schmuck brothers were old-timers in the airplane business and built several planes of that day. This particular plane was a parasol monoplane with two open tandem cockpits and was powered by a one hundred horsepower Kinner five-cylinder engine that gave it exceptionally good performance. I helped Wayne service it and maintain the engine, for which I was paid in flying time.

One Sunday when there wasn't much going on I went up for a short flight, and when I landed the owner ran up, saying he would like to fly the plane himself and asking if I would ride along. As it was a chance to get another flight I readily assented. He got in the back seat and started the engine, and we took off in a steep climbing turn.

When he started his turn I knew instinctively something was going to happen, because his air speed was too low for such a maneuver, but he was much older than I and I hesitated to take the controls away from him. But I had a feeling we were in for trouble, and sure enough, right in the middle of his turn the engine quit cold.

Shouting to make himself heard over the rush of air, he yelled, "Take it, Tony, it's all yours!" I immediately took the controls, which I was going to do anyway, and put the nose down to establish a glide. We were at a dangerously low speed and very close to the ground. It looked at first as if I could make the cross runway and land downwind, but by the time I had regained flying speed we were just skimming the tree tops, while ahead of me I could see rows of high-tension lines, and I could tell from the feel of the controls and the response of the airplane that I would be unable to get over them.

Nor was it possible to go under them or turn aside. A row of houses parallel to the wires blocked my escape in both directions. There was only one thing left to do, and I hit the wires square on the nose. They almost stopped me in midair, and then the airplane fell nose first across the road. The wires slowed us up before we hit the ground, and luckily we didn't catch fire. We both jumped out unhurt.

Not long afterward I had another close call that almost cost me my life.

I was flying a Velie Monocoupe with a passenger in the other seat. He was a big boy and had long legs, and the monocoupe was a very small, cramped airplane. The dual controls for this plane were pretty makeshift, with the stick on the left between the pilot's legs, and a sort of cross bar like a crank handle serving for the right-hand control on the other side. My passenger's knees were under this bar, and before landing I suggested that he put his feet in the corner of the cockpit and keep his knees down so there would be no possible chance of interfering with the controls.

I had just started my last turn into the field when suddenly the plane snapped into a left spin. Almost instinctively I jammed the stick forward and pushed with all my might on the right rudder. We were now less than four hundred feet from the ground, extremely low for such a maneuver, especially in a plane like the Monocoupe, which was known to spin if a pilot breathed too hard. Wayne Merrill, who had just arrived at the airport, was familiar with this airplane, and when it snapped into the spin he knew the jig was up and turned away so he wouldn't see me crash.

At the very instant the airplane snapped out of control my passenger realized what had happened. Unconsciously he had brought his knees up under the lateral bar, moving the control stick back and stalling the plane. He straightened his legs at once, releasing the pressure, and I was able to recover from the spin within a quarter of a turn. We cleared the ground by a few feet and then had telephone wires to get over, missing them by inches.

Narrow escapes seemed to be catching up with me now, and it wasn't long before I had a third brush with death. This time, however, it was no one's fault but my own.

I was flying a Fleet Trainer owned by John Nagel, a new operator at our field, and one of the best friends I have ever had. John was a very generous man and let me fly his airplane in return for maintenance work. It was built by the

Consolidated Aircraft Company and named for Reuben Fleet, the president. A small biplane with two open cockpits in tandem, it was a junior version of the Consolidated PT3, the primary trainer of the Army Air Service in the late 1920's. The Fleet had a top speed over one hundred miles an hour and was one of the most popular planes of its day.

John asked me to give a flying lesson to his friend Harry Fromm in this airplane and we took off for Alhambra to visit the local airport. In those days there wasn't much doing and we always had time to drop in at the many little flying fields around Los Angeles and see our friends. There were about thirty fields in operation at the peak period before the depression, twice the number in use today, but they were almost all dirt and grass airports without runways or facilities for handling commercial traffic.

Kenny Brooks and Dick Allen, now a pilot for Northwest Airlines, were operating at Alhambra, along with several other friends. When we got ready to leave after our visit Dick came up and said how about a whippersnapper, which meant some kind of stunt. I said well, maybe, and upon taking off I decided I would make a climbing turn and at about seven hundred feet do a snap roll, which is a forward roll in horizontal flight over on your back and on around to an upright position again.

I had done plenty of snap rolls before in the same airplane, so the maneuver didn't worry me. However, I failed to take into consideration the fact that we had recently changed from a metal to a wooden propeller, which was lighter and influenced the center of gravity of the airplane. Moreover, Harry was a big boy, and being in the rear seat increased the tail heaviness even more.

I did a snap roll to the right and went through the usual procedure at about the right position to recover, but the plane made no attempt to right itself whatsoever and entered a power spin. Recognizing the predicament I was in, I immediately chopped the power and took corrective action. We made two complete turns and recovered just a few feet from the ground; luckily it was the lowest part of the field, as we would have hit the ground and crashed if we had been over any other part. After leveling off I had to apply full power to clear the telephone wires south of the field. When I finally looked back at Harry to see how he was taking it his eyes were big as saucers. I didn't tell John Nagel how close I came to busting up his airplane, but he heard the story from the boys at Alhambra, who thought the spin was part of my demonstration.

Encouraged by my ability to fly an airplane under emergency conditions and get out of trouble, I decided to train myself for stunt flying. In those days many pilots did acrobatics for fun and it was also a way to earn money at air shows. This was the part that interested me, and not long afterward I entered the acrobatic competition in the Long Beach junior air show—my flrst venture in professional flying. I used John Nagel's Fleet Trainer, which he very kindly loaned me for this occasion.

The air show was limited to pilots under twenty-one years of age, and I guess that was pretty young to be a stunt flyer, as there were only two entrants in the acrobatic event. My competitor was a Long Beach boy named Clyde Schlieper, still in his teens like myself. Clyde was a good acrobatic pilot and had the advantage of being on home ground, and to beat him I knew I would have to do something special.

My ace in the hole was an English pun, a half outside loop followed by a half roll to a right-side-up position. At that time an outside loop was pretty new, and as airplanes weren't designed for it there was a chance of a wing coming off, which made it a fairly dangerous maneuver. However, the Fleet was a stout plane and had been used for outside loops before and it was just a matter of me getting up enough nerve to try it.

The common type of safety belt in those days was a simple strap that buckled around the pilot's waist and held him in his seat. For this occasion, however, I installed a special shoulder harness for extra safety. We flipped a coin to see who would go up first and Clyde won the toss. While he took off and began his routine I buckled on my parachute and crawled into the cockpit, where I made ready to go when he came down. After I was securely fastened in my seat and had checked my cockpit I watched him go through his maneuvers; he was an excellent flyer and I realized he had a top-notch routine.

I had flown all these maneuvers too, but this was my first air show and I had never done them in competition. Without previous experience of that sort, it seemed my best bet was to follow his lead and do everything he did, turn or turn, and let the judges decide who did it better. When it was my turn to go up I did just that, climbing to four thousand feet and repeating his maneuvers, with some snap rolls and a few aileron rolls thrown in for good measure.

My grand finale was the Enghsh pun, which I expected to be my clincher. Back at four thousand feet again, I slowed my airplane down to about sixty miles an hour. Then I pushed the stick all the way over and pointed the nose straight down. The wires holding the wings together began singing as I picked up speed and the engine and propeller were howling like mad. My eyeballs seemed to be hanging on strings, but I held the stick forward until the little Fleet was upside down, when I rolled out and immediately pushed over again.

This time I was even lower and going faster than before, and the little airplane was really screaming. Again I nosed over and under and pulled out, leveling off so close to the ground I was sure my maneuver had clinched first place for me. When I landed I could tell the crowd liked it. The race announcer was so surprised by my stunt he was practically speechless, and one of the race officials had to remind him to tell the customers what was going on.

I taxied up to the stand and got out of the airplane, glad it was over, but sure I had won. Clyde came up and shook my hand and told me how much he liked my act. Even Milo Burcham, a famous Long Beach stunt flyer, came over to congratulate me; he was a great acrobatic pilot, and coming from him praise really meant something.

Assuming I was the winner and would get the prize, I returned to Long Beach after dinner for the official announcement at a public meeting at the Fox Theater. The auditorium was filled and I was nervous and shaking, but never doubting that I would get the prize, I waited proudly for the program to begin. Not until it was finished and the audience began leaving did I realize the acrobatic event had been ignored completely.

Turning to Roy Patten and his wife, who were with me, I said there must be some mistake. Roy told me to go up on the stage and ask for an explanation. But I was too dejected to do anything and sat ashamedly in my seat until the theater was almost empty, when there was nothing left to do but go home. John Nagel telephoned the race committee the next morning to find out what happened but didn't get much satisfaction; they told him there was no acrobatic trophy. However, the Long Beach paper listed me as the winner, which was some consolation.

I liked acrobatics, and despite the disappointment of my Long Beach experience I did more stunt flying and was always ready to try something new. In this way I learned to do an inverted spin, which was considered to be a very dangerous maneuver in which the pilot usually bailed out or cracked up. We were sitting around the airport when somebody asked me if I could do one, and I said I never had but I would try if they would buy the gasoline.

They collected $2.50 and I took off in a borrowed TP Swallow, an open-cockpit biplane. I figured the best way to do my spin was to go up to two or three thousand feet, roll over on my back, push forward on the stick and kick the rudder. That is what I did, and lo and behold, it was the most beautiful inverted spin you could imagine. My recovery was easily within one-eighth to one-quarter of a turn, and I did several of them, much to the delight of the spectators.

It was much the same accidental way that I made my first parachute jump. I had the privilege of getting my instruction from H. E. "Spud" Manning, a local boy who made his living jumping at air shows and circuses, and undoubtedly one of the greatest jumpers in the history of this highly hazardous profession. His specialty was delayed jumps, opening his 'chute at the very last moment before hitting the ground. Spud spent a lot of time at our airport and we were good friends.

On this particular day there wasn't much doing and Spud

asked if anyone would like to jump. Vernon Castle, another boy at the field, and I both said we would. We flipped a coin and I won. One of the other boys took me up in his Waco 10 and Spud went along to comfort me.

At about three thousand feet I crawled out on the wing beside the fuselage, and when Spud had me spotted just right he said "jump," and I fell off backward. He wanted me to fall about a thousand feet before opening my 'chute to get the thrill of a free fall. My first sensation was not much different than you get in a fast elevator or diving from a high board, but as I fell farther the wind pressure increased and I was conscious of the rush of air over my face and body. I had dreamed of falling in my sleep many times and I was always frightened, but this was pleasant and not like a dream at all.

Now I was face down above the hangar I had slept and worked in for so many years, and I thought this was a good place to open my 'chute. It snapped me into an upright position but the shock wasn't too bad. The strange thing I noticed now was the eerie feeling you get from the complete silence. The shrill whistle of a train was the only thing I heard until I had almost reached the ground. Spud had spotted me very well, and I landed right in front of the hangar. The next time I jumped was from a jet during the war and it saved my life.

I recommend acrobatics to anyone who wants to be a pilot, because they give you a different outlook on the art of flying an airplane. Young people should have acrobatic experience, and of course it is a "must" for military pilots, as it provides a complete understanding of the capabilities of an airplane. Stunting is not dangerous if done correctly within those limits, but flying itself can be dangerous without acrobatic training. That is one of the problems in military flying today. Military pilots should have a greater feeling for an airplane. They are not taught enough acrobatics, and as a result they sometimes get killed in relatively simple maneuvers.

The trend is away from acrobatics because there has been a fear of stunt flying—not because it is dangerous, but because it puts the pilot and his plane in positions which are unnatural. It is a deviation from the normal and the familiar. You don't need to know how to do spins, loops, snap rolls and upside-down flying to get a private license today, but you will never be a fully-qualified pilot if you have never done them. The airplane is a man-made bird, and the pilot can never understand it fully until he has flown it through its entire range of maneuvers.

Although I did not get paid for teaching until later in my flying career, when I felt qualified I began giving flying lessons to friends, and one of my first students was the wife of one of my early friends in aviation, Jimmy Karnes. I looked after his Wallace Touroplane for him and in return he let me fly it. One day while I was teaching his wife to fly we went to San Diego for her first cross-country flight, accompanied by John Nagel and a student in another plane.

The day was very foggy, with visibility about one mile and a ceiling between two and three hundred feet. In those conditions our flight was in violation of the air traffic rules, but many pilots flew in such weather by simply staying contact and never getting into the clouds. We reached San Diego with some difficulty, continually weaving in and out of the canyons and going around the hills by way of San Juan Capistrano. The last few miles were flown along the coast just above the breakers, and it was still foggy when we started back on the trip home.

Looking for better weather, we took a return course inland, but conditions were not improved. We were flying along the mountain range when suddenly John's plane broke formation to the right and started spiraling down. I thought he might be in trouble, so I swung around and followed him. He broke through a hole in the overcast and made a safe landing in a very small field, flanked by hills on two sides. As I came in the ground rose suddenly to meet me, and before I could apply enough power to pull up over it my tail wheel hit with such force it broke off, and I landed dragging the tail on the ground.

John's engine was out cold. After an inspection it was found to have dropped a valve and needed a new piston and cylinder assembly. I took off without a tail wheel and flew to the airport, where I picked up the necessary parts and returned in one of John's planes. The fog having lifted, I found him without much trouble and landed safely this time. After we made the necessary repairs to his engine we both took off again and got home before dark.

It was after this trip that John said he thought I was ready for my transport license, although I had tried for a limited commercial license the year before and failed the written examination. The limited commercial required only fifty hours of solo flying, but it permitted you to carry paying passengers only on local flights; by comparison, the transport license qualified you to fly anywhere, and this time I studied hard.

The written examination included navigation, meteorology and air traffic rules and regulations. Then I took the flying test, consisting of take-offs and landings, including spot landings within two hundred feet of a marker; figure eights around pylons at eight hundred feet, followed by vertical banks without loss of altitude; and stalls, spins and forced landings. This I accomplished with I presume average proficiency, and on July 6, 1932, I was granted my transport license after 201 hours in the air.

I was now a professional pilot and could enter aviation conducting any type of flying for pay, providing I was qualified in the class of aircraft concerned. My next goal was to get more flying time and experience, with the hope that eventually I could become an airline pilot. I was equipped to go ahead at a faster pace than I had been for the last four years.

5

Barnstorming

I got my transport license when I was only nineteen years old, and with an early start like that it seemed that I could quickly realize my ambition to be a full-time pilot. But this was 1932, with the depression getting worse every year, and my ambitions had to wait like those of millions of other people. Most pilots were driving trucks and I was lucky I could stay with flying at all. I did everything from barnstorming to teaching, just to keep my hand in. Many of my ventures failed, but I was used to wearing a tight belt. Perhaps my previous experience in lean living pulled me through the depression years, where somebody in the habit of eating regularly might have given up.

During the years after the First World War nearly everyone who entered aviation barnstormed at some time or other. The term ''barnstorming'' as applied to aviation was taken from the slang expression for theatrical performances in barns and similar improvised halls in country districts. In the same way, a barnstormer originally meant an actor who traveled from town to town, performing wherever he could find an audience. The name applied equally well to pilots of that era who made their living in the carnival atmosphere of itinerant air shows and flying circuses.

When I first began to fly most pilots had barnstormed around the country at some time in their flying career, making a little money and getting a lot of experience. Before the depression, some of the old-timers did very well financially in this business. It wasn't unusual for a pilot to go out to some small country town and set up shop in an open field adjoining the highway, and during a Saturday and Sunday make as high as $400 to $500 doing stunts and flying passengers. In a few lucrative months like that a man could make enough money during the spring and summer to live on the rest of the year, and if he salted his money away and invested it wisely he could be wealthy when he retired.

In the 1930's, after the stock market crash, that kind of money disappeared, but you could still manage to make enough to buy gas and oil and a meal or two and pay for your lodgings. There was seldom any left over to put in the bank. Most of the pilots as I remember them were easygoing fellows, and the old saying about "easy come, easy go" certainly applied to them. There was usually a party after the day's work and the cash flowed freely, with the barnstormer usually footing the bill.

By the time I learned to fly and accumulated enough flying hours to get my transport license, the depression had set in and there was hardly a dime to be scraped out of the public. However, I took every opportunity to go barnstorming anyway, mostly in the little towns away from the metropolitan area, where people weren't in such close contact with flying. You could always get a little money from an audience like that, but in most cases I just wanted to get away from the everyday life around Los Angeles and see the people out in the country.

There was always a big difference when you flew into a small community. You would be greeted by the local aviation enthusiasts within a few minutes after landing, and in most cases you were invited to someone's home for the evening. You would have two or three offers for dinner and in many cases lodgings for the night. If you stayed several days in the same town it was not unusual to have most of your meals given to you by invitation.

My weekend visit to an air show at Lompoc, a little farming community in the Santa Maria Valley, was one barnstorming trip that will always stand out in my memory. I had the use of Jimmy Kames' Touroplane and Spud Manning and I flew up Saturday to see what we could do to earn a little money. Lompoc was quite wealthy as farming districts go and in normal times it would have been a good place to go barnstorming, but this was the week all the banks were closed. We didn't think about it until the next day, when I realized we had hit a dud.

On Sunday morning we were out at the airport and I went through the crowd trying to sell rides in my airplane. It seemed nobody had any money. When the time came for Spud's jump I went around again to take up the usual collection. Generally speaking, from a crowd like that we would get at least $100 the first time around, but today I finished my collection with less than $1 in my hat. I told Spud of our plight but he said he was going to jump anyway. He was that sort of fellow, and he would go on with the show if he didn't make a dime out of it.

In desperation I passed the hat once more. The airport manager graciously donated $5, which was probably the last he had, but I kept telling myself it would get us back to Whittier. With this $5 bill in my hat I went through the crowd again. Instead of just asking for a donation, this time I begged the people for any change they had, no matter how little. I explained our predicament, saying we were going ahead with the show in spite of our failure to collect enough to make it worth our while, and we would appreciate any amount at all to help us get out of town and get home again. If it was only a penny it would help.

They started to go into their pockets and bring out the pennies and I never saw so many in my life in one heap. Some of the people also fished out their last few silver coins when I reached their hearts with my pleading, and my hat was almost full of loose change when I got back to Spud again. We took off and flew to 10,000 feet, where he jumped off the wing and plunged earthward. He carried a twenty-pound sack of flour in his arms, opening the sack and trailing a white streak of flour behind him as he plummeted toward the ground. By arching his back and using his head to steer he always spotted himself to land directly in front of the spectators, the only man I ever saw who could maneuver his body in a free fall.

As he approached within 1,000 feet of the ground a gasp went up from the crowd. It was always from 1,000 feet down that people would start to scream, especially the women. Then around 500 feet the first trickle of the parachute would be seen and at 350 or 400 feet it would blossom out and Spud would swing gently to the ground. In those days he was undoubtedly the world's greatest delayed parachute jumper, just through stunts like this.

When I landed we thanked everyone who had helped us and went back to our hotel, where I dumped the money on the bed and started counting. There were hundreds of pennies and nickels, a few dimes and a handful of quarters and half dollars. I think it totaled about $35, just enough to pay our expenses with no profit. In other words, the following week would be lean living.

Spud's fame got around the country, and early in 1933 some businessmen from Uniontown, Pennsylvania, arrived in Whittier to see him. They wanted him to make a jumping tour of the East under their auspices, and they were also looking for an airplane to use, preferably a Ford Tri-motor. This plane was powered by three Wright Whirlwind J-5 engines, had dual controls and carried twelve passengers. It was o its way out of general use by now, but one of the early models was in storage at Grand Central Air Terminal in Glendale, and they bought it for $4,500. Spud signed up for the tour and I went along as co-pilot. My duties also included servicing the engines and selling tickets for rides.

The plane was named "Mac's Air Palace," after Bill MacAfee, one of the owners, and we took off for Pennsylvania. We couldn't have picked a worse time. Our first stop at Banning, California, was a financial failure, and our next stop at Palm Springs wasn't much better. The inhabitants of these communities seemed to have little interest in scenic rides in our airplane, while Spud's collections never amounted to more than a few dollars. At Tucson, Arizona, we ran out of money and were stranded two weeks until we could earn

Ford Tri-motor

enough to get out of town. Then it was only by the providential intervention of a local millionaire who liked flying. The state's aviation enthusiasts were guests at his ranch, and he invited us to put on our show and also take them up for rides. As he paid the bill, quite a number went up with us, and it was through this windfall that we got back on our feet. After further delays caused by dust storms and other bad weather, we reached Uniontown two weeks later.

We began barnstorming through western Pennsylvania, and by this time I had become quite annoyed with our pilot, an eastern fellow, who seemed to lack the knack for getting the airplane on the ground. On almost every landing he overshot the field and had to stop the plane by ground looping. As we were now operating out of some very small airports, mostly on top or on the side of a hill, this method of landing became fairly hazardous, and I began wondering what would happen. I soon found out.

On our first flight at Indiana, Pennsylvania, the pilot's inability to get the plane on the ground caught up with us again, but this time he came in too fast and too far down the field to stop even by ground looping. At the end of the airport the ground dropped sharply to a dirt road and a ditch crossing our path. Would the landing gear stand the strain when the wheels hit the ditch, or would the plane nose over and push the engine back into the cockpit on top of us? I could see all this happening, and at the last moment I closed my eyes and pulled back on the control wheel with all my might. The Ford Tri-Motor lifted off the ground just enough to clear the ditch and then settled back down again on the far side and slid to a grinding halt. Apparently unconcerned by our narrow escape, the pilot taxied back to the field and took off again with another load of passengers, not even bothering to check first for possible damage to the airplane. This was too much even for me, and it was here that I parted company with Mac's Air Palace.

I next took up with a new friend I called Bob, a former coal miner and farmer who owned a Great Lakes trainer painted orange with a large dragon on the fuselage. He made many of the local air shows, taking up passengers and doing acrobatics. Bob always wore a parachute, which I thought was odd, because he did his stunts near the ground where a 'chute wouldn't help him if he had to bail out.

Bob took a liking to me and let me fly his plane, which was excellent for acrobatics. In fact, many passengers requested stunt rides, for which they paid up to $5 each. We took this plane on tour with good results; for some reason people wanted to fly in the little orange airplane that made so much noise. On such flights I would often go behind a hill to avoid being seen by airport officials and do my acrobatics with the passenger in the front seat.

One of Bob's habits was drinking, and when he got drunk he always had an urge to fly. One day he took off in this condition and I have never seen a wilder demonstration of crazy flying. The airport was on a plateau between hills next to a river. Bob delighted in tearing down in a near-vertical dive on the airport, where he would clear the edge of the field and continue out of sight down to the river several hundred feet below. This left the spectators in hysterics and I have no doubt he thought it was great fun.

Another time at Du Bois, Pennsylvania, where I was putting on an acrobatic demonstration, Bob had been drinking and insisted on coming with me. This could well have been the last flight for both of us. My last maneuver was a split S, a half roll to your back and pulling through like a half loop. As I entered this maneuver and retarded the throttle to reduce power to complete my half loop without gaining too much speed, Bob suddenly shoved the throttle wide open again. Before I could pull it back once more, considerable altitude had been lost and considerable speed gained. Now instead of clearing the ground with a safe margin we were down in a ravine.

I went right down to the tree stumps in my pullout, and on the way up I encountered high-tension lines ahead. My first impulse was to go over them, but fearing my speed was too great to pull up and clear them, I chose to go under them instead. There appeared to be ample room, but I had failed to see two telephone wires low on the poles. I hit them just about square with a slight shudder and a singing of the wires as they broke and spun around the struts. I think this accident sobered Bob up. The next morning we left town early before the telephone company caught up with us.

The airport at St. Mary's, Pennsylvania, had one of the most interesting landing strips I have ever encountered. It was quite narrow and on top of a ridge, bordered on one side by trees about thirty feet high. As the day wore on the wind shifted from parallel to the runway to crosswind, putting the strip on the leeward side of the trees. This made landings very difficult, for the air was extremely turbulent on the leeward side. As an alternative, I tried landing uphill into the wind on a steep knoll adjoining the airport.

I paced it off and figured out approximately where I should touch down. Here I put a little flag on a stick and flew the plane right up to this spot, where I chopped the power and landed. I found that landing on a hillside is a cinch if you come in with enough speed to pull up and flare. I was becoming bolder all the time, and while I was no match for Bob, his influence was creeping up on me.

Perhaps it is just as well I left him when I did. By now the Great Lakes was getting very tired and could not pass its annual inspection without overhaul, and being without funds to repair it, Bob put it in storage. I picked up some odd flying jobs around town the rest of the summer and barnstormed south of Uniontown to augment my funds, which were generally less than $10. Toward the end of August I made plans to rejoin Spud Manning in Chicago.

Spud had quit Mac's Air Palace about the same time I did and spent the summer jumping at air shows on the East Coast. Now he was booked at the air races during the Gordon Bennett International Balloon Races in September. With $10 in my pocket, I got a ride into Pittsburgh on a bread truck and thumbed my way from there to Chicago, where I found Spud at race headquarters. We went out to the airport and I got odd jobs working around the fleld.

Spud was sponsored by the Pennzoil Company; he had top billing at the races and put on some of his best jumps. At this time he was suffering from a double hernia, possibly brought on by his jumping. In any event it was so painful he had to wear his leg harness loose, putting an extra strain on his shoulders, which were black and blue from the straps.

Many famous pilots of the day took part in the air races at Chicago that year, including Jimmy Wedell, Steve Wittman and Art Chester, some of whom I raced with in later years. There was also a woman's race which was saddened by several accidents. May Haizlip nosed over on landing, and Florence Klingensmith was killed after her GB Racer started shedding parts in the air and her parachute failed to open when she bailed out at low altitude. I was the first to reach the scene in the Pennzoil crash truck and helped remove Florence's airplane from the field.

On September 5 Vincent Bendix invited the air show participants to his home in South Bend, Indiana, for a house party; Spud went while I waited for him to return to Chicago the next morning. I shall never forget that day. A strong wind was blowing from the west and the hours passed and no Spud. Then we heard he had accepted a ride in an autogiro and was last seen heading west across Lake Michigan. I was ready to borrow an airplane and go looking for him when the sad news came. Flying against that headwind they ran out of gas and the Coast Guard found their bodies floating in the lake. I can imagine Spud's feelings when they started out over that lake; he had a fear of water and could not swim.

With Roy Johnson of Whittier, who was traveling with Spud by automobile, I made arrangements to ship his body home, then drove back to Los Angeles with Roy. After the funeral John Nagel and I organized a benefit air show for Spud's widow, whose second child was born the day he drowned. We had bad weather, and despite an excellent program we raised only $225.

The next thing I turned my hand to was teaching and it worked out pretty well.

One of the pilots around Los Angeles Eastside Airport was Don Reece, a young fellow my age who had learned to fly about the same time I did at the Aero Corporation in Los Angeles. Aero Corporation was founded by Jack Frye, who later formed Standard Air Lines and eventually became president of Trans World Airlines. Don and I had been around some time now, doing handsprings for hamburgers, and getting in what flying we could. To interest more students in aviation, Don decided the cost of lessons had to come down. His solution was the E-Z Flying School which we started.

Regular flying instruction at our field cost $9 an hour, which was standard for the Los Angeles area. Lessons were broken down into fifteen-minute periods, during which time the student usually got a little air work and three takeoffs and landings. It was Don's idea to give five-minute lessons, cutting the unit price accordingly, and in that way attract more customers. We didn't know how much a student could learn in five minutes but we decided to find out.

It worked surprisingly well. John Nagel let us use his Fleet Trainer and we advertised flying lessons for seventy-five cents.

We split it up fair and square by dividing five minutes into one hour which is twelve and then dividing twelve into $9. About twenty students showed up for opening classes. We had ground school two nights a week to acquaint them with the fundamentals of flying, followed by flight instruction in which we tried out our new teaching method.

Instead of taking them up for a joy ride the first time, I allowed them to follow through on the controls from the beginning. I considered the possibility that some students might get frightened and freeze on the controls, but I felt I was probably as strong as they were and I could take the controls away from them if I had to. I was young and took that chance. In the many months we conducted the E-Z Flying School I encountered several students who were frightened but only one who was stronger on the controls, and that wasn't from fright; he was a wrestler and was so strong he just couldn't help himself.

Since low cost was what we were selling, we gave lessons without student permits until our students had a chance to try it out and see if they had an aptitude for flying. This enabled them to start lessons without spending $10 for a permit, which would have stopped a lot of people in those days, and the ones who dropped out saved that money. They got six lessons before they had to decide if they wanted to continue, and in that event we flew them to Long Beach to get their permits. The CAA inspectors knew what we were doing, and although it wasn't exactly according to the rules it made sense to them and they did not object. They agreed that people were entitled to know if they wanted to fly before investing $10. Of those who did go on, we found they were ready to solo in about four and a half hours.

While I was out barnstorming around the country, my sister Nancy had stayed home in Los Angeles working at a regular job and saving her money. Through a friend she met George Weedon, a neighbor who was interested in aviation, and told him about me and the E-Z Flying School. Not long afterward she telephoned me to talk about airplanes, a subject which had never impressed her particularly, and I got the impression that Mr. Weedon might back me in a new flying school. This seemed too good to be true and I rushed right over.

Mr. Weedon turned out to be a partner in Crowell, Weedon & Co., the Los Angeles stockbrokers. He told me he and Mr. Crowell had a little extra money and would like to give it a whirl in aviation. They were interested in backing a new low-price flying school like ours and asked me to suggest a suitable airplane to use for instruction. I recommended the Porterfield, a small, inexpensive plane with high performance. It was good for teaching and I also thought it had sales possibilities in Los Angeles. They bought one of these planes through the local distributor and I took delivery in Kansas City and flew it home.

We formed the Coast Flying Academy, with myself as president and Crowell and Weedon as secretary and treasurer, operating from Alhambra airport south of Pasadena. It was a popular field at the time and looked like a good place to get students. But the new school was a failure and it was my fault. I wasn't much of a businessman and my heart wasn't in it. I loved to fly too much and that occupied my thoughts most of the time. In a few months my partners decided to liquidate the business. We didn't lose money, but there was no profit in it either, and they turned their attention elsewhere. The Alhambra venture was only a small part of my flying career, but it showed me I was definitely not suited to manage an outfit.

By 1935, when my first business venture folded, aviation was pretty well along the road to recovery from the economic hardships that plagued it earlier. People went crazy about airplanes after Lindbergh's flight to Paris in 1927 and it was easy to promote money to build new planes, but the depression hit flying hard. Within a year after the stock market crash in 1929 aviation was on the rocks, with the government about the only remaining customer for the nation's aircraft manufacturers. Most of them went broke, including the Lockheed company, and receivers sold new planes for ten to fifteen cents on the dollar.

Beginning in 1932 there was another steady growth in aviation as airplanes improved and customers reappeared in the market. The new planes of the 1930's were not radically changed in appearance but they were better designed and made of better materials and had improved performance. In addition, the cabin plane came into general use and brought new comfort to flying. In this way the airplane began to interest people who did not want to dress to fly. All I ever had was my regular clothes, finally saving up enough money to buy a leather jacket, but the fancier boys who could afford it wore high leather boots and riding breeches. We all wore helmets and goggles, but even these were superfluous in the enclosed cabins of the new planes now flying.

Perhaps the biggest advance in aircraft construction of the 1930's was the all-metal airplane. The German Junkers low-wing monoplane built shortly after World War I showed us how superior metal was for wear and tear in an airplane, but it was several years before Henry Ford built his all-metal plane, the Ford Tri-Motor, better known as the Tin Goose. Metal was a more expensive type of construction, but it soon caught on as its long-term economy became apparent. Boeing, Douglas, and Lockheed all brought out their first metal transports—the Boeing Monomail, a streamlined, low-wing monoplane; the Lockheed Electra, a twin-engined, high-performance monoplane; and the Douglas DC-1 and DC-2.

Meanwhile smaller manufacturers went into light personal planes like the Piper Cub, Taylorcraft and Aeronca. Through their efforts in bringing low-cost aviation to the public, nearly everyone who had a desire to fly could afford it. For example, the Porterfield we bought for the Coast Flying Academy cost only $1,800. Slowly the old wooden-wing, open-cockpit airplanes of the 1920's disappeared from the nation's expanding air fields. They were too expensive to fly in comparison to the new planes that could get a guy up in the air cheap.

6

The Firecracker

The year 1935 had come and gone and I was still hungry—
for some of the bare necessities of life as well as for fame.
My clothing was pretty threadbare and my general appearance
was that of a bum. Of course I had to eat to fly, so my first
problem was still making a living. This could always be done
by teaching, but it offered only a minimum income, and I felt
that I should do better than that. Besides, my failure in the
Coast Flying Academy showed me that I wasn't a businessman, and if I continued teaching I would have to work for
somebody else. I considered this a step backward, and although I did it again to support myself, my chief interest and
main effort were soon given to a new venture. It was professional air racing, and this time I succeeded.

Although air racing is almost as old as the airplane itself, it
gained its first real impetus in the United States when the
national air races were inaugurated in 1926. At first the
participants were mostly military pilots and planes, and there
was little chance for civilians to win against the superior
aircraft flown by the armed forces. In the next few years,
however, several commercial manufacturers entered the racing field with personal planes especially designed for that
purpose. Travel-Air, long a leader in commercial aviation,
came up with the Travel-Air Mystery, a low-wing, wire-
braced monoplane in the two-hundred-mile class. Matty Laird

built the Solution and Super-Solution, very small, thin-wing biplanes flown by men like Jimmy Doolittle and Charles "Speed" Holman. Even pilots who built their own planes competed successfully, such as Benny Howard, a captain on United Air Lines, who placed third in the Thompson Trophy Race in 1930 with a little low-wing monoplane of his own design and construction. For the next ten years, until the war turned the spotlight on military aviation again, civilian planes and pilots dominated air racing in the United States.

They took over the national air races, which by now had becoming the leading event of their kind. A whole new breed of racing planes appeared on the scene, such as the famous "Gee-Bee" monoplanes; Keith Rider's low-wing monoplanes with metal fuselage and retractable landing gear; Jimmy Wedell's Wedell-Williams racer that set a new land-plane speed record of 305 miles an hour in 1933; Larry Brown's famous monoplanes, and Roscoe Turner's Turner-Laird Spe-

Gee-Bee

cial. The national air races offered pilots a good choice of events, including the Bendix cross-country race; the Greve Trophy Race for planes of limited engine size; and winding up with the big event of the show, the Thompson Trophy Race for all who could qualify for its sizzling speed and the tough, grueling course.

It was during the 1930's, when money was scarce, that air racing and aircraft performance made their biggest strides. Undoubtedly the chance to hit it rich in big-time racing, which offered sizable purses even during the depression, attracted both designers and pilots. With top flyers like Jimmy Doolittle and Roscoe Turner taking up serious air racing, they could call on the best aircraft designers in the aviation industry for the planes they flew. In fact, the racing planes built during the depression served as models for several of the nation's top fighter planes in World War II.

Most racers were built on tight budgets, often in the designer's backyard in his spare time, and because of this shortage of time and money many of them didn't get in the air until the races were ready to begin. Things reached a point where planes were completed only a few days before they were shipped to Cleveland and they were often tested after they arrived at the races. The test usually consisted of one flight around the field, and if everything looked all right the plane was gassed up and entered for the qualifying run. In such a situation there were bound to be accidents on test flights, which was a hazard in the congested areas around metropolitan airports where races were usually held. For example, I cracked up at Cleveland in a little racing plane with a new wing that had never been tested, almost killing myself and wrecking the plane. Things finally got to the point where race officials had to require all planes to be test-flown before they were brought in.

After closing my flying school at Alhambra, I went back to Los Angeles Eastside Airport, where I found work flying for Roy "Mac" McCreery, an oldtimer in aviation who ran a used-airplane and spare-parts business at the Whittier field. Roy owned a J6-9 Travel-Air like the one I used to fly for John Nagel. We took his plane to local air shows around southern California, and although it wasn't a racer, I entered it in several contests with good results. I got racing experience, and my share of the prize money helped buy groceries and pay the rent.

My first race in Mac's Travel-Air, at the annual air carnival at Prescott, Arizona, was also my first real air race in adult competition. I was reluctant to enter, not knowing how Mac would feel about racing his plane, and also doubtful that I could beat several other fast entries, but Mac thought we had a chance and he was interested in the prize money too. Much to my surprise the six-passenger Travel-Air outclassed the field.

Winning a race or any kind of competition is very thrilling and satisfying. It makes you feel that you have done something a little better than the other fellow, and the limelight is on you for a while, which always makes you feel good. This feeling has grown on me for a number of years. I have never deliberately stepped out and tried to show off, but I have always enjoyed putting on a demonstration for anyone who might care to watch. It was on many an occasion such as this that I would take great joy out of performing.

My next race was at Ontario, California, where I flew two Travel-Airs, including a racing version equipped with a speed cowling and pants on the wheels. My main competition turned out to be John Sheasby, an old friend from Pomona who is now a captain on Western Air Lines. Johnny was flying a Travel-Air biplane with a souped-up engine, the same kind Lindbergh used in his Ryan monoplane on his famous flight to Paris. It probably developed as much power as I got from my J6-7, and with a much lighter airplane he jumped out in front of me at the start. It was a short race and I was afraid that I wouldn't have time to catch him, but finally I passed him on the last lap. My share of the prize money was quite a help in those lean days. Mac didn't have too much work, and sometimes I supplemented my earnings by helping Don Reece instruct students at his flying school.

In the fall of 1936 I flew a small experimental plane built by Gene Mendenhall, a young Los Angeles designer, who asked me to be the test pilot because I was the only one who seemed able to get it off the ground. It was a clever little plane with gull wings and tail booms like the Lockheed P-38 fighter plane a few years later. The pilot sat in a small cockpit nacelle in the nose of the plane, and the engine was mounted in the center section of the wing, with a pusher-type propeller between the tail booms at the rear of the engine nacelle. The landing gear consisted of one wheel under the cockpit, with a tail and wing skids instead of wheels.

Because of the experimental nature of this airplane, we wanted to know more about it before flying it again in populated areas, so the first Sunday in October we trucked it to Muroc Dry Lake in the Mojave Desert, now a test center for the U. S. Air Force. However, the engine wouldn't start and our trip was a waste of time. To save going back to Muroc we decided to conduct any further tests at Rosamond Dry Lake, which is closer to Los Angeles.

It was here on two succeeding Sundays that we made several flights, all of which were cut short by engine failures. The little two-cylinder, two-stroke-cycle engine in this plane was a pretty sad affair, and on every flight it conked out after just a minute or two in the air. After several such forced landings I had a dim view of the airplane. Gene was satisfied with his creation, however, and we concluded our test program on a note of triumph.

After coming home, however, we found skeptics at Gene's airport who refused to believe the plane had flown, and he felt obliged to meet this challenge to his reputation as an aircraft designer by demonstrating the plane for them on one more flight. He asked me to take it up again and I accepted, but the first thing I did was look for a course to fly that offered the best place for a safe landing if the engine quit.

Telegraph & Atlantic Airport, where Gene was operating, was in east Los Angeles adjacent to the Southern Pacific Railroad yards and shops. I planned to take off across the railroad tracks and fly over a narrow strip of land in the yards to a point where I could turn and come back to a large field on the other side. If the engine was still running at this point I would circle the field, retrace my flight path and return to the airport.

The flight worked out as planned except for one small detail which I overlooked. As I reached the end of the strip of ground in the railroad yards, the engine conked out as usual, but as I turned toward the field across the tracks for another deadstick landing I had an unpleasant surprise. A railroad siding ran through the corner of the field over which I had to make my approach, and this area on both sides of the spur track was now filled with large piles of broken concrete.

My air speed was dangerously low, but I stretched my glide as best I could, hoping to get past this dangerous area before stalling out. My luck was still with me. I cleared the last pile of concrete by scant inches and then the teetering little racer stalled and dropped helplessly to the ground.

The field was soft, which helped break my fall. As the nose of the plane struck the dirt it came to such a sudden stop that my safety belt snapped and I shot forward in the cockpit. My feet went right through the nose of the plane and dug two deep furrows in the soft earth, while my body was wedged so tightly in the wreckage I was unable to free myself. Fortunately for me, it did not catch fire. I sat that way about five minutes, trying vainly to pull myself out of the cockpit, until the first spectators reached the accident scene and pried me loose. Except for a few cuts and bruises I was all right, but the plane was a complete loss. That was the end of the Mendenhall Special.

My aim was now set on the national air races in Los Angeles. I wanted to get another racing plane and compete. I had found an airplane, an old cracked-up Brown racer that was wrecked on a test flight at Mines Field, but I thought I could repair it and I could buy it for $150. A friend put up the money and I drove over to Los Angeles to take delivery of the wreckage, including a trailer to carry it.

As I carted the parts out on the driveway to load on the trailer, I saw these bent and mangled bits of airplane, and it made me sick to my stomach, thinking that I had only two months to actually rebuild this plane. I sat down a few minutes until I felt better, when encouraged by the thought of working hard and setting a fast pace, I regained my composure and felt I could win.

Because time was so short, several friends came over from Whittier to help me rebuild the plane. One drew up a new set of plans and another did the welding on the fuselage, while my old friend Frank Bolman offered to repair the wings. This project took all of my time, day and night, and there was no time left to make a living. Once again my mother came to my aid. Knowing my heart was in this venture and to succeed I had to eat, she gave me $150 on the condition I spend it all on food and nothing else. I willingly took it and that is exactly what I did.

My next problem was getting an engine for the airplane, which cost more money I did not have. Hoping someone would come forward to help me out again, I continued working on the airframe right up to race deadline, but it was a waste of time. Even though Cliff Henderson, managing director of the national air races, tried to get me a sponsor to buy an engine, the Brown racer never flew again until after the war. All I got out of the races that year was a couple of tickets and a chance to meet the top pilots of the day, such as Earl Ortman, Art Chester and Roger Don Rae. When the races were over I put the Brown in storage and went back to work for Don Reece and his flying school.

Except for my illness as a boy, I had always enjoyed good health, but now my eyes started bothering me, and I found myself squinting to see clearly. They were checked at my next physical examination, which all pilots are required to take semiannually, and I was told I had astigmatism and must wear glasses. This was a blow at first, as I was afraid that glasses would hurt my flying, but they have never held me back. My pilot's license remained in force with a waiver stating I must wear glasses, and I certainly could see a lot better when I had them on. So far as I could tell I flew just the same. Later on I had sunglasses ground to my prescription and I wear them all the time, indoors as well as out. It's probably vanity, but I kid myself into thinking people don't know I need them.

My next venture into air racing came in 1937, and this time I got to Cleveland. By now I was pretty well known around Los Angeles as a speed flyer, even though I hadn't made much money at it, and I was offered a chance to go to Cleveland in a new midget racing plane. It was built by several employees of the Consolidated Aircraft Company in San Diego, from designs of Claude Flagg, an old-time aircraft designer and now in the inspection department at Consolidated. With a fifteen-foot wing span in its original design it was probably the smallest racing plane in the world, but the one-hundred-horsepower British Pobjoy engine gave it a top speed near two hundred miles an hour.

Flying it for the first time from Lindbergh Field in San Diego was as big a thrill for me as it was for the hundreds of Consolidated employees who gathered to see the new plane take to the air. Never before had I flown anything quite so small and with so much power. As I opened the throttle the little plane leaped forward as though shot from a cannon. I had often dreamed of such an airplane, but I never thought I would fly one.

Additional test flights followed at Los Angeles municipal airport, where I flew the plane all summer in my spare time. Meanwhile Flagg's boys began work on a new and even

Pobjoy Special

smaller wing, designed to make the plane fly still faster. When time came for us to leave for Cleveland the new wing had not yet been flown, so there was nothing to do but wait and test it back there.

Even in those days, the atmosphere of the national air races was pretty much as it is today. A summertime sport, air racing is normally conducted in hot weather before shirt-sleeve crowds. The air of mixed excitement and impatience that marks any public competition is evident, and mingles with the holiday mood of the spectators and the carnival cries of the concessionaires. Back in the hangars where pilots and their ground crews are whipping their planes into final shape, the excitement is even greater. There are plenty of bugs to be ironed out of a racing plane before it is ready to fly, and every small detail must be cared for in advance. The engines are especially important, as they take a terrific beating when they run wide open for a long period. The struggle to get them running smoothly is always a major headache before the race begins.

We had an additional problem, installing and testing a new wing that had never flown. Before my first flight I knew the reduced lifting area would affect my take-off, and with the short span and smaller ailerons, control would be marginal. Even so, I was taken completely by surprise. Starting my take-off run, I reached a speed of one hundred miles an hour and lifted the little plane off the ground. It immediately rolled to the right and almost turned upside down before I knew what had happened. I never felt so helpless in all my life. I retarded the throttle to reduce torque and get it back in level flight again, but lateral control was extremely poor and it felt as though I had no ailerons. I had read about planes wavering around out of control, but thought it was just a story; now I was flying one—or was I?

Again I applied just enough power to continue to fly and again the plane began rolling, this time to a vertical position. I decided the best place for me was on the ground. Righting the plane with difficulty, I chopped the power and came in. The nose of the plane was low and the right wing was still down. Control was sloppy and I was on the edge of a stall.

With the stick all the way back in the left corner and full left rudder I hit the ground with a shattering crash. The nose plowed into the ground and there was a sharp crack like a pistol shot as the right wing broke off. The whirling propeller came apart as it dug into the runway and I had a fleeting glimpse of one blade sailing through the air. I hung on to the controls as the plane skidded crazily along the ground, praying that it would not flip over. Spinning to the right and left, it stayed right side up as its momentum slackened and then slid to a stop, and taking a deep breath I unbuckled my safety belt and stepped out unharmed. Thus ended my first attempt at big-time air racing.

The following year I had a better plane and came back to score my first successes at Cleveland and Oakland, California.

The plane was a Keith Rider racer named *The Firecracker*. C. H. "Gus" Gotch, a West Coast pilot, flew it at Cleveland in 1937, winning third in the Greve Trophy Race at an average speed of 231 miles an hour. The owner was Bill Schoenfeldt, a Los Angeles aviation enthusiast, whom I knew through Vernon Dorrell. Bill offered me the chance to fly his plane in 1938, with the understanding that I would take it over and put it in shape and he would back me in the Pacific International Air Races.

This was an act from heaven, a thing I had been dreaming of for years. Now I was going to get my chance in a real racer, a plane capable of more than 330 miles an hour, which at that time was a fantastic speed. After visiting Bill's shop on Western Avenue and getting acquainted with the airplane, I set up a schedule to do the job, as I was the only person who would work on it. Bill bought all the parts and supplies needed for overhaul and I paid for my own labor.

The Firecracker looked like its namesake, with a long, barrel-shaped fuselage, a small, low wing and a couple of small fins for a tail. But it was powered by a Menasco Super-Buccaneer inverted six-cylinder engine developing 550 horsepower, and it was the fastest plane in the world for its size and engine displacement. I completely reconditioned this airplane and overhauled the engine, and made my first test flight early in May at Long Beach municipal airport.

Up to this time I had not flown a really fast airplane. Sitting in the tiny little cockpit, I started the engine and listened to it roar. I am a fairly large man, and as there was not room for both me and my parachute in the cockpit, I had removed the cockpit canopy for the first flight. I was squeezed in so tightly that Don Reece and Roger Don Rae had to buckle me in my seat.

Roger had flown *The Firecracker* before and he was at the field this morning to tell me what to do. He had not yet given me a word of instruction, and finally I turned to him and said, "Roger, I'm ready to go and you haven't told me a single thing."

He bent down so I could hear him over the roar of the engine. "Look," he said. "As you apply power to the engine the nose will want to go down. Hold the nose up by pulling the stick back. The plane will swing to the left. Move the rudder and make the necessary adjustment to keep it straight and hang on to your hat. That is all I know."

That is all he said. I pushed the throttle forward and the plane leaped ahead. It was like being tied to a rocket. This made the Pobjoy feel like a tired old horse. In four or five seconds I had left the ground and was streaking upward. The next time I looked at the airspeed indicator I was going over two hundred miles an hour. After half an hour of tests I landed, thrilled by the performance of this airplane and confident we had a winner. At once I telephoned Bill to tell him how well it flew, and he was so excited that words failed him.

We took the airplane to Oakland on May 24, where we assembled it and prepared to qualify. This was a big day in my life. I had never even qualified, much less flown in a big race before, and had never competed against famous pilots like Roscoe Turner and Earl Ortman, who were among the professional flyers participating in the Pacific International Air Races that year. Some of them knew me but had yet to see me perform, and I have no doubt there was considerable speculation as to what kind of bird was this Tony LeVier.

We were able to do a favor for Roscoe which paid off later for us at Cleveland. When he reached Oakland he found a bad gasoline leak in his plane and half the fuel was in the bottom of the fuselage. We happened to have a supply of the special rubber hose he needed to fix the leak, which we gave him, and through no fault of his own he missed winning the main event by a narrow margin.

There were three main races over a period of three days—the first two for planes in the 550-cubic-inch class and under, which were open to planes like mine, and the final event which was unlimited. I qualified on my first attempt and Roscoe qualified in his Turner-Laird Special. Art Chester was flying the *Jeep,* a midwing monopane with external bracing, and Steve Wittman was on hand with two planes, the D-12-powered *Bonzo* and the veteran *Chief Oshkosh* with a new Menasco engine. Gus Gotch was entered flying a new midwing monoplane with a good racing record, the *Folkerts Special.*

I knew from previous flights in *The Firecracker* that in order to get the landing gear up after take-off I had to climb out very steeply at a high angle and slow the plane up by pulling the power back. As my first race got under way I performed this maneuver, which slowed me up and permitted the entire field to get in front of me. But once my gear was up I immediately took off and began catching the pack.

I passed Steve Wittman, who was leading, but he put on a little more power and passed me. Then I put on a little more and passed him again. Finally I ran him out of power. He had no more to call on and I was out in front going away when his engine blew up. He was out over the water, but Steve was a good flyer and he got back to shore, where he landed in a potato field. His plane was a wreck but he escaped serious injury, and he raced again in *Bonzo* on the final day.

The second race was very much the same except for Steve. It was here that Gus Gotch ran into trouble out over No. 2 pylon in San Francisco Bay and actually went out of control and spun in. I also won this race easily, as the competition wasn't up to the speed potential of my airplane. *The Fire-cracker* was certainly living up to its name. With two victories under my belt, all my friends were pulling for me to win the main event and make it a clean sweep. I got one telegram reading, "Congratulations make it three straight we are all for you," and signed, "Boys Los Angeles Eastside Airport." Another said, "Dearest Tony love and best wishes for your success God bless you," and was signed "Mama."

Now, however, I was up against the big boys, such as Roscoe Turner, three-time winner of the Thompson Trophy Race, and Earl Ortman in a Keith Rider Special built for the London-Melbourne international air races. But the thing that bothered me most was the fact that I could not wear a parachute in the cramped cockpit of my airplane and still close the canopy over my head. When I sat on the 'chute there just wasn't room for both of us. Another problem was a gasoline leak behind the engine firewall that developed at the last moment. There was no time to fix it before the race, so I stuffed rags around it to soak up the leaking gasoline and said another prayer.

Bill and I had planned that I would hold a certain speed and allow Turner and Ortman to lead if they chose, up to the fifth lap of the eight-lap race, when I would make my spurt and catch them. Turner, Ortman and I all left the ground at the same time. I had to slow up to retract my gear as usual and the whole field got ahead of me. Then I took out after them and quickly passed everyone but Earl Ortman. I was holding my own against him when Turner went by me and we continued in this order through the fifth lap.

As I entered the sixth lap I opened up my engine for the first time and began gaining on the leaders so rapidly I knew that in another lap I would catch them. At that moment my oil pressure suddenly dropped to nearly zero. Faced with a quick decision to reduce power or go ahead and possibly damage the engine, I decided to take no chances and throttled back to my earlier power rating. I finished the race that way, winning third place.

After the total points were counted I had the highest score for the three-day meet and was awarded the trophy for champion pilot. This so encouraged Schoenfeldt to shoot higher that he immediately entered *The Firecracker* in the national air races. They were held at Cleveland again in 1938, and interest as usual centered about the Thompson, Greve and Bendix trophy races, the first two of which we planned to enter. Bernarr MacFadden was entered in the Bendix that year but cracked up before the race shooting landings, and Jacqueline Cochran won it in her Seversky low-wing monoplane, the only woman in the field of ten who started. Total prize money at Cleveland increased from $82,000 to over $102,000, and Schoenfeldt had visions of making a real killing. *The Firecracker* carried extra fuel for the Thompson race, which was longer than any we had flown previously, and our plane was nothing but a flying gas tank when we left for Cleveland.

We had also increased the engine power, and it blew sky-high on my first qualifying flight; only luck saved me from a bad accident. Inspection revealed that the No. 2 piston had a hole the size of a silver dollar blown through the head. The No. 2 cylinder was badly scored and required honing before it would be fit for use. There seemed no possibility of repairing it that afternoon and the deadline to qualify was the next morning.

It was only a few minutes before Roscoe Turner heard of our predicament. In return for our assistance at Oakland he offered the services of his entire crew to help fix our plane. While we dismantled the engine he took Bill and the cylinder in his Packard and drove madly across Cleveland to find a machine shop before closing time. After working all night on the engine it was ready the next morning, and I flew and qualified for the Greve trophy race a few minutes before the deadline.

As race time drew near on Sunday I became excited and very tense. An air race with a racehorse start is considered one of the great spectacles of competitive sport. Unlike other forms of racing that take place on the ground, air racing is in the third dimension and requires great alertness on the part of the pilots to avoid flying into one another.

We were lined up at the starting line—Art Chester in his new racer, the *Goon,* powered by the Menasco C6S Super-Buccaneer engine, the same one I was using; Joe Jacobson in Keith Rider's new creation, a sleek all-plywood Menasco racer called the *Eight Ball*; Earl Ortman in a Marcoux-Bromberg, the *Jackrabbit*; George Dory, a newcomer, in the

Bushey-McGrew Special, another Keith Rider racer called the *Bumblebee*; and Harry Crosby in a brand-new all-metal plane of his own design. Harry had crashed in a similar plane in the 1936 races and had been laid up for two years with a broken back. He designed this new plane while in a plaster cast in the hospital.

I was strapped in my seat with the engine running when the one-minute flag went up. Bill Schoenfeldt was on the field helping the crew hold the plane down. He tried to hide his excitement to ease my own tension, but it wasn't hard to see he was jumpy too. He shook my hand and called good luck over the roar of the Menasco.

As the seconds ticked away I had my eyes on the official starter with both flags high in the air. My heart was beating so hard I could feel it pounding above the vibration of my powerful engine. Then the flags came down, and my throttle was already forward before they touched the ground.

We took off north toward Lake Erie and the first scatter pylon about one mile away. As *The Firecracker* leaped ahead I caught a glimpse of Art Chester's cream-colored *Goon* to my left and slightly behind me. At the take-off halfway point I was still in front of him and gaining. The runway was smoother than I had expected, and I bounced only a couple of times before leaving the ground.

Now I pulled up sharply in the familiar maneuver to get my landing gear retracted; if my speed was over two hundred miles an hour the wheels would fail to close into their wells against the tremendous pressure of the air. I had to crank them up by hand in that airplane, and as I slowed up the other planes flashed past me, with Chester leading. I was momentarily dejected, but then I reminded myself that *The Firecracker* had enough speed to catch all of them if my engine would keep going.

The crank handle turned hard and stopped. With my gear finally up, I banked sharply to the left around the scatter pylon, a striped tower sticking one hundred feet into the air. Leveling out from my first turn I moved the throttle forward again and pointed the nose of my plane down the No. 1 straightaway.

The five other planes were bunched together about half a mile ahead, with Chester still in the lead. My Menasco engine was almost wide open and I caught and passed George Dory and Harry Crosby on the back stretch. Earl Ortman and Joe Jacobson were just beyond them.

I pulled up slightly at the No. 3 pylon and passed Ortman as I rolled into my turn in a near-vertical bank, swinging in with my eye on the pylon to cut it as closely as possible. My plane was still gathering speed as I passed Jacobson on the far side of the turn.

Only Chester was in front of me now, his engine spewing black smoke, and I knew he was "coaling" it, but I had the speed to catch him. No. 4 pylon was still half a mile ahead when I passed him going into my next turn. As I crossed the white starting line I took the No. 1 adhesive tape tab from my instrument panel and stuck it on my metal seat. One lap completed. 10 miles flown—19 laps and 190 miles still to go. This was my first long race—twice as long as Oakland. Could I stand the strain? Even Oakland was an effort in this airplane. It was not designed around a frame as big as mine, and I sat hunched over in the cockpit even without a parachute.

I went by Chester so fast I saw no need to burn up the engine unnecessarily and I throttled back from 3,350 to 3,000 rpm's. I was in the back stretch on the second lap when he passed me. Easing the throttle forward to 3,100 rpm's again, I gained just enough speed to stay with him; if I flew closer to the pylons on my turns I would be able to conserve the engine still more.

I turned inside of him at the next pylon, using elevators and ailerons, and passed Chester again. The laps flew by. At the ninth lap we had both lapped the field. As I entered my eleventh lap he passed me for the umpteenth time, when suddenly without warning my engine misfired.

I snapped to attention and scanned my instruments for signs of trouble—3,200 rpm's, oil pressure 45, oil temperature 205 degrees, fuel pressure 12 pounds. I wobbled my auxiliary fuel pump and the pressure surged to 14 pounds, but the engine was still rough and continued misfiring. I checked the cylinder head and base temperatures for each cylinder. The heads were cool at 495 degrees, the bases running much too hot at 230 to 250 degrees. But what could I do about it—no Bill to consult with up here. Just me and *The Firecracker*.

I looked at the stubby little wings as they quivered and shook from the rough air and engine vibration. There was no other choice—I had to reduce power and try to stay in the race by flying a tighter course. There was an oil scum forming on my windshield from the engine, making forward visibility poor, and it was going to be touchy business trying to tighten my turns around the pylons.

As I throttled back I held my own in the turns, but I lost a little on each straightaway. At the end of the fourteenth lap Chester had a substantial lead. My engine was getting rougher every minute, and looking forward over the long nose of the engine cowl I could see the entire assembly twist and shake from the violent power interruption. Would the engine mount stand up under this beating? It was well designed, but the side bracing was light. Grimly I kept on flying.

Chester was more than a mile in front of me, going into his turn around the No. 2 pylon, when I saw him suddenly pull up and veer sharply to the left inside the race course, then pass me going in the opposite direction about three-quarters of a mile away. Was he pulling out of the race? As I followed him into the turn I looked back and saw him get back on course. He must have cut a pylon and had to go back and try it again.

With this lucky break I now enjoyed a comfortable lead, and I eased the throttle back still more to reduce power and save my engine. It was still rough but it didn't have to work quite so hard. Now I devoted all my attention to my course from one pylon to the next—flying each straightaway just right, turning smoothly into the pylon and then tightening my turn, and after passing the pylon picking up the next landmark as I eased out of the turn. There was a turn every thirty seconds at the speed I was flying, and each one had a slightly different problem because of a changing wind blowing across the race course.

After each turn I looked left to check Chester's position.

He closed the gap steadily until at last I could not see him and I knew he must be very near. I eased the throttle forward again to 3,200 rpm's and the engine roughened noticeably. I was in the nineteenth lap, coming up on the No. 4 straight-away, when I sensed Art's nearness, and as I banked into the home pylon I saw him flash past me.

One lap to go—two minutes to fly—less than ten miles and it would all be over. A sudden urge to win came over me, and I shoved the throttle forward with such force that the engine choked and stuttered for a moment. Then it let out a roar never before equaled. I felt a tremendous surge forward and I knew it was now or never.

My windshield was so smeared with oil I was unable to see through it. I was peeking through a small hole on the left side of the canopy, not daring to start my turns until the pylons came in view. Chester was nowhere to be seen as I rounded the No. 2 pylon. Then I eased into the No. 3 marker and caught a fleeting glimpse of his plane as I crossed his path and turned inside of him. He went wide around the turn and I knew I would win if my engine would stay in the airplane.

Now I was around the last pylon and on the home straight-away. As I roared over the finish line I saw the checkered flag waving for me. I had a wonderful feeling of elation and relief, glad to be the winner, but at the same time happy the race was over. I pulled up into a victory zoom in front of the grandstand, then retarded the throttle and eased the power off my engine.

Circling around the field several minutes to slow up and cool off, the engine got smoother, and I lowered my landing gear and wing flaps to enter the landing pattern and come in. I was ready to come down. My back felt like a pretzel and I was exhausted by the events of the last half hour. I came over the fence a little too fast, going about 110 miles an hour, and slipped off a little speed but not enough.

The Firecracker settled to the ground in a nice three-point landing, but as it began to roll it hit rough ground. It lurched and pitched completely out of control, first right and then left, and I heard the sound of metal ripping and tearing and wood splintering as the wings broke open. In front of the grandstand the landing gear collapsed and the overwrought little plane crashed into the ground and came to a grinding halt.

Bill rushed up to help me out of the cockpit—I have never seen a happier guy in my life. He told me I beat Chester by four seconds in the most thrilling race ever staged at Cleveland. Roscoe Turner couldn't have been more pleased if he had owned the airplane. *The Firecracker* was in bad shape—much too bad to fly the next day in the Thompson Trophy Race, but no one seemed to mind.

I had set a new record of 250 miles an hour and won $12,000, of which I got 30 per cent. Schoenfeldt was delighted with our victory and quite satisfied to rest on his laurels. It was disappointing to miss the Thompson race, but he said we would come back the next year, which we did. But that is another story.

7

The Thompson
Trophy Race

While fame is sweet, I realized that life goes on, and the high spots are few and far between. Perhaps it is better that way. Air racing was a thrill and it was great to be a winner, but these thrills come only two or three times a year; in the meantime there was work to be done. The purse from Cleveland was money in the bank and took the urgency out of my other jobs, but I still had to make a living. So I returned to Los Angeles and went back to teaching and flying charter trips.

Up to this time I had been handicapped in commercial flying by lack of an instrument rating. I had never scraped together enough money for instrument training, yet without it I could not become an airline pilot. I knew enough to realize that racing could never be a full-time job, and anyway I wanted to fly for an airline. Now that I had a little money in the bank I decided this was the time to learn instrument flying.

The vital importance of this training was brought home to me in a local flight one day from Mines Field in Los Angeles to the Alhambra airport in the San Gabriel Valley. There was a layer of fog covering the entire area with a ceiling of three or four hundred feet. I took off anyway on the chance that the fog would be breaking up inland, and assuming there would be plenty of holes along the way to come back down if I wanted to, I decided to climb up on top of the overcast for the short flight.

When I broke through on top, however, I was surprised to find another cloud layer above me. I had planned to navigate by the mountains and hills sticking up through the fog, but now they were hidden from my view, and I was confronted with the problem of guessing at the right direction to fly. The ground below was completely obscured, and as I was flying without instruments there was no way to steer a course except by the reflected rays of the sun filtering down through the upper cloud layer.

After fifteen minutes of this kind of flying I became extremely alarmed. The glare of sun reflecting from the intense white fog beneath me was rapidly becoming unbearable and I knew I could not stand it much longer. There was nothing to do but go down.

I did not dare turn north, for in that direction lay the mountains. Nor could I continue east any further, for I knew by this time that I must have passed over Vail Field and the Whittier hills lay ahead. My only choice was to turn south toward Long Beach and the ocean, hoping to make contact with the ground before my fuel ran out.

I had no navigation instruments whatsoever, having removed even the compass for repairs. Guessing at my direction, I headed in what I thought was a southerly direction away from the highlands and toward the sea, at the same time throttling back and starting to descend. As the fog closed around me I had that terrible feeling of being completely lost. I dropped lower and the light grew less, until I reached a point beyond which I dared not go.

Suddenly the fog darkened beneath me and I knew the ground must be terribly near. Should I continue on? Would I strike something? Then all at once I broke into the clear about one hundred feet above an orange grove and was flying contact with the ground once more. A minute longer and I would have let down over Santa Fe Springs, an oil field with derricks well over one hundred feet high reaching up into the fog where I had been blindly flying. I knew I couldn't keep pulling boners like that and stay healthy.

In January I enrolled in the instrument school at California Flyers in Los Angeles under the excellent tutelage of Robert Buss, who later became a captain for Western Air Express (now Western Air Lines) and today is in charge of their ground school. It was expensive but I completed most of the course. It seemed to me that pilots should be able to learn instrument flying without spending all that money. Considering myself qualified by this time to teach the subject, I decided to open an instrument school of my own along the lines of the old E-Z Flying School, and depend on low rates to attract students in large numbers.

Don Reece, my first flying school partner, came in with me again. Working out of the old Monarch airport in East Los Angeles, we bought a side-by-side Piper Cub coupé, fitted it with dual instruments and a home-made radio for student instruction and opened for business. Because our prices were low the school caught on at once. Where other schools were charging at least $20 an hour for instrument instruction, we were using a small airplane we had modified ourselves, and the low operating cost enabled us to give lessons for $8 an hour. The Cub was slow but this made it better for student instruction, as it gave the student more appreciation of the wind drift required to fly a radio beam. Although I still didn't have my own instrument rating, in the process of teaching others I became extremely proficient myself.

That summer I took another crack at air racing with Bill Schoenfeldt and *The Firecracker*, this time concentrating exclusively on the national air races. With a brand-new wing and a completely overhauled engine, the airplane was in excellent condition again, and when I took it up for its first test flight at Long Beach airport it ran like a clock. In September we were back in Cleveland for another gamble with fame and fortune.

War broke out in Europe that weekend, and these were destined to be the last national air races for seven years. It may well be that they would have ended permanently if the war had not occurred at that time. The cost of building the high-performance airplanes that were beginning to dominate air racing was reaching the point where few private individuals could afford it. In 1946, when the races were resumed, cheap war-surplus planes like the P-38 I got for $1,250 brought racing costs back down to the place where the pilots could afford it.

This year Schoenfeldt and I were shooting for two races, the Greve and the Thompson, with combined first-prize money totaling almost $30,000. The Greve came first and I found myself matched against a field of four other contestants, one of whom failed to start. That left Art Chester in the *Goon,* a sleek, midwing monoplane powered by the popular Menasco engine; Harry Crosby in a low-wing monoplane of his own design, the CR-4; and Lee Williams in a Brown B-2 racer named *Miss Los Angeles.*

I drew the pole position with Williams on my right. He pulled ahead as we started down the runway and cut in front of me, forcing me to swing hard left to avoid a crash. This put me in very rough ground in front of the grandstand, and I nearly cracked up before I could get airborne. He was in the air too and headed straight for the No. 2 scatter pylon, apparently mistaking it for the first one; I was following close behind him, unable by this time to maneuver and get back on course.

His racer was obviously tail-heavy from too much gasoline, and as he whipped into his first turn at the pylon his plane stalled out and fell out of control, tumbling end over end into the ground. I was right above him when it happened, and as I turned in a near-vertical bank around the pylon I saw him falling almost straight down.

I was saddened by his death but now I had a job on my hands, having missed the No. 1 scatter pylon and being a mile off course. I banked steeply to the left and swung around hard to retrace my path. As I did so I caught a glimpse of Chester and Crosby flashing by on course, at least two miles out in front.

By now I was safely around both scatter pylons, and I crossed the starting line with the throttle wide open. I had to catch Chester, who I knew was pushing the *Goon* to the limit.

I was confident *The Firecracker* had a lot more speed, but a two-mile lead was a lot to overcome.

Finishing my first lap down the home straightaway, with the No. 4 pylon ahead, my engine was laboring too hard, and suddenly I remembered that my landing gear was still partly extended, creating extra drag on the airplane. I eased the throttle back and pulled up in a steep climb. A last tug on the hand crank and I was satisfied the gear was fully retracted. Now I opened the throttle wide again and dropped the nose of the plane in a shallow dive.

I could tell by the smoothness of the plane and the easy way the engine was running that the gear was up and I was really traveling. Ahead of me I could see Crosby and Chester well in the lead. I caught Crosby on the back straightaway, his landing gear still down, and was coming up fast on Chester. As the fourth and fifth laps spun by I throttled back slightly to 3,200 rpm's. Chester was only a few hundred yards in front now and I was fast closing the gap.

I passed him on the No. 1 straightaway crossing Rocky River, going by him very fast, and I throttled back still further; no need to make the engine work harder than necessary. My lead increased as the eighth and ninth laps went by. Automatically I checked my instruments but everything looked all right. Then on the home straightaway in the tenth lap my engine misfired sharply twice in succession.

Instinctively I pulled the throttle back and made another instrument check. The fuel valve and mixture control checked okay. What could it be? Should I continue the race or play it safe and land? The engine was getting rougher every second and my speed had dropped off sharply; if I stayed in the race I would probably come in last anyway.

I didn't really think the engine would last five more laps, and if it quit on the back stretch I would never make the airport. I saw visions of a crash landing in some small field. Others had done it but still I didn't want to take the chance. Better to land now and find the trouble while the engine was still running, and fix it for the Thompson Trophy Race if we could.

With my mind made up, I pulled out of the race going into

the eleventh lap and landed. As my little plane rolled to a stop I looked up and saw Chester and then Crosby flash by. Crosby was flagged down two laps later by landing gear trouble, and racing against time, Chester went ahead and set a new record for the Greve of 263 miles an hour. It just wasn't my day to fly.

Back in the hangar, an engine check failed to disclose anything wrong, but I was close to the situation and I knew there was trouble somewhere. Steve Wittman, against whom I flew in the Thompson race the next day, gave us our clue. Steve had experienced the same kind of trouble once before, and it came from the high-tension coils in the magnetos breaking down under the intense engine heat. Sure enough, this was our trouble, and with new coils and cooling ducts the engine was ready again the next morning.

There were six other starters in the Thompson Trophy Race, including Roscoe Turner, shooting for his third win; Steve Wittman in the familiar *Bonzo*; Earl Ortman flying his low-wing Marcoux-Bromberg with a Pratt & Whitney Twin Wasp Jr. engine; and Harry Crosby and Art Chester in the same planes they had flown the day before. It was my first Thompson race, and I was determined to make a good showing or I wouldn't dare be seen around Cleveland again.

We were lined up ready to go, strapped in our seats with our engines running, as the final minutes slipped away. Now the white one-minute flag came up and the engines began revving up still faster as the seconds ticked by. My propeller was spinning, and without wheel brakes on the plane it took three men to hold me at the starting line—Bill Schoenfeldt on the left wing tip with Young McClure on the right and Roy Grubaugh holding the tail. I was tense and excited and my stomach seemed to be turning over, as it had all afternoon.

The starting flags came down in front of me with my throttle almost wide open. The boys released their grasp on the plane and it leaped ahead. But I had extra gas behind my seat for the 300-mile race and almost at once I could feel the difference in my acceleration. *The Firecracker* was dangerously tail-heavy. This was what had killed Lee Williams and I was in the same boat.

My center of gravity was way behind the rear limit, but my reputation was at stake in this race and I was determined to keep going. I glanced to my left ad saw Roscoe Turner even with me neck-and-neck as we sped down the runway. My airspeed indicator showed eighty miles an hour. The stick was jammed all the way forward against the gas tank in front of me but the tail of my plane was still dragging on the ground.

As I hit a rough spot in the field the front end of the plane bounced into the air and then settled heavily back again, lurching from side to side. I was really worried now. At ninety-five mph the wheels skipped a couple of times and the nose rose in the air but the tail was still dragging. It was too late to cut the engine, as I would crash into the crowd at the end of the runway. I had to stay with the plane.

At the very last moment the tail came up and I left the ground in a dangerously nose-high attitude, with the stick all the way forward. As the plane climbed steeply I began cranking up the landing gear—this time I wasn't going to forget. The air was very rough and the plane pitched crazily, but there was nothing I could do about it except try to fly it; if the engine quit I was a goner. Only brute power and a good airplane could pull me through such a condition of unbalance.

At five hundred feet I eased the stick back slightly; I had a semblance of control but I had to be extremely careful, for if I overcontrolled the plane would stall out and that would be the end. The scatter pylon was off to my left and I thought my gear was up. At about one thousand feet I finally leveled off and started my turn into the race course.

Looking left I could see a number of planes off in the distance, and I wondered how I could ever hope to catch them. As I rolled gently into the turn I had to push the stick forward to maintain control instead of pulling it back. What chance did I have to win a race in a plane that could barely make a turn without running out of control? I thought of Lee Williams again and wondered if he suspected what was wrong; probably not until it snapped on him, and then it was too late.

Now I dropped my nose a little to gain speed, at the same time easing the throttle back a bit; it was wide open before I

Schoenfeldt "Firecracker"

started my turn and I was so busy I forgot to retard it. Then I switched my fuel valve to the rear tank—I had to get that tank empty if I ever expected to win this race. My turns were still high and wide until I could burn off some gas.

Looking for the other planes again, I saw two of them clear across the course on the home straightaway. As I came around the No. 4 pylon my tail began to lighten and I readjusted my stabilizer for a more normal trim. The plane leveled off and the cg moved slowly forward, and I began tightening my turns a little more at each pylon. *The Firecracker* was really rolling. The engine was running beautifully and I had it nearly wide open. One by one I began passing the field, until by the end of the fifth lap only Roscoe Turner was still in front of me. The engine was throwing oil on my windshield now, making it hard for me to see out, and I was unable to find him.

Inside the cockpit my back felt as if it were going to break. I was wearing a parachute for the first time in this airplane, specially-designed to fit on my shoulders. The 'chute had jarred loose in the rough air and was pressing down on my neck, and every time I hit a bump the shock went right through me.

I checked off the laps on my counter each time I passed the grandstand, and eight laps had passed and still I could not see Turner. Then streaking down the No. 1 straightaway in the ninth lap I got a glimpse of a silver plane flash past my left wing, and rolimg my plane slightly to see better I knew it was Turner. He had lapped me! Even though I knew it was impossible I immediately set out to catch him.

Again I eased the throttle forward until it was almost wide open. My manifold pressure was 65 inches of mercury and the engine was turning 3,200 revolutions per minute. My airspeed indicator was jumping back and forth around 310 miles an hour. The engine never ran so well—oil pressure 50 pounds and oil temperature 95 degrees. But still I knew there was no hope of beating Turner and I felt like quitting. Only plain stubbornness kept me going. Bill wanted the Thompson trophy pretty bad; maybe Turner would slow up.

Finally I decided to hold my own and save my engine. I lapped Joe Mackey, flying Turner's old Wedell-Williams racer, and then I lapped Steve Wittman and Harry Crosby. I was glad to see Harry got his wheels up after two years. The race was almost over and I was just holding on.

In the twenty-seventh lap Turner passed me again—he was really pouring it on; a great guy and he deserved to win. He had more hard luck than anyone in the business except the real unlucky ones. As I entered the home straightaway on my last lap I saw the checkered flag and No. 70 on the finish line; that was mine. The race was over for me, and I didn't even bother to fly a safety lap—I was sure I hadn't cut any pylons anyway. I throttled back and circled the field to slow down and entered the landing pattern, careful not to get in the way of the other planes still in the race.

Now I was over the edge of the field—gear down, flaps down. I was still a little fast and I slipped off my excess speed. The engine was idling fast—should I cut the switch and run the risk of another crackup like the one last year? I decided I could make it. As I cut the switch the engine slowed up and I touched down before the propeller had stopped. *The Firecracker* bounced a few times, then settled down and rolled to a halt.

For a minute I just sat there, unable to move; I was sure my back was broken. Bill and Mac were the first ones to reach my plane and helped me get out. I could hardly stand up. They were telling me I won second place and asking me if I saw Turner when he caught up with me in the ninth lap. Caught up with me—good Lord, I thought he had lapped me! It was then I learned that I had held the lead for several laps without knowing it. Had I known it I believe I could have made more of a race out of it. Oh, well—that's racing!

Like so many other pilots, this was my last air race for the duration. Returning to Los Angeles, I resumed my work at the instrument flying school. By this time most of our students had daytime jobs and took their lessons in the early morning or evening, which left me a lot of free time. In this situation I called my old friend Claude Flagg, who now was working for the CAA at Douglas Aircraft Company in Santa Monica, to ask about a daytime job myself. He told me Douglas might be looking for pilots and suggested that I apply.

Claude arranged for me to see Jake Moxness, at that time the company's chief pilot. With war in Europe, I thought aircraft production would increase in this country and there might be a test pilot opening for me. Jake said no, they weren't much busier than they were before the war, but if I wanted to start as a mechanic I would have a chance to become familiar with Douglas airplanes, and when he needed more pilots he would get me a transfer to flying duties.

This sounded all right to me so I followed his suggestion, starting work that fall as a mechanic on the flight line. I guess it was the first real job I had ever had. After a few days I began to meet other pilots around me in overalls and I asked Rudy Birch, one of several I knew, how many pilots Douglas had on the payroll. He said about six hundred—most of them mechanics like myself hoping they could get a transfer to flying.

Since I was brand new, naturally I was at the bottom of the list, and with six hundred ahead of me my chances for promotion looked pretty remote. I finally came to the conclusion that my best chance to be a pilot was to stay in the flying business and not get sidetracked in other jobs. The thing I have found over the many years is to stick with what you want to do to the bitter end if you expect to get the rewards that every man must desire.

About that time a letter from my old friend Vernon Dorrell, with a job offer as co-pilot on Mid-Continent Airlines, ended my brief career at Santa Monica. Vernon was now vice president in charge of operations for this airline, which flew out of Kansas City through the Middle West. If I could get my instrument rating, which I still lacked, and pass the airline physical examination, I could at last realize my ambition to be an airline pilot.

The instrument license was no problem, because of my experience in teaching instrument flying, and I was probably better qualified for this examination than any I have ever taken. I expected my eyes to be a problem in the physical, but to my surprise my heart turned out to be the stumbling block. I failed to pass the Schneider test.

I had survived several years of rough living and some close calls in airplanes, and when the doctor told me I had a bad heart and shouldn't be flying I didn't know whether to laugh or cry. Thinking it over later, I came to the conclusion that I was all keyed up and so anxious to get this new job that my pulse beat faster than normal when I took the test. I went to another doctor and he passed me, but I made a mental note to relax when taking physical examinations in the future.

In March, 1940, Don Reece left Monarch Airport and leased a strip of land next to the old Vail field in Montebello. Here he established a new airport which later became known as Montebello airport and subsequently was taken over and operated by Edgar Bergen, the ventriloquist. I was helping Don drag the field for a runway when I got a telegram from Vernon Dorrell saying I had a job with Mid-Continent as a co-pilot.

I arrived in Kansas City on TWA, flying on a pass, and was checked out by R. L. Brown, the chief pilot, in a Lockheed Electra. This was a twin-engined, low-wing, all-metal monoplane that was the forerunner of the famous Hudson bomber in World War II. Brownie said I was deficient in several things but he liked my style of flying and he thought I would make a good airline pilot.

Although I spent only six months with Mid-Continent, they were probably among the most enjoyable of my flying career. The regularity and precise manner in which airline flying is conducted intrigued me. Some of the little things we got into, although slightly irregular, were interesting too. When we took delivery on a new and larger plane, the Lockheed Lodestar, I was checked out again by another pilot, Captain Harris. I was doing a series of stalls and fast recoveries for him, but I didn't recover quickly enough, I guess, and he asked me to speed it up a little. From the way the plane handled I felt sure I would wind up in a secondary stall and a snap roll, but I did what he told me. Sure enough, on my third stall the plane snapped over on its back. Captain Harris looked at me as we turned upside down and said, "Well, we will learn something about this airplane, won't we?"

I had dropped my early ideas of being a test pilot and was quite happy in my airline job when one day I again met Claude Flagg, who by now had transferred from Douglas to be CAA plant representative at the Cessna Aircraft Company in Wichita, Kansas. It seemed that General Motors research laboratories in Detroit were buying a Cessna Airmaster as a flying test bed for a new experimental aircraft engine and they might need a pilot to run the tests. I was only mildly interested, but I agreed to give it some thought. In the meantime my regular semiannual physical examination came due and to my surprise and concern I again got a bad report on my Schneider test.

It seemed to me that if this sort of thing went on I would be faced with the possibility of failing the test and losing my job every six months. After much deliberation I decided I shouldn't take that chance, so I handed in my resignation with great reluctance and applied for the job at General Motors, which by this time had opened up.

I started work the middle of August and made the second test flight with the new engine at the Cessna factory. It was a very peculiar design. Charles F. Kettering, head of the General Motors research laboratories, was in charge of the project and gave it much of his personal attention. He hoped to develop this engine as a power plant for guided missiles like the V-1 buzz bomb which the Germans used later in the war.

After a number of test flights at Wichita proved the engine was airworthy I flew to headquarters of General Motors in Detroit, where my job consisted of putting hours on the engine and collecting flight data during numerous tests. While working in Detroit I had the pleasure of meeting Avery Black again.

Since leaving Whittier Airways years before, Avery had held various positions and now was working as a ferry pilot for Lockheed Aircraft Corporation. Lockheed had a contract with the British government for a large number of Hudson bombers, and Avery's job was to take the new planes off the production line and fly them to Canada, which was legal at that time. They were delivered via Detroit city airport, which was my operating base, and this is where we met. Avery says I was sitting in the lobby of the Fort Shelby Hotel starving to death, but this must be wrong because I wasn't hungry for a change. I just looked hungry.

After work we adjourned to the Embassy Club downtown for a little party with the other ferry pilots and I asked Avery about Lockheed as a place to work. I knew the company, which had a reputation for building good airplanes, but I had never applied for a job there because I did not feel myself qualified. Now I had more experience, however, and as my General Motors job probably would end when the engine tests were completed, it looked like a chance to get back to California.

Next day we both returned to work and I didn't see Avery again until December. At that time I asked permission to fly the Cessna home for Christmas, mostly to spend the holidays with my family, but also to visit Lockheed and see about a job. As we were just putting time on the engine it didn't matter which way I flew, so my boss said okay. I took the opportunity to visit Burbank and renewed my acquaintance with Milo Burcham, who now was a Lockheed pilot too.

It was only a couple of months before Avery sent me an application blank and wrote that I practically had a job waiting for me if I could get to Burbank. Nothing was definite, but I was so anxious to get back home I gave notice anyway and left General Motors two weeks later. When I reached Burbank the first man I saw was Marshall Headle, Lockheed's chief pilot. Avery and Milo must have given me quite a buildup, because he hired me. Two weeks later I began work as a ferry pilot at Lockheed. It was April 25, 1941, and I have been there ever since.

Looking back to my early years of flying, it is easy to see that 1941 was a turning point, not only for me but for aviation. The old planes I had known and worked with were changing, and some of them were already gone. Airplanes would never be the same again.

Test flying in particular has come into its own in just the past ten or fifteen years. Looking back, I can see how the art of designing and flying airplanes went hand in hand. As planes became faster we learned more about them, and today our vast amount of knowledge about flying is probably in direct proportion to the speed of the airplane.

It wasn't until about 1925 that the first real commercial planes were designed and built. One in particular that I remember as being outstanding for its day was the Travel-Air biplane, designed and built under the leadership of Walter Beech, who later founded the Beech Aircraft Corporation. It closely resembled the German-built Fokker of World War I, and for many years it was called on to play the part of this famous German airplane in motion pictures of that day.

The monoplane came into the aviation picture about 1925 too, with planes like Claude Ryan's M-1, similar to the plane Lindbergh flew across the Atlantic. The big manufacturers like Boeing and Douglas built mainly for military customers, but they also found time to bring out early commercial planes that were forerunners of their later successes in the airline field. Douglas planes were used to carry air mail on the first regular service between Los Angeles and Salt Lake City, and Boeing also built mail planes that replaced the British de

Havillands which pioneered air mail service in the United States.

Curtiss and Packard were the big aircraft engine manufacturers until the Wright company entered the field with the air-cooled radial engine that started the trend away from liquid-cooled power plants. Pratt & Whitney soon came on the market with the Wasp, another fine air-cooled engine. Lindbergh's flight to Paris in 1927 really put the radial engine in business. It had the advantages of simple design and easy maintenance, and by 1941 it was firmly established as the leader among airplane power plants. World War II, which brought so many other changes in flying, only served to confirm that fact, until a new and revolutionary power plant, the jet engine, came along to change the airplane itself.

8

Test Pilot

Two California brothers, Allan and Malcolm Loughead (pronounced Lockheed), built their first airplane in 1912, less than ten years after the Wright brothers flew. Allan designed it without prevous training or experience. It turned out to be a practical, efficient biplane amphibian that made money, and it was followed by a distinguished line of successful airplanes that proved it was no fluke. They included the Model FB-1 seaplane, the largest in the world at that time, which was launched in 1916 and sold to the U. S. Navy; the S-1 sports biplane in 1919, the lightest, most economical private plane of its day; and the brilliant Vega, in 1927, a high-wing, streamlined monoplane that made many of the nation's great pilots famous and set thirty-four world records before it passed into history.

Sir George Hubert Wilkins and his pilot, Carl Ben Eielson, proved its greatness when they made the first flight over the North Pole in the No. 2 Vega on April 15, 1928. They picked up their plane at the new Lockheed factory in Burbank that month and flew to Point Barrow, Alaska, where it was fitted with skis. Watched by a few Eskimos, they took off from a snow-packed runway headed for Spitsbergen, Norway, twenty-two hundred miles away. Nearly a day later they landed at Green Harbor, Spitsbergen, having completed the first flight across the top of the world. Wilkins dispatched the following cable to the Lockheed company:

Lockheed Vega

"Twenty and one half hours flying time Vega monoplane handled load splendidly congratulations. Wilkins."

On December 31 the same year, in another Vega, Sir Hubert flew over the South Pole, making history again. He was the first man and the Vega the first airplane to fly over both poles. While mapping Antarctica from the air during that expedition he discovered a lofty new peak in Graham Land and named it "Mt. Lockheed" as an expression of the esteem in which he held his airplane.

These two flights established the Vega as a pilot's plane, and it proceeded to set new records almost every time it flew. Speed, altitude and distance marks were shattered in the next few years by famous flyers like Art Goebel, Frank Hawks, Roscoe Turner, Amelia Earhart, Wiley Post, Ruth Nichols and Jimmy Mattern. Wiley Post and Harold Gatty flew the immortal *Winnie Mae* around the world in eight days in 1931. Amelia Earhart became the first woman to fly her own plane across the Atlantic in 1932, the year that Mattern and Bennett Griffin flew a Vega nonstop from Newfoundland to Berlin. Wiley Post became the first man to make a solo flight around the world in 1933, winning a place for his Vega in the Smithsonian Institution.

Lockheed soon built bigger, faster planes in which more records were set. In the Sirius, a new low-wing monoplane equipped with water skis, Colonel and Mrs. Charles Lindbergh pioneered the Great Circle route from the United States to Tokyo in 1931, and two years later made their 29,000-mile survey flight from New York to Europe, coming home by way of Africa and South America. Their plane is now in the Museum of Natural History in New York City. Jimmy Doolittle flew to racing fame in another Sirius with an all-metal fuselage. In 1934 Sir Charles Kingsford-Smith and Captain P. C. Taylor made the first west-east crossing of the Pacific Ocean from Australia to California in a Lockheed Altair. In 1935 Wiley Post flew *Winnie Mae* to altitudes above thirty thousand feet to test his theory that planes could fly faster in the thin air of the sub-stratosphere. Proving his theory was

"Winnie Mae"

right, he flew from Burbank to Cleveland, Ohio in eight hours, averaging 253 miles an hour in a plane built for a top speed of 165.

In 1929 the Detroit Aircraft Corporation bought controlling interest in Lockheed and when Detroit Aircraft went into bankruptcy in 1931 it took Lockheed down with it. Carl B. Squier, now a Lockheed vice president and "the best-known airplane salesman in the world," was then general manager. He filed a separate receivership in Los Angeles and was named liquidating agent. However, instead of closing Lockheed down, he kept production going almost single-handed, even mortgaging his home in 1931 to meet the Christmas payroll. He mortgaged his automobile so many times he never knew when he would go out and find a deputy sheriff in it.

Squier knew that Lockheed planes had a future and he looked around until he found somebody with money to buy the company and keep it running. The man he found was Robert E. Gross, president and chairman of the board for the past twenty years, who also knew a good airplane when he saw one. Gross first heard about Lockheed when he ran across its Orion flying airline schedules between Los Angeles and San Francisco in an hour and a half—faster than today's airplanes. "I began to see that speed was important," Gross said later, "and when Lockheed folded I wondered how it would be to pick up the bricks."

Then only thirty-five years old, Gross was a Boston boy who played baseball at Harvard and learned investment banking with Lee Higginson and Co. in Boston after the first war. He left State Street in 1928 to found the Viking Flying Boat Company in New Haven, Connecticut, and "give the flying boat business a whirl." His first plane was delivered in October, 1929, and after that Gross said "people didn't want boats, they wanted collateral."

He came to San Francisco in 1931 and soon afterward flew to Burbank in an Orion to see the Lockheed factory, where he met Carl Squier. He liked what he saw, and with five associates, all under forty years old, bought the company for $40,000. It had eighty employees and its assets consisted principally of a ranch-house office, an unpaved flying field covered with tumbleweeds, and four partly-built airplanes.

Lloyd Stearman became president, with Cyril Chappelet, now a vice president, as secretary, and Gross as treasurer. Squier stayed on as sales manager. With Hall Hibbard, a Kansas boy with a knack for designing good airplanes, as chief engineer, the new management buckled down to the job of putting Lockheed back on its feet. Its first job was raising cash to meet an $800 payroll, Squier having reached his absolute borrowing limit.

After a short time Stearman dropped out and Gross took over as president. He drove a $200 second-hand Ford, and much of his time in the early days of the company found him touring the Los Angeles financial district in his Model T, selling Lockheed stock. Of those days he says "all we had was ourselves, the RFC and Mr. Brashears"—a reference to G. Brashears & Co., a small local investment firm which between 1933 and 1937 sold some $1,500,000 in Lockheed stock, mostly in the Los Angeles area.

Lockheed had only one company garage, and until Gross arrived Squier had the only car in it. Hibbard rode to work on a bicycle. A dog named Contact made his home in the office, where packages for Lockheed were delivered C.O.D. "or else." One girl and five dictionaries made up the foreign sales department. Marshall Headle, the company's test pilot, was also employment manager. There weren't many job applicants, so they really didn't need him, but he was on hand in case a good man came along.

Headle loved airplanes and baseball with an almost equal passion, and as the company's employees had their own ball team, most of his early, interviews with job seekers touched on their athletic qualifications. A good shortstop who could hit .300 (and operate a rivet gun too) was a good bet to land the first available opening.

The Orion was Lockheed's last wooden airplane, and the two-engined Electra, which flew in 1934, was its first all-metal plane. Like many of Gross's decisions, the change from wood to metal planes was arrived at in an informal, almost offhand way, although the success story of his management indicates that he seldom guessed wrong.

One mid-morning in the fall of 1932 found him in the coffee shop at the little Burbank airport, dunking a doughnut and watching the planes outside. They included both the single-engine Orion and a new twin-engine Boeing flown by United Air Lines, one of the first all-metal transport airplanes. Gross asked himself which plane he would prefer to fly in if he were a passenger. Having answered the question to his own satisfaction, he went back to the office and immediately put his staff to work designing a two-engined all-metal plane. The result was the Electra, which eventually was purchased by twenty-six foreign countries, developed into three other successful models, and put Lockheed in the black.

An Electra took Prime Minister Chamberlain of Great Britain to Munich in 1938. The same year Howard Hughes, the movie producer, set a round-the-world speed record of three days and nineteen hours in a Model 14. About the same time a British purchasing commission arrived in the United States looking for a new bomber for the war they felt was imminent. Lockheed invited them to Burbank, and in the ten short days before they arrived built a full-scale mockup of a bomber version of the Model 14 without designs or blueprints, using magazine illustrations as models for gun turrets and bomb bays.

When the mission reached Lockheed they liked the mockup but the plane still had to be sold to the British Air Ministry. A company sales team headed by Courtland S. Gross, Robert's younger brother and now executive vice president, Clarence L. "Kelly" Johnson, then chief research engineer, and Carl Squier went to London for a month and came home with a $25,000,000 order for 250 airplanes. It was the largest single order ever received from any government by any American aircraft manufacturer, including his own.

Up to this time the company had built only 290 planes in all six years under the new management, and had never built a combat plane. It had only 2,000 employees and 240,000 square feet of factory floor space. Nothing daunted, however, the youthful management set to work with characteristic vigor to meet the deadline, which called for all 250 planes to be delivered by the end of 1939.

To speed up production, the new Hudson bombers were built with standard airline windows. Someone said the plane was designed so the crew could have tea in flight, but as a matter of fact the Air Ministry felt the windows would be especially useful in a reconnaissance and patrol plane. Hudsons were the first American-built planes in action in World War II and covered the evacuation of British forces from the beach at Dunkirk in 1940.

When Congress passed the Neutrality Act which forbid U. S. citizens to deliver arms to the European belligerents, the British government became extremely concerned that the flow of Lockheed bombers would be cut off. Gross waved away their fears with characteristic aplomb and began looking for an airport. He found what he was after near Pembina, North Dakota, an air strip lying jointly in the United States and Canada, and he bought it. Until provisions of the Neutrality Act were eased, Lockheed pilots flew their Hudsons to North

Lockheed "Hudson"

Dakota and mule teams pulled the planes up to the international boundary, where they sort of rolled across the border into Canada.

The rapidly-expanding Lockheed factory in Burbank was already bursting at the seams in 1939 when the U. S. Army ordered the new P-38 fighter plane, and more floor space became imperative. It was soon found down the road in a whiskey distillery. Over lunch one day Gross bought the plant for $20,000, and early P-38's were built in the former 3-G Distillery.

The first Hudson order for the British was completed ahead of schedule and was followed by additional orders for this airplane from both Britain and the U. S. armed forces. The personal plane of King George VI of Great Britain was a Hudson known as the *Royal Chariot*. In 1941 the British came to Lockheed again with a large order for a bigger bomber called the Ventura, a military version of the company's last prewar transport plane, the Lodestar, which was a larger version of the model 14. By the time the United States entered the war Lockheed employed fifty-three thousand persons and was the nation's largest aircraft manufacturer.

Its peak employment during the war was over ninety thousand. At peak production 30 per cent of its airplanes were built outdoors because of the shortage of floor space, with employees working in raincoats in bad weather. Lockheed built twenty thousand airplanes in World War II, including three thousand Hudsons, five thousand Venturas and B-17's, and ten thousand P-38's.

This was the company where I really began my flying career. However, I was there some time before I knew much about it; all I was interested in was flying airplanes. Of course, there are many kinds of test flying, and because of my youth and inexperience I had to start at the bottom and work up.

Like most aircraft manufacturers, Lockheed had a production flight test department to fly the planes it built. Marshall Headle, who hired me, ran the department and was the company's chief pilot. His staff of production pilots tested each new plane as it came out of the factory to check its performance before it was turned over to the customer. In addition, Lockheed was building bombers for Britain, and Headle had a special group of ferry pilots who flew these planes to Canada and delivered them to the Royal Air Force.

Unlike other manufacturers at that time, however, Lockheed also had a flight test section in the engineering department, which specialized in testing new airplanes before they went into production. Rudy Thoren, who is head of this outfit and my boss, set it up as a one-man office in 1938. I began work in production flying and spent a year in that department before I became an engineering test pilot.

Milo Burcham joined Lockheed in 1938, and I often ran across him flying the Hudson at Mines Field back in those years. When I came to Lockheed he was doing experimental flying for Rudy Thoren, although he was still classed as a production pilot. The engineering department required a lot of test flying and senior pilots like Milo got this assignment. In addition, he was world-famous as an acrobatic pilot, which helped him get an early crack at the P-38.

Many years before as a boy wandering in the Whittier foothills, I had seen airplanes flying overhead and wished some day I would be a pilot too. Later on, as I grew older and actually started to fly, I thought it would be thrilling to be a race pilot, and then a transport pilot on an airline. And oftentimes, after reading the stories of the test pilots of the 1930's, I thought this too would be a great and interesting profession. Now I was at the door and was entering into a new life.

I arrived at the Lockheed pilot house in Burbank on May 2, 1941, to start work. After paying my respects to some old friends like Nick Nicholson and Kendall Benedict, whom I had not seen for a number of years, I was escorted into "Pop" Headle's office. Here was a truly great man in the flying business. He was quiet and soft-spoken, but when he spoke it was with authority and wisdom, and everyone respected Marshall Headle.

He introduced me to his two assistant chief pilots, Elmer McLeod and Curry Saunders, who were in charge of checking out new pilots like myself, and within an hour I was assigned to a Lockheed Lodestar for my initial check flight. Joe Towle, later Lockheed's chief pilot and now our director of flying, was my first check pilot.

In those days Lockheed had a system for checking out pilots whereby a new candidate would be assigned to one pilot for his transition work, and after passing that check he would be turned over to a second pilot. If he passed his second check he would then make a final check flight with "Pop" Headle, who personally approved the flying of all new pilots.

I worked about an hour and a half with Joe and he passed me on to Harry Downs, another check pilot. Harry took me up in a Hudson bomber for my second check flight, together with Tom Brown, now a pilot for Trans World Airlines, and Allan Russell, who later became the private pilot for William Randolph Hearst.

The Hudson was a twin-engine, all-metal monoplane, with the typical Lockheed twin tail. Instead of passenger seats it had crew stations and fuel tanks in the cabin, with a bomb bay in the floor and a gun turret in the rear, in addition to nose guns. It cruised around 250 miles an hour, which was excellent performance for that time, and was probably the fastest bomber of its day. It also had good range, and with extra fuel tanks the RAF flew Hudsons from Canada to England throughout the war.

The Hudson was similar to the Lodestar, except for a shorter tail, which many pilots thought made it harder to land and take off. While I was working in Detroit I often noticed that pilots ferrying this plane came in with what appeared to be excess speed, and instead of rounding out and landing on all three wheels it seemed they shoved the stick forward in order to get the front wheels on the ground first. After I went to Burbank they elaborated on their landing problems for my benefit, and when it came my turn to land on this particular flight I pushed the nose down so hard we bounced back into the air.

"What's the matter?" Harry yelled. "Are you trying to crack us up?" After I managed to quiet the Hudson down he suggested I try landing it like any other airplane. I told him this was good news to me, and from then on I got along fine. Flying Hudsons later, however, I noticed that you could usually bounce one fairly easily if you weren't careful; but this only served to jack you up and get you back on the ball.

After about an hour's transition time from Harry I made a check flight with Elmer McLeod in a Lodestar. Apparently I didn't show him much, as he turned me down, saying I couldn't keep the airplane straight on takeoff. I went back to Joe Towle for half an hour, who got me straightened out and then sent me up with "Pop" Headle. I have never in my life flown with a more pleasant individual. He seemed to sense the right thing to do at the right time to put a pilot at ease. I didn't come in with the rudder quick enough and hard enough when he cut one engine, but a word from him was all I needed to correct this trouble. As I look back now I see that many pilots who have had trouble with an engine failure on a multi-engine aircraft could have used some advice from Pop Headle.

When we landed he told me I could stay at Lockheed and assigned me to ferry flights on the Hudson. My first trip was May 13 from Burbank to our Nashville, Tennessee, modification center, and I will never forget the wonderful feeling of success I had when I got my orders. I spent a month down there ferrying Hudsons on final delivery to Montreal.

When I returned to Burbank the Army took over ferry flying from the aircraft manufacturers and I was transferred to production flying. After taking the Hudsons up and checking their performance we delivered them to the Air Corps' new Ferry Command base at Long Beach municipal airport. It was on one of these flights that I nearly lost my job, and I had no one to blame but myself.

I had a crew of three on board and we were doing the usual stall tests prior to landing. Overwhelmed with a sudden urge, I asked if there was any objection to my spinning the airplane. Not hearing any objections I assumed everyone was agreeable and put the airplane into a spin to the right, recovering after a couple of turns. Although I was sure the Hudson would spin very well, it was a foolish thing to do, and I was reprimanded the next morning for taking a chance with other people on board. However, I had the satisfaction of knowing the Hudson could spin and recover, and reports to the contrary were untrue.

Despite its size, it was a very maneuverable airplane, and it proved on many occasions to be very well built. One time a German Messerschmitt jumped a British Hudson over the English Channel, and going into a steep dive to get away the Hudson pulled out just over the water, while the Messerschmitt failed to recover from the dive and dove in. Back at base inspection showed the bomber's wings so badly bent from the pullout the airplane had to be junked. Through many occasions such as this the Hudson got the name "Old Boomerang," because it always came back.

We were now flying six and seven days a week, and on Sunday, December 7, I reported for work as usual, making a production test flight in a Hudson bomber. It was a morning flight, and I had landed the airplane and was driving home when I heard a bulletin on my car radio announcing the Japanese raid on Pearl Harbor. The office was on the phone when I got home, requesting me to return immediately and stand by to evacuate aircraft.

The day passed without evacuation orders from the Army, and late Sunday night I went home again. Monday passed the same way; the weather was bad and there was no flying of any kind. Tuesday we went home once more without flying, but late in the afternoon I got a call to return to the field, where I received orders to fly a Hudson to Ontario, California, about forty miles away. The weather was still bad and contact flying was difficult, but I knew the route well so I took off with three other planes.

Setting a compass reading I knew would take me over Ontario, I flew east through clouds all the way, finally spotting the field through a hole in the overcast. The ceiling was about two hundred feet but I broke through and landed safely. We waited quite some time and rain began falling. It was almost dark when the other planes arrived, having flown over the entire San Gabriel Valley looking for the airport.

The emergency evacuation of aircraft ordered by the Army in southern California fell hardest on Lockheed, which was the largest producer of aircraft in that area. Our pilots took off for destinations in all directions, many of them just landing strips out in the desert. But despite more bad weather the evacuation went on. Because the situation was considered so critical we flew the planes without any of the customary preflight checks. They were serviced with gas, oil and hydraulic fluid, and if they showed fuel, oil and hydraulic pressure on the gauges we took off right from the production line. This was a real test of efficient manufacturing, for we evacuated literally hundreds of airplanes in this way and not one Hudson cracked up.

In January, 1942, I began flying production tests on the advanced version of the Hudson called the Ventura. It was similiar in design, with the same wing and twin tail, but was a bigger and heavier airplane with more powerful engines and improved performance. Ralph Virden conducted the engineering tests on the Ventura under the direction of Rudy Thoren, and after it went into production I was one of three pilots assigned to production testing.

We always started with a walk-around inspection on the ground to check the plane externally. After a cockpit check we warmed up the engines and took off, climbing to ten thousand feet, where we reduced power and checked the flight characteristics and performance of the plane. Then came speed runs to check out engine operation at various power settings. The radio equipment and other flight instruments were checked next, and on the way down we tried out the landing gear warning horn, usually at five thousand feet. The horn is very important on an airplane with retractable landing gear, and if a pilot forgot to lower his gear the horn would blast him in the ears to warn him. Many pilots who have accidentally landed with gear up said later if it had not been for that damned horn blowing in their ears they could have heard the control tower on the radio calling to tell them their wheels weren't down.

We had been flying the Ventura nearly a month when I ran into landing gear trouble. One day on a production test flight over the San Fernando Valley, I had just completed the warning horn test and was ready to return to the field, when my instruments indicated the landing gear was not fully extended, and on looking out the window we saw the right wheel was only partly down.

This was not too alarming, but after several unsuccessful attempts to get it all the way down we decided the gear system was out of order and called the factory for advice. As we lacked direct radio communication with our flight operations office, our message had to go through the airport control tower and operations had to come to the tower to communicate with us. We continued around the field waiting for instructions, and finally operations called us over the tower radio and told us to stand by while Pat McCarthy and Rudy Thoren flew alongside in a Lodestar to look the situation over.

I throttled the engines down to lowest possible power in order to conserve fuel. The time was growing close to the proverbial belly landing that I already had in mind. My plan was to come in as slowly as possible under power until the fuselage touched the runway, then turn off the engines and skid to a stop. I asked permission to prepare for a belly landing but operations wanted to wait a little longer. It was due to this final delay that we crashed.

We were quite low with flaps partially extended to obtain the most efficient flying attitude for the low power. My fuselage tank was empty and I switched to my auxiliary tanks in the wings. However, in order to draw fuel from these tanks the cutoff valve from the fuselage tank had to be closed, and the crew member assigned to close it apparently failed to do so. The fuselage tank began feeding vapor and air to the engines, causing them to start cutting out, and I was unable to get fuel into them from the auxiliary tanks even though they were turned on.

I was flying due north, just east of the Burbank airport, in a position where I could have turned and made it. Realizing my predicament, I called the tower to stand by for an emergency landing, which meant clear the runways of aircraft and vehicles. My altitude was less than five hundred feet and my speed was down to about ninety miles an hour. The engines were coming in and going out in large surges of power, and I throttled back to prevent any uneven surge of power that would throw me into a stall.

As I started my left turn to the field I was suddenly aware of the engines letting out a mighty roar right and left, causing the airplane to almost spin off in one direction then the other. Looking back in the cockpit to see the reason, I discovered the flight mechanic with a throttle in each hand, pumping them back and forth. I said to hell with the throttles, get the flaps down, and I hit both throttles in the closed position. Again I gave my attention to my approach for the landing, but I was quickly aware that I had lost my chance ever to make the airport.

Now there was only a mass of buildings, high tension lines and revetments where I would surely crash, and I swung hard to the right to get away. As I turned back toward the hills north of the airport I spotted an open field, and I knew instinctively I could make it. Faced with an emergency of this kind, I have found my senses become extremely acute and my judgment is far more accurate than usual. In such a case I think the total skill of a person comes out to his command to aid him in saving the situation.

As I approached this patch of open ground I was nursing the airplane for all it was worth, realizing I had to clear the last row of houses ahead of me and trying to judge where I would touch down. As I crossed over the last house I pulled back hard on the stick to raise the nose for contact with the ground. It was then I saw, some hundred yards farther out in the field, pile after pile of wooden boxes and stacks of wood. It was too late now to try to turn aside. As we drew closer I saw a narrow road through the piles of lumber, going in my direction, and I aimed the plane at this tiny opening in these acres of boxes and touched down.

My main right wheel was still partly retracted and the right wing immediately hit the ground. As we struck the woodpile the wing was dragging and it started to pull the airplane around. The first pile sheared off the left wheel. With the left wing acting like a surfboard on rough water, we porpoised up and down over the stacks of wood, the left engine out in front as a battering ram. The plane was pitching like a boat running against a heavy sea. We went about one hundred yards like this, finally grinding to a halt turned almost completely around, and with the warning horn on the airplane blasting furiously in the sudden silence. I didn't notice it until we were out of the plane and a safe distance away. Then it annoyed me and I went back to the plane and shut it off. There was no fire, but on the chance that leaking fuel might become ignited I took all movable equipment and our tools out of the airplane. A few bruises were the extent of our injuries, but the plane was badly damaged and didn't fly again for another year.

In a few minutes we were surrounded by the entire pilot staff and many of our ground crew. Harry Downs and Swede Parker put me in a car and drove me to the local pub, sometimes referred to as the "Bucket of Blood." It is probably ill thought of that anyone would take a drink of whiskey at a time like this, but when the nerves have been taxed and you are keyed up to the very top, a letdown might leave you with apprehension and a thought as to what could have happened.

That is why Swede and Harry took me down and proceeded to give me what turned out to be three triple Scotch and sodas, although they said it was only double. After the time required to consume this amount of whiskey they took me back to flight operations and I was bouncing on my heels. Although I was only partly there, the boys said I sounded very funny, and apparently I described the entire incident to their gleeful satisfaction.

When the airplane was inspected we found the main actuating strut on the righthand gear had actually come apart inside and jammed. I could have flown forever and never got the wheel down. This cleared me of any responsibility for the accident, but I still felt it was a black mark on my flying record at Lockheed. Perhaps I thought the company would let me go. In any event, TWA came around looking for ferry pilots on the North Atlantic, and I signed up for an interview.

I talked with the TWA pilot who visited the factory taking applications, telling him the many things I had done in aviation, including the fact I had been a test pilot for General Motors. He said I must have a fine education, and with this I merely smiled, as much as to say your guess is as good as mine.

If Harry Downs had not happened to glance in the door as we were talking, it is quite possible I would be doing something else today. He nodded for me to step outside, and in the hall he took me by the arm. "Look, Tony, you're not on the list to leave," he said. "We are figuring on keeping you." Needless to say, that ended the interview so far as I was concerned.

In March, 1942, I was selected to be a check pilot. My first job was checking out a group of co-pilots who had been with the company some time and had acquired considerable experience, but had not yet been checked out as captains. They turned out to be excellent pilots. Dual controls had been eliminated from the Hudson by this time, so I gave them check time in a Lodestar.

I was still waiting for a chance to fly the P-38 Lightning, the fastest plane of its day. It was a midwing monoplane, with a center nacelle housing the cockpit, guns and radio equipment, and flanked by two engine nacelles followed to the rear with booms connected by the horizontal stabilizers. Milo Burcham did most of the experimental flying on this sleek, fast fighter, and when it went into production he was named to pick the pilots to do the production testing. Although it was a wonderful airplane and very easy to fly, it had very high performance, and Pop Headle felt that production flying should be assigned to men who liked to fly fast. I was that kind of a flyer, and was one of the fellows that Milo picked.

Much to my disappointment, this plan fell through. To prevent possible hard feelings among older pilots, we were assigned to the P-38 according to length of service with the company, and I was so far down the list I gave up hope of ever flying this airplane.

Then late one afternoon, with the pilot house deserted, a call came in for a production flight on a P-38. Johnny Myers, now a vice president and sales manager of Northrop Aircraft Company, and one of our test pilots at that time, walked in as I got the call and told me to go ahead. I was pretty rusty on

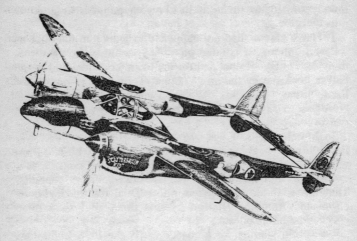

Lockheed P-38

the airplane, having long since given up hope of flying it and forgotten the cockpit procedures, but at his urging I made the flight.

I must admit I didn't feel at all at home in the airplane with which I later became so familiar. However, this ride broke the ice for me, and made it easier to fly again. I went home that night and brushed up on the P-38, and the many things I had previously learned about it came back to me. The next morning I was eager and got to work early. Being the first pilot at the office my name was at the top of the list for a P-38 production flight and I got the first plane that came off the line. It was a far different flight than the day before and this time I thoroughly enjoyed it.

All that spring I flew production tests on P-38's, Hudsons and Venturas, with Army acceptance tests now and then to change the routine, but my heart was always with the Lightning. This was the kind of plane I had always dreamed of flying. It was the world's first really high-performance, high-altitude tactical airplane, with a top speed over four hundred miles an hour and a service ceiling over forty thousand feet. I dreamed of specializing in this kind of airplane, and unknown to me, that day was close at hand.

Two tragic accidents about this time badly hurt the Lockheed flying organization and saddened everyone in the company.

The P-38 was now flying at altitudes where few men had ever been. Pressure and oxygen were the two great problems for human beings six and seven miles above the earth, and although we had an airplane now that could go that high, it was another matter for the pilot to stay there.

Without a pressurized cabin he was subject to the bends, a vapor lock in the bloodstream that caused excruciating pain and forced him to come down. Moreover, his oxygen equipment was still meager and rudimentary because the need for it had never existed previously. We were trying everything now that gave promise of being helpful, simulating high-altitude conditions in our pressure chamber and testing every device that made sense.

Marshall Headle was trying out one of these new devices, a breathing vest that was a forerunner of today's pressure suit. It was an effort to aid the pilot's natural breathing mechanism in the thin air of the stratosphere. He had the vest on in the chamber one morning when it got out of cycle with his own body needs and he began to pass out.

Recognizing he was in difficulty, he reached for the emergency breathing aid, but apparently shut it off instead of turning it on. We found him unconscious in the tank at very high altitude, and the only way to save his life was to release the dump valve and immediately drop him to sea level. The abrupt change in pressure caused a shock to his heart and nervous system from which he never recovered.

About the same time Ralph Virden was killed by compressibility in a dive test in a P-38. This was an Army demonstration, and at the end of his flight he was to come down in front of the hangar and put on a show. Suddenly we heard the terrible sound of an airplane in a steep dive, followed by a dull thud and then silence. We realized that an airplane had crashed, and the only plane it could be was a P-38. Who was flying a P-38? It wasn't long after that we found out Virden had made his last flight. Diving at high speed he apparently got into trouble in his pullout; the tail failed and came off and he was at too low an altitude to bail out and save his life. With him we lost our only experimental P-38, and vital tests had to wait until we could replace it.

Rudy Thoren was now chief flight test engineer, with Milo Burcham as chief engineering test pilot and Joe Towle as his assistant. The separation between engineering and production flying was complete, and as the wartime demand for newer and better planes increased the engineering workload grew constantly heavier. With Virden gone and Milo involved in new administrative duties, he and Joe looked around for help. On Rudy's recommendation Milo offered me the job and at once I accepted. Flight operations approved the transfer, and on July 1, 1942, I made my first P-38 flight as a Lockheed engineering test pilot, a job I've had ever since.

This was really test flying, the thing I wanted—flying new planes and planes that had never flown before. I guess Rudy hired me because he knew I liked acrobatics and speed flying. In addition, he says I have good co-ordination and calm nerves. I was able to handle emergencies. I didn't know anything about engineering, but I was eager to learn, and I kept trying till I got it. Most important, I loved to fly, and speed was only part of it. I liked to get away from the earth, and now I could go higher than ever.

9

P-38

From the day I entered the engineering department in July, 1942, I have specialized in experimental test flying. Beginning with the P-38 and on up through the jets I have devoted myself to the problems of new airplanes, many of them never encountered before. During this time I have done my share of flying in transports and bombers and other large airplanes, but fighters became my specialty. I have been only one of many pilots who did their work in fighters, at Lockheed and elsewhere, but any success I have had in flying was achieved in high-speed aircraft. I was just lucky to get the opportunity to do what I liked best.

Upon arriving in the engineering flight test section I found myself immediately thrown into an unremitting test program on the P-38 Lightning fighter plane. Although it was now in production and in service with the British and American air forces, it was so advanced and ahead of its time that it encountered situations which had never arisen previously.

Some of these problems, like high-altitude flight, were anticipated and could readily be overcome with things like cockpit pressurization and engine supercharging, both of which we pioneered on the P-38. But other problems like stability and control of the airplane at high speeds were completely unexpected and much harder to lick.

The problem of compressibility in particular, which had not been encountered previously because the P-38 was the first airplane capable of approaching the sonic barrier, required nearly two years to solve after our engineers found the source of the trouble. An airplane flying through air sets up pressure waves which influence its flight. As its speed increases the air flows faster around the thicker parts and thus accelerates unevenly around the plane. If the plane reaches high subsonic speeds the air flow becomes fast enough to form shock waves, which can cause shock stall. In the case of the P-38 they caused a considerable loss in wing lift in high-speed dives, which resulted in a tendency of the airplane to nose under and sometimes go out of control.

As a test pilot, I was just the means used to investigate problems like this, but the job was important because the airplane was too. The P-38 was one of the major weapons in the air war against Germany and Japan, and its success or failure had a direct bearing on the prosecution of the world-wide conflict. With a few minor exceptions, I spent the next two years testing this airplane, going on to other planes only when a faster and better fighter—the jet—came along.

The man who designed the P-38 was Clarence L. Johnson, at that time Lockheed's chief research engineer. "Kelly" Johnson, as we all call him, is a big Swede from Ishpeming, Michigan, who joined Lockheed more than twenty years ago. Like m , he was crazy about airplanes as a boy and they became his sole interest. Unlike myself, however, he stayed in school and got a college education; Kelly's interest was building airplanes, not flying them, and he studied aeronautical engineering at the University of Michigan, where he made straight A's and paid his expenses by tutoring in calculus.

Before he graduated in 1932 he had won two engineering scholarships and was elected to several honorary engineering societies. Jobs were scarce that year, and even Lockheed turned him down, so he went back to Ann Arbor and took his master's degree in aeronautics, specializing in boundary layer control and engine design. The next year he tried Lockheed again and made it.

Kelly designed the P-38 in 1937 in response to an Army Air Corps requirement for a new single-seat fighter plane. The P-38 won the Army's design competition and the first airplane flew in January, 1939. It was much faster than anything else flying, and, eager to set a new transcontinental speed record, the Army flew the prototype airplane to New York City before it was dry behind the ears. Coming in for a landing an engine failed and it fell short of the airport and cracked up, setting the development program back nearly two years.

Starting over again, Lockheed began engineering on the second prototype airplane in April, 1939, and it flew in September, 1940. Thirteen of this model were built. In the meantime work began on a third prototype airplane, incorporating structural and design changes learned from earlier models. Engineering began late in 1939, after war started in Europe, and the first airplane was delivered in July, 1941. Armed with a 20-mm cannon and machine guns, the P-38 was in production and operational when the United States entered the war in December.

Not until after it was rolling off the assembly lines and was in combat did we start running into many new problems, the most serious being compressibility. We encountered this phenomenon in high-speed dives in the P-38, which was the first airplane capable of approaching the speed of sound. It was like a giant phantom hand that seized the plane and sometimes shook it out of the pilot's control. Men and planes were being lost, and high-speed flight was stopped in its tracks until this problem could be licked.

Milo Burcham had already spent a lot of time in dive tests to find the answer when I joined him. In addition to going through the rigors of compressibility, we were working out several other problems such as more engine power, boosted controls and pressurized flight. On my first test flight my cockpit canopy came off in pullout from a high-speed dive. This was old stuff to me, and if it was a sample of experimental flying I felt that my new job was going to be quite interesting, which in fact it turned out to be.

When testing military aircraft it is not uncommon to press the engines continually to their maximum performance. As a matter of fact, practically all of our flying in those days was at maximum engine power. A test usually consisted of a flight at certain altitudes, generally thirty or thirty-five thousand feet in the case of the P-38, and the climb to altitude was always at maximum power. It was common to have an engine flare up at this extremely high power and start to detonate, a form of violent explosion in the cylinders that was extremely detrimental to the pistons, rods, and crankshaft. Often this detonation would occur so quickly and so severely that the engine would actually explode and tear itself apart.

These engine explosions also occurred in level flight. On a speed run at war emergency power one day at twenty-five thousand feet the engine started to detonate without warning, and before I could reduce power it blew up. After feathering the engine I returned to Burbank and landed. When the mechanics removed the bottom cowling, parts of the engine actually fell to the ground. Flailing connecting rods had cut the crankcase completely in two and the engine was hanging by the cylinder block. When this happened to an engine Jim White called it "jumping naked." It was actually just like that; it exploded and flew apart. As I look back it amazes me that in all the years of experimental flying we did on this airplane we never had any serious engine fires.

The P-38 was highly maneuverable and I quickly took the opportunity to get in a little acrobatic flying between test flights. It was common practice for our P-38 pilots to spend fifteen or twenty minutes in acrobatics or mock combat after the day's testing was completed. We usually had dogfights with each other, but often we engaged military pilots who were in the air and wanted to play. Milo Burcham was a famous acrobatic pilot in his own name and could put a show with a P-38 you would never forget. I wanted to follow in his footsteps and be like him, and I took every opportunity to improve my own acrobatics.

One such occasion arose when I was running P-38 gunnery tests at Muroc Dry Lake, later the Air Force test center in the California desert. For nearly a month I flew to Muroc daily to fire my guns, and on the way home I would practice acrobatics, particularly at low altitudes. Over the Mojave Desert in the vicinity of Lancaster and Palmdale I set up a small program of my own to acquaint myself with low-level aileron rolls, single-engine maneuvers and upside-down flying in this airplane.

I began by rolling it upside down at a safe altitude around five hundred feet and flying it inverted until I learned how to hold it in level flight in that position without losing altitude. Then I repeated this maneuver closer to the ground, finally doing it at fifty or seventy-five feet. When I had mastered inverted flying with two engines I turned one off and repeated the maneuver on a single engine. Pretty soon I was able to do my stunts practically on the deck.

While I enjoyed this kind of flying as a sport, my chief purpose was to become completely familiar with the airplane. I wanted to train myself in case I was called on to demonstrate it, and I felt it was important to be able to handle it under all flight conditions. After I considered myself fairly proficient I sometimes conducted my practice sessions in the vicinity of the Polaris Flying School at War Eagle Field, where John Nagel and Bob Downey, one of my students at the E-Z Flying School, were now instructors. Sure enough, an invitation to demonstrate acrobatics in the P-38 arrived in short order.

I asked Milo if he would object and he said no, anything like that I could do would be more than appreciated. Next I needed permission from the Air Corps plant representative at Lockheed, Colonel Clarence Shoop, who is now employed by the Hughes Aircraft Company, manufacturer of airborne radar. Colonel Shoop was profoundly interested in anything that would help aviation and the Air Corps, and when I presented my plan he endorsed it 100 per cent and assigned one of our flight-test airplanes to me for the demonstration.

I was extremely happy. This was a chance to get out and test myself a little bit and maybe sell the P-38 to the pilots; the air cadets at Polaris were ready for advanced training, and if they liked my demonstration it might encourage them to request assignment to P-38's. Many Army pilots had found the transition to P-38's difficult because it was a big airplane and had two engines, and I wanted to show the graduating class at Polaris that despite its size and high performance it was extremely easy to fly.

My demonstration might have ended in a crash had it not been for my good luck and the fact that the P-38 was a fine airplane. It had a reputation among many pilots for being treacherous on one engine, and when the students asked me to demonstrate a stall on one engine I agreed because it was a chance to prove this report was untrue. I had stalled the airplane a number of times on one engine, although I had never noticed how much altitude I lost before I regained flying speed, and if I stalled this time at one thousand feet I assumed that I would have ample altitude to recover. However, I was completely mistaken.

In order to get into a stall I had to reduce speed to eighty miles an hour and reduce power on my good engine; as I did this I immediately fell several hundred feet before I could get the nose down again. I then applied power to my good engine but I continued falling. There was only one thing left to do at that point, fly the plane toward the ground and continue to apply power, and hope to gain sufficient speed to resume level flight. About one hundred feet from the ground I extended my wing flaps, which gave the wings enough lift for me to pull the nose up and level off. This incident taught me to do my stunts at a safe altitude until I knew what would happen. When I landed I told the students frankly that I had made a mistake and stalled too low.

The P-38 had many fine qualities: unsurpassed altitude, speed and range; but we were constantly plagued by the problem of compressibility. Although our engineers were well aware of this condition, to fix it was another matter. After many experiments, including the use of counterweights on the elevators and raising the tail, Kelly Johnson and Ward Beman, his research assistant, found the answer in the Lockheed wind tunnel.

Their solution was the compressibility dive brake, known today as a dive flap or speed brake. Used for the first time on a P-38, these brakes were attached to the main wing spar under the wing, where they offset the loss in lift in high-speed dives and enabled the pilot to remain in control of the airplane. Because of the urgency of the problem, Milo and I immediately began a series of daily test flights to prove these flaps were the answer we had been seeking.

We had been in this test program three or four weeks when we learned through official channels that an Air Corps colonel in England had power-dived a stock airplane 780 miles an hour without dive brakes, and he and the airplane had both landed in one piece. It seemed the Air Corps thought we weren't getting any place in our tests, so they were sending this colonel over to tell us how to dive the airplane.

Milo and we other test pilots, together with Kelly and Rudy, met with him when he arrived, and we talked with him the better part of an hour. I must admit that at first I was completely taken in by his story. But I was still puzzled by the fact that he could dive the P-38 at such a speed without dive brakes and still keep control of the airplane, and when we went back to the office I asked Milo about this.

He came around with the most disgusted look on his face and I think at that moment he would have liked to knock my head off. "Don't let me hear you being taken in by such a story," he exclaimed, and nothing more was said about it. Why this colonel made such a statement and what his motive

Raised Tail P-38

was we never learned, but we knew from our own experience it could not be true.

We continued our own tests with the new dive brakes, pushing the speed up a little higher on each dive and watching for the first signs that trouble was near, but the Air Corps still felt we weren't going ahead fast enough. The Army pilot who cracked up the first prototype airplane trying to set a transcontinental speed record was now the P-38 project officer at Wright Field, and he was still eager, so a few days later he took up the only plane we had equipped with dive brakes to run some tests of his own.

Instead of the airplane returning when he was due back about an hour later, we began receiving telephone calls from various people in the western part of the San Fernando Valley, saying that a P-38 had been seen falling in pieces, and the pilot had parachuted and had fallen to the ground. Not long afterward we were notified that he had lost the airplane and bailed out, receiving a broken ankle when he hit the ground.

Investigation showed that he broke the tail off in a vertical dive, the same as Ralph Virden. When he tried to get out of the dive the tail loads went up so high they exceeded the design limits of the aircraft. He admitted later that his seat cushion got in the way of the dive flap lever, which was beside his seat on the right-hand side, and he failed to use the dive flaps, which undoubtedly would have saved the airplane. The worst part of his accident was the loss of the only plane equipped with dive brakes, and our test program was delayed several months until another plane could be fitted out with this equipment.

When it was ready we resumed our dive tests, and in addition we began evaluation tests on a new hydraulic boost for the ailerons, designed to improve the maneuverability of the airplane. The P-38 had always been considered heavy on the controls, especially on the ailerons, and after trying various fixes Kelly decided to incorporate a hydraulic control boost for the first time on a fighter plane. When Milo took the boost up for the first time he outrolled any known airplane. I later conducted many of the evaluations, and after we made necessary changes in the control mechanism to reduce adverse yaw effect, or the tendency of the airplane to turn when it is rolled by the ailerons, we standardized the installation and it was built into production airplanes on the assembly line.

The new tests on the dive brakes began at thirty thousand feet and consisted of a series of progressively steeper dives to twenty thousand feet, where we started our recovery. In those days we lacked any cockpit instruments to indicate the mach number of our dive, or the speed of the dive in terms of the speed of sound; as a result we were diving pretty much hit or miss until we thought of using a directional gyro as a dive indicator. Turning it ninety degrees in the instrument panel, we caged the gyro and set it at zero in level flight before pushing over.

By observing our dive angle on the gyro indicator we could hold it until we reached the desired altitude, where we could recover, pulling maximum G's possible up to the design limit of the aircraft, one G being the equivalent of the pull of gravity. By this method we were able to chart the constant increase in the dive angle, which produced a corresponding increase in dive speed, without endangering the airplane unduly. On each flight we photographed our instruments with a special motion picture camera known as an automatic observer and measured the stresses on the airplane with strain gauges.

We had progressed well into our second dive program when the Air Corps notified Lockheed they desired to increase the airplane weight two thousand pounds for the dive tests and specified that we make all further dives starting at thirty-five thousand feet. The purpose of course was to meet more demanding requirements. However, it made both Milo and me shudder and we went into a huddle to figure out the best approach to our new problem.

We knew this extra weight would accelerate our speed in a dive, and coupled with the higher altitude would undoubtedly push us to our critical mach number much sooner, or the per cent of the speed of sound which this airplane was capable of sustaining without breaking up. In other words, the hazards were increased. We were agreeable, however, and we increased our weight and began diving at forty-five degrees from thirty thousand feet, repeating this for each thousand feet until we reached thirty-five thousand feet, at which point we would increase the dive angle five degrees on each flight until something developed to stop us.

Milo and I were swapping flights now, taking turns on the dives; he would make a dive at a certain angle and then I would duplicate it and raise it. We alternated in this fashion every day, as our dives got higher and faster. The system was new to us, but it enabled two pilots to share the daily strain of the dive program, and we both were getting valuable information and experience. It was probably the first time in the history of flight testing that two pilots conducted dive tests together on the same airplane.

It was on Milo's fifty-five-degree dive from thirty-five thousand feet that we thought we had reached the limits of the airplane to go faster and we were over the hump. As a double check I repeated Milo's dive and then raised the angle five degrees, and it was this day that I had my first serious trouble in flight testing.

I had reached thirty-five thousand feet just south of the Muroc Dry Lake and turned north, intending to enter my dive in the vicinity of the new Air Corps test center. My cameras and recording instruments were operating and my two engines were turning at twenty-six hundred revolutions per minute. With my dive brakes extended I pushed forward on the control wheel and headed earthward.

Our tests had been going well up to now; even the engineers were satisfied. If the results to date meant anything the rest should be a cinch. I reached a sixty-degree dive angle within two thousand feet after pushing over and everything appeared normal. This dive should wrap it up. Then at thirty-one thousand feet I thought I noticed a different feel in the airplane, as if it wanted to get away from me.

Before I had time to do anything the plane started to nose under abruptly and entered a steeper dive. This was what killed Ralph Virden, but now I had dive brakes, and the plane was still under control. My first instinct was to pull out of the dive, and I fought the control wheel back with all my might.

As I did so the nose came up, and I found I could maintain my original dive angle by pulling hard on the wheel. In this fashion I continued downward, the airplane getting rougher every second and the tendency of the nose to tuck under more pronounced.

As I passed thirty thousand feet I was again tempted to pull out of the dive, but I was still flying the airplane, and I decided to ride it down. There was only a bare increase of three miles an hour on my airspeed indicator over Milo's previous dive, when the P-38 behaved normally, but these extra three miles had transformed it into a mad demon.

I rode the bucking plane down to twenty thousand feet and started my recovery. Now I pulled back on the wheel nearly all the way and the nose barely responded. I continued down to thirteen thousand feet, pulling out of my dive very slowly, until the plane was again in level flight. My strain gauge instruments were set for 100 per cent of limit load, and they were all over 100 and all the red warning lights were on when I finally got out of the dive.

Thinking the plane might be overstressed, I flew back to Burbank at extremely low speed and power. An instrument check revealed I had exceeded the limit load of the airplane, but it had successfully withstood the strain and escaped damage. This was final proof to us that the P-38 could dive up to its design limits with dive brakes before going out of control or breaking up. It meant that the dive brake had licked the problem of compressibility control on the P-38, and brought our tests to a successful conclusion.

Milo Burcham was a great flyer and a good friend, but he ruled with an iron hand, as I had reason to find out on several occasions. We had another P-38 modified for two seats, with an extended center nacelle which gave it a long nose, and this plane was called *Nosey*. One day on a test flight in *Nosey* I was carried away by the excellent way this airplane behaved in dives. Although I had completed my test on that flight I decided to dive to low altitude at the critical mach number, for no reason except that *Nosey* dove so well.

This time I really hung one on. I held the plane right at the mach limit at an extremely steep angle, reaching a top speed of 530 miles indicated, which was 100 miles over the maximum allowed for that airplane at low altitude. Then I pulled out of my dive about one thousand feet from the ground and went on home, thinking no more about it until the next morning, when we gathered in the projection room to view the movies of my test.

A recording camera in the nose of the plane had faithfully photographed the test instrument panel throughout my dive. We watched the altimeter drop at an extremely high rate, with the speed going up and the altitude going down, until it dropped under ten thousand feet and suddenly I realized what I had done. Milo started to take on a queer look and make unpleasant glances at me, and when the film showed I dove to one thousand feet and pulled 7½ G's getting out, he blew his top. It was not pleasant there at all for a while, until Joe Towle told Milo in a quiet way that he had no one but himself to blame, as I was just trying to follow in his footsteps. At this Milo said we must remember we were in an extremely dangerous business, and to do more than was normally required might end disastrously. We all agreed to take it easy in the future and he more or less laughed it off.

Another incident for which I was reprimanded wasn't my fault, but it showed that Milo would not let any of his pilots go over his head. This time he really hit the ceiling and I offered to resign.

I was testing a production installation on an experimental airplane, and after I landed the production boys asked me to take it up again the next day. I told them to come down and ask Milo, he would assign a pilot, and forgot about it.

We were sitting in the office the next morning when they came in, and instead of addressing Milo they asked me if I was ready to make the flight. I told them to ask him, but by that time he had already exploded. If it had not been for Joe again, I think I might have been kicked out of the department. Milo and I went outside and I attempted to square things up. I explained the best I could that I had made no attempt to go over his head, and if he thought for one moment I had I would prove he was wrong by resigning. With that he felt that maybe he was wrong in his decision and shook hands and we made up. That was the last time we ever disagreed on anything.

This was late in 1943. There were large numbers of P-38's in England by this time, starting to go operational against the German Air Force as fighter cover for our bomber sweeps over Europe, and reports of trouble with our airplane, such as range, fuel consumption and engine performance, were coming back to Burbank. Meanwhile many pilots were being transferred to P-38's from slower planes like the Bell P-39 and the Republic P-47, and were encountering compressibility for the first time.

P-38's in the field had not yet been modified with dive brakes, and the dive problem was getting serious in many fighter groups. In an effort to work out some of these problems, Lockheed sent Ward Beman and Phil Nelson to England to visit P-38 bases in the Eighth and Ninth Air Forces. Ward came through the office before he left, and I told him if

Republic P-47 "Thunderbolt"

he needed a pilot I was eager. Little did I realize that a few months later word would come from Ward Beman through General Doolittle's headquarters that one A. W. LeVier was wanted in the United Kingdom to demonstrate airplanes.

We were still having our troubles at Burbank. For several years we had been plagued by improper regulation of the engine turbo-supercharger on the P-38. The regulator was a very tricky device, developed from an automatic manifold pressure regulator and adapted to the turbine feature of this airplane, and it was definitely inadequate.

In theory the turbine was a combination gas turbine and compressor, using energy from the engine exhaust gases to turn a compressor wheel, which compressed or supercharged the engine air at altitude. About the highest you could fly without a supercharger was twenty thousand feet, and we used this device on the P-38 in order to fly higher. However, its operation was very irregular, resulting in surging that caused the engines to act up in a most erratic fashion, and in the final months of 1943 I flew many tests to find a fix for this condition.

One such test involved a night flight at thirty thousand feet. While flying back and forth over the coast between Los Angeles and San Diego I dreamed up a most diabolical scheme to have fun and startle some people, and after the test was completed I headed down to do a little buzz job.

I began by giving my home town of Whittier a good rousing welcome, descending at 450 miles an hour with propellers in low pitch, which made the P-38 howl like a scalded cat. After giving Whittier a good trouncing I flew west toward Los Angeles along Whittier Boulevard, where a ground searchlight picked me up. I turned the airplane down again and headed directly down the beam, keeping my head lowered in the cockpit to avoid being blinded by the light, and held my dive until the searchlight crew turned the light out. At five hundred feet it went out and I pulled out of my dive and headed home.

On the way back I buzzed Montrose, where I was living at the time, dodging the searchlights in that area that were trying to pick me up. There remained one more neighborhood I thought should have a little sport, where old Jim White lived, my buddy at flight test. I gave him my last buzz job, and the next morning he told me I went right over his house and broke two windows next door. At least that's what his neighbor said, but when Jim asked to see the windows he was told they had already been repaired.

On New Year's Day, 1944, I had a midair collision in a dogfight with a Marine fighter plane.

I was on my way home from a routine check flight near San Diego, flying over the sea a few miles offshore, when I spotted five Chance Vought Corsairs going in my direction. These were a type used by the Navy and Marines, and it was a great delight to tangle with them, as the P-38 had superior performance and it was usually quite easy to defeat them in mock combat.

They were flying a V formation and I came up beside them and attempted to suggest a little combat, but they paid no attention to me and kept on going. I circled around a couple of times, making passes at them in a friendly manner but to no avail, so I decided to go on home. By now they had turned and were flying south, and the urge came upon me to make one last pass.

I came in from the rear, zooming down under and in front of the leader and continuing up in an Immelmann, and then started for home. For some reason I looked around once more to see if they had changed their minds about playing, and I saw all five of them fast on my tail. I knew then they were eager and out to get this wise guy in a P-38.

I immediately put on additional power and began a circle to get in position to pick up and attack one of the planes. I made two or three passes at various planes in the formation, including a mock pass at one which had turned me slightly into the sun, when suddenly out of the sun appeared another plane, not more than two hundred feet in front of me and coming toward me head on.

I thought this was it. The big R-2800 engine on the nose of that Corsair looked awfully close, and I knew a false move now would be fatal. I waited to see what he was going to do. When I saw he was trying to pull up to avoid me I shoved forward on the control wheel with all the energy I had in store and passed under him, our wingtips striking as we passed.

This sobered me up considerably and made me realize how foolish I was to provoke this dogfight. I turned again for home, thinking how I could explain the damage to my airplane, when another Corsair came alongside and motioned to me, as if to ask if I had had enough. I pointed over to my left wingtip and he took one look and peeled off like a frightened eagle. He was probably thinking the same thing I was, how would they explain the damage to the airplane?

At first I thought I might tell a lie and say I had struck a fence post or something silly, but then I decided the best thing was to tell the truth. To save my neck with the Air Corps, however, I submitted a slightly cleaned-up report. I said I was flying home minding my own business when I was jumped by five F4U's, and in attempting to avoid a collision with one of these planes our wingtips touched slightly in passing. There was a twinkle in Colonel Shoop's eyes when he read this report and he said no further action would be taken.

F4U "Corsair"

It was that same afternoon, as I was about to leave this civilian court-martial, that I was called to Hall Hibbard's office. Kelly and Rudy were there, and they kidded me a few minutes about my dogfight and then got down to business. Ward Beman had asked for me in England and I was needed just as fast as I could get there.

10

Fighter Tour

Flying out of bases in England, the Army Air Forces began their attacks against Germany early in the war. The Eighth Air Force under General Eaker mounted the first bombing raid in August, 1942. It pioneered a new concept in aerial warfare, high-altitude precision daylight bombardment, which was endorsed and continued in January, 1943, by the Combined Chiefs of Staff meeting at Casablanca. They in fact wanted to bomb Germany for at least another year before invading Europe, and in April, 1943, the Eighth Air Force and the RAF Bomber Command, acting under orders of the Combined Chiefs, began the Combined Bomber Offensive. Its objective was to destroy and dislocate German military, industrial and economic strength, and to undermine the morale of the German people in order to weaken their will to resist. It was a round-the-clock offensive, and it continued right up to the invasion in June, 1944.

These raids did not go unchallenged by the Luftwaffe, which reacted strongly. Fighter cover for our bombers was essential from the start, and as the months passed it became apparent that we did not have enough. The Republic P-47, which was used initially as fighter escort by the Eighth, had a combat radius under four hundred miles, and many important targets lay beyond its reach. Not only were our bomber losses prohibitive when we went farther, but German fighter strength in the west continued to grow. More escort planes with greater range were needed to take our bombers all the way to their targets and bring them home.

In this situation the Army Air Forces turned to the P-38, which was already favored among fighters in the Mediterranean and the Pacific. It had more range, and with the addition of external fuel tanks it was converted into an escort for B-17's and B-24's operating out of England against targets in Europe.

P-38's flew their first mission with the Eighth Fighter Command on October 15, 1943, and equipped with two 165-gallon fuel tanks on the wings, they took the bombers more than five hundred miles from base and brought them home. On November 2 they flew escort to Wilhelmshaven and on November 13 to Bremen, again demonstrating their ability to go all the way to the target and meet the German fighters on more than even terms. Outnumbered five to one,

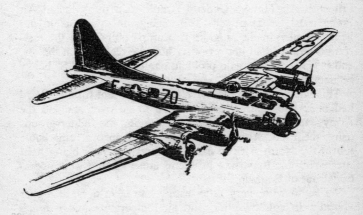

B-17

only seven P-38's were lost out of forty-seven that went to Bremen, although sixteen returned to base with battle damage, including one plane that took more than one hundred hits and came back on one engine.

Most important, the P-38's were proving that long-range fighters could hold bomber losses to an acceptable level, and gave the Air Force reason to hope that with a larger escort losses would be even less. Aided by North American P-51's, which were now being diverted from ground support to bomber escort, thirty-five P-38's went back to Bremen on December 20 and performed creditably at what was then considered extreme fighter range. On December 30 they flew their longest escort to date to Ludwigshafen and again proved their value over long distances.

Despite the success of this new method in reducing our bomber losses, the German Air Force was still a formidable opponent and had to be reckoned with in Allied plans for the invasion of Europe. In fact, at the beginning of 1944 there was serious doubt among American airmen that an invasion could succeed against German air power, and in a New Year's message to the commanding generals of the Eighth and Fifteenth Air Forces, General Arnold said the German Air Force must be destroyed. This change in emphasis in our heavy bombardment program in Europe pointed up the realization that we had not seriously hurt the Germans in the air, and it was now the main problem confronting the U.S. heavy bomber forces.

This was the picture when Ward Beman sent for me. Ward had been chosen by Kelly Johnson to go over and aid the Army with the many problems confronting the fighter groups using the P-38. Although this plane had done a remarkable job in the North African campaign and was now being used successfully in Italy, new problems arose when it went operational out of England.

To begin with, very little testing had been done at higher altitudes in cold weather, and air temperatures were much colder in that part of the world compared with southern California. What had caught up with us, as well as with others, was the fact that the P-38 was primarily designed as a

North American P-51 "Mustang"

short-range fighter-interceptor and not as a long-range escort fighter. Like other fighters, it had great capabilities, but it would take time to develop them.

Ward found the morale of the pilots was the biggest problem. There were a lot of sharp boys but they were spread too thin through the ranks, and even many of them had much to learn about the P-38. Some of the problems confronting us in England were a sudden increase in engine failures, malfunctioning of the turbo-superchargers, and most dreaded of all, the compressibility dive that was almost sure to cause a crash and often kill the pilot. If an engine quits that's bad; a troublesome supercharger is almost as bad; and if the poor pilot freezes because of a poorly-heated cockpit you are defeated before you start. It was these and many other things that troubled us.

Ward made his request for me through the Army and it came back from England signed by General Doolittle, who had just taken over from General Eaker as head of the Eighth Air Force. I had met Jimmy Doolittle twice before and I don't know whether he remembered me, but if I could be of help I was ready. Kelly said there was no time to wait for the many inoculations required for overseas assignment, which normally would have taken three weeks. The Army was waiving all formalities and I would proceed with the least possible delay. In less than a week I was on my way.

My first stop was at headquarters of the Air Technical Service Command at Wright Field, Ohio, where I got my credentials and a telephone number to call if I got stuck along the way. It came in handy. My next stops were Washington and New York City, which were the big bottlenecks going overseas. I was bumped in both places, but I called this number and was immediately put back on the airplane.

I flew all the way, riding as a passenger in a very cold Army C-54. Our first stop out of New York was the big Army air base at Stephenville, Newfoundland, where I landed with influenza and a 102-degree fever. I went to the base hospital, where they loaded me down with medication to deaden the fever, and we took off again for our next stop at Prestwick, Scotland. Here I changed to an overnight train to London, arriving early the next morning.

My instructions were to stand in front of the Grosvenor House, a big hotel on Park Lane, where I would be picked up. I stood there on the sidewalk about half an hour, wearing an Army officer's uniform without insignia, which was the standard dress for manufacturer's representatives in combat theaters. After several minutes a military policeman who had been watching me with growing suspicion came over and challenged me. By doing some fast talking I convinced him I wasn't a spy. Finally my escort arrived, an officer from Doolittle's headquarters, and assured the MP I was legal.

He drove me to Eighth Air Force headquarters a few miles northwest of London. After drawing my flying equipment I was immediately driven to Nuthamstead, headquarters of the 55th Fighter Group, which was the first P-38 group in England to go operational the preceding October. Ward Beman and Phil Nelson were waiting for me, together with Glenn Fulkerson, one of our most experienced P-38 crew chiefs, who was on loan from Lockheed Overseas Corporation at Langford Lodge in northern Ireland. The airplane assigned to Major Webb, a squadron commander, was waiting for me, and within an hour after arriving at this base I made my first test flight in England.

Ward had already outlined the test to be made. It required a cruise climb to thirty thousand feet, drawing fuel from 165-gallon drop tanks, and upon reaching altitude continue to cruise at best power setting for maximum range.

After a certain period of time the engines were to be run at war-emergency power for five minutes, then reduced to military power for fifteen minutes, and finished off at a low-power cruise condition, returning to base with fifty gallons of fuel remaining. The purpose of the test was to find out how long I could fly and how many air miles I could go under these conditions.

During the test I had to record certain data at each five thousand feet in my climb and each fifteen minutes during my cruise—engine rpm's, manifold pressure, oil pressure and temperature, and carburetor and coolant temperature. With this information, Ward would be able to estimate how much the performance of the airplane had already been improved, and what still needed to be done.

At twenty-nine thousand feet the right engine blew up and fell apart. As I had already had ten Allison engines blow up on me in the last two years, this was nothing new; usually I could feel it coming, but this time it just went "wham" and that was it. I switched from my drop tanks to regular wing tanks. My drop tanks were not yet empty so I kept them with me, although I was pretty heavy and on one engine it was sort of cutting it close. However, we had done this quite often in California and I didn't figure I would be in any sweat.

I had been flying due north toward Scotland, figuring this would keep me over land. Being on top of a heavy overcast, I did not know my position, so when I turned south toward my base I asked for a radio fix. They immediately came back with my exact position and distance from home so fast I thought this was going to be wonderful; you couldn't get lost over here with this kind of service. I flew the heading they gave me and figured out I should be there in about fifteen minutes.

About ten minutes passed when they came back on the air with landing instructions; if I was west of the perimeter I should turn hard left and land on runway 29, into the wind which was blowing about thirty miles an hour. At once I looked down and there was the field right below me. I thought to myself this was peculiar, as I hadn't figured on being there yet, but everything was just like I left it and the tower had a green light on me. I swung around left but as I looked at runway 29 the wind was across it, so I called the tower and asked them again what runway to use.

Getting no answer this time, I picked an alternate runway with a headwind, which was the logical thing to do under the circumstances. I turned left into my good engine and with my landing gear down I entered the base leg for runway 24. I was still extremely heavy with drop tanks on, and as I turned the airplane started to buffet. I had partial flaps down at the time, but even so I realized I was making too tight a base leg. I opened the throttle and pulled the gear and flaps up and made a wide circle to the right, and this time I came in and landed with room to spare.

Again I called the tower on the radio, requesting taxi instructions, and again there was only a deep silence. Then I looked around to see if anyone was waving at me, and for the first time I realized this was not the field I had taken off from. I could see now it was a B-26 bomber base, laid out identically to the fighter base I had just left. There was nothing to do now but roll to a stop off the side of the runway and get out of the airplane. A jeep came out on the field to get me and I was driven to base operations, where I identified myself. The boys said they sure were sweating me out. They saw me with a dead engine, and the idea was general in the Air Corps over there at that time that a pilot with one engine out on a P-38 was a sad sack.

B-26 "Marauder"

In a couple of hours an ambulance from Nuthamstead arrived to pick me up and we drove home in the blackout. I had to buy the drinks at the officers' club that night, taking quite a ribbing for getting lost on my first flight in England. It didn't yield much information, but I probably saved Major Webb a ride home on one engine, because he was going out on a fighter sweep in that airplane the next morning.

I still had the flu and was running a fever again. The next day 1 went to the base hospital and the flight surgeon put me to bed for a week. When they let me out Phil Nelson and Glenn Fulkerson picked me up and we drove to the 364th Fighter Group at Honington, another P-38 outfit.

This was a base where we could really do some good, because they had all just arrived from the States and there were plenty of green pilots. Few had ever flown above twenty thousand feet. Ward Beman arrived a few days later and we prepared a series of lectures covering the best operating procedures for the P-38, and dealing in particular with high-speed flight, with emphasis on the evil of compressibility.

It was here that I was first challenged as to whether the P-38 could be dived safely. Hadn't a colonel made a vertical dive from forty-one thousand feet and recovered okay? Other pilots had made similar claims—what about it? In every crowd there are always a few skeptics, and this gang was no exception.

I tried to be completely honest with them, saying that they were going into combat very soon, and not to get any wild ideas about chasing the Jerries when the German pilots peeled off at altitude, because if they tried to follow suit their goose was cooked. At low altitudes and on the deck they could take on anything, as there was no match for the P-38 down low.

I explained, however, if they ever did get into dive trouble there was only one way to save themselves, so far as I knew. The first thing to do was to pull the power off the engines, put the props in low pitch to create lots of drag, take a firm grip on the wheel and pull back carefully. If the elevator load became too heavy, use the trim tab a very small amount but don't overdo it, because when you get down to lower levels where the air is dense and powerful, the trim tab becomes very effective and can overstress the airplane. Just ride the thing and try to keep the dive angle from getting any steeper; if you pull too hard you increase the loads on the tail and it might come off. An airplane can only stand so much.

From Honington we continued to Bovingdon, the headquarters of the Eighth Fighter Command, for a series of engine tests and dives. Here I demonstrated how well the P-38 could fly on one engine. I wasn't in England to sit in a corner, and I stuck my neck out farther than I ever had before, just to get the work done. On altitude flights to collect test data here and at the 20th Fighter Group at Kingscliff, I went up daily in heavy weather, flying as high as thirty-five thousand feet without seeing the sun, to get information on engine performance. One week I pumped the landing gear down by hand three times because of poor maintenance on the airplane. Everyone was doing his best, but there was a war going on and they were shy of everything.

While at Bovingdon the P-38 pilots told us of their trouble doing a split S. This was a tactical maneuver required at high altitude, and it was from this maneuver that many of them crashed. It was simply a half roll to your back and pulling through like a half loop, but it was often done when they were attacking an enemy plane, and if he did it you would have to follow. When we left Bovingdon, Ward, Glenn and I went to Langford Lodge, the Lockheed modification base near Belfast, to pick up a special P-38 equipped with dive brakes, and I set out to see for myself if I could do a split S in this airplane.

To do this maneuver you have to commit yourself to it, which meant getting into a dive, and committing myself in a marginal airplane was what worried me. I didn't commit myself until I knew it was safe, and this is how I did it:

Starting at twenty thousand feet, I pushed the control column forward until I was in a vertical attitude, headed straight down, and then pulled out immediately and recorded my altitude. Then I went up to twenty-one thousand feet and repeated the same maneuver, and continued to do this in increments of one thousand feet until I was able to do it from thirty thousand feet, at which point I knew the airplane would take it. I was getting up to mach numbers around .71 and the true speed of the plane was up around 550 miles an hour.

The new dive flaps on this airplane made it possible for the P-38 to do a split S in perfect safety. They changed the characteristics of the wing in compressibility toward a normal subsonic condition, and also increased drag which permitted the plane to take on steeper dive angles without accelerating too rapidly. Later on I was able to prove to the Air Corps that the P-38 would do a split S; I actually had mock combat with several other planes and did it very well.

When the airplane was ready, I flew back to England to take the new dive flaps on a demonstration tour. Bovingdon was weathered in, so without waiting to start my tour at command headquarters I began my rounds, visiting all the P-38 bases in England as weather permitted. It was April now and winter was over, and the flying conditions improved steadily. The Ninth Air Force was now operational from England, flying medium bombers in raids on the Continent and building up a tactical air force to furnish ground support for the coming invasion. In addition to Eighth Air Force P-38 bases, the Ninth Fighter Command had three P-38 groups, with squadrons dispersed at several air fields in southern England. I visited them all during April and May, demonstrating the good features of the airplane, and emphasizing its vastly improved safety and performance with compressibility dive brakes.

I paid a return visit to Nuthamstead, the first base I had visited when I came to England. From there I went to Kingscliff again and gave them a lecture on the P-38. When I was finished they didn't seem too impressed and I wasn't getting the interest I had hoped for, so after supper I went out to the field while it was still light and took off. I climbed to twenty thousand feet and then came down in a vertical dive straight over the officers' club. When they heard me coming they all rushed outside, expecting to see me auger in, and now that I had their attention I came down on the deck and did some slow rolls across the field on one engine, and after landing I had plenty of fellows to talk with.

They were all interested in what I had on my airplane, and the next day I let the squadron leaders fly it and find out for themselves what they could do with dive brakes. I told them to go up to thirty thousand feet and dive it at a sixty-degree angle and see what a tremendous improvement we had made, and they all came down bug-eyed at what they could do with this airplane.

I was next sent to Goxhill, a transition base, where a most deplorable situation had arisen over the past week or ten days. They were losing an enormous number of pilots in transition training that was going on up there—more than was even conceivable; even if you didn't know what you were doing you shouldn't lose them like that. I went up there immediately and the things I found out amazed me.

To begin with, the base commander didn't like P-38's. He admitted at the bar that night that he was strictly a P-40 man, and we thought to ourselves it was a fine state of affairs to have the instructors against the airplane they were teaching people to fly. As a result, he had the most misinformed group of pilots I have ever come in contact with, and their feelings toward the P-38 weren't fit to print. In view of this situation, when I gave them my demonstration the next day I really poured it on.

It included things I normally don't do. I went all-out to prove that any young man with average intelligence and courage could fly the P-38 just as well as myself. These kids were young, twenty or twenty-one years old on the average, and all they needed was good leaders.

Before I went up I told them the maneuvers they were going to see would prove to them that their mistakes were uncalled for, and their buddies were killed because they were not trained properly. When I came down I had never seen such enthusiasm; it was just like they had been saved from hell. After that I think they were all convinced that the airplane had real possibilities, even the base commander, and was far from being the killer it was tagged for.

My next stop was a P-38 base at Andover, which was headquarters of the Ninth Fighter Command under General Pete Quesada, who is now a Lockheed vice president and manager of our missiles systems division. The Andover pilots came from a P-47 outfit in the States and had just gone operational. The change from a single-engine to a multi-engine airplane was more far reaching than most of them realized, and what with one thing and another their morale was pretty low.

I came in over the base at twenty thousand feet and gave them the old razzle-dazzle to wake up the countryside, starting with a nice vertical dive, and when I came down across the base I got real eager. The air was clear and nobody was flying, so I decided to give them the works. I really beat up the joint. I flew upside down on one engine in front of the hangar and then got into some accelerated stalls circling the base with my dead engine hanging down, which usually had them jumping. When I landed almost the whole base turned out to greet me, and I have never seen such a bunch of eager pilots in my life.

Engine failures were always a big problem on the P-38 because of the jobs assigned to it, and I devoted a lot of time on my tour to explaining and demonstrating single-engine performance. The P-38 used liquid-cooled engines, made by Allison Division of General Motors Corporation, and they would frequently blow up and tear themselves apart. During the four months I spent in England the Air Corps made almost two thousand engine changes on the P-38's based there; in other words, practically every P-38 in England at that time had at least one complete engine change. That was the seriousness of the engine trouble. It was partly due to the various problems we had with the engine that General Doolittle finally made his decision to transfer the P-38 out of the Eighth Air Force.

Knowledge of P-38 single-engine performance was extremely helpful in getting home, and it was the pilots who were not familiar with it who often ran into trouble. Despite the many problems confronting them they did a good job, however, and when things got tough they really learned fast. They were all operational within a month after I reached England, and they would often fly missions in weather that shouldn't happen to your worst enemy.

One day I flew into Kingscliff under a very low ceiling about two hundred feet, with low scattered scud around one hundred feet, and as I approached the base I could see P-38's all over returning from a cross-channel sweep. They were coming back all over England at that very moment in that kind of weather, and landing with very few accidents. I had to circle fifteen minutes before I could squeeze into the traffic pattern and land too. I ran across them quite often over there, coming back or going out, and to this day they can't be praised enough for the way they flew.

They had victories at high altitude, but they really shone down low. Often after these fighter sweeps they would drop down on the deck on the way home and beat up enemy installations. The P-38 could make very tight maneuvers at low altitude, and when the pilots found the Germans on their tail all they had to do was turn hard right or left and get behind the enemy plane. They used to pull hard turns to the left, for instance, which often caused the German ME-109 to stall out and snap-roll into the ground.

I never ran into the German jets but I talked to several P-38 pilots who did. These jets didn't give the boys any particular trouble while I was there, but it was easy to see it wouldn't be long before they did. They had at least two hundred miles an hour speed advantage on us, and performance was out of this world. Several pilots had the little ME-103 make passes

Me-109

at them without firing. Apparently the Germans were just playing around. Maybe they weren't ready to call our hand or didn't have guns to fire, maybe they were just testing the new airplanes. At any rate, there was nothing we could do to stop them. They would come from high above and dive through our formations and go jazzing back and forth like a yoyo. There wasn't any sense trying to catch them, that was obvious.

It is apparent now that when we started large-scale air raids on the jet factories we cut a vital link in the German war machine. That was where our bombers really saved the day. If the Nazis had been able to get enough jet planes built they could have riddled our bomber forces to ribbons and the whole course of the war would have been changed. They could have picked off our bombers at will and knocked down our fighters if there was any time left.

We had nothing whatsoever, not a single thing, to combat their jet fighters at that time. The Lockheed P-80 was flying back home but it was still experimental. A few of these planes reached Europe before the war ended but never flew in combat. If the war had continued the P-80 would have seen action, and in my opinion would have been the deciding factor.

After completing my P-38 demonstration tour I flew back to Langford Lodge to await the first bulk shipment of dive brakes for installation on combat planes in the European theater. While I had been in England demonstrating this modification, the Lockheed factory back home was building several hundred special kits on highest priority, with new planes coming out of the factory getting them installed right on the production line.

Early in May about four hundred sets of dive brakes were loaded on an Army C-54 cargo plane and dispatched to Langford Lodge for field installation in Europe. We were looking for them, as we knew they would lick the dive problem for Army pilots and save lives and airplanes. Joe Johnson, Lockheed's P-38 project engineer, came over on another plane to set up the modification line.

The days passed and no kits. Joe moved heaven and earth trying to find them, only to learn the worst—the C-54 was shot down by mistake by a British plane over the North Atlantic and its precious cargo of dive brakes for combat airplanes was lost at sea. Through lack of time and press of other matters, they were never replaced.

Using a few sample kits, we were able to modify only twelve P-38's, but they saw combat and did an outstanding job. Even without dive brakes, this airplane could still be counted on when the chips were down. The invasion began a few days after I left England, and to the P-38's of the Eighth and Ninth Air Forces went the assignment of flying fighter cover on D-Day for the great invasion armada.

Late in May we got word from the factory that it would be best for us to return, for they had the feeling that if the invasion started we might be unduly delayed in getting back to the States. Ward Beman and I went home together, taking the local transport from Langford Lodge to Prestwick, where we caught a TWA ferry flight to the U.S. We flew to Reykjavik, Iceland, stopping to eat and refuel, and from there flew nonstop to Washington, D.C. I got a good look at the Atlantic Ocean on the way home and it was a mighty bleak expanse of water. When I tried to visualize myself flying across it instead of Lindbergh in that little Ryan monoplane back in May, 1927, it made me shiver all over, and I realized the tremendous gamble he took and what a wonderful flight he made.

Like most people returning from a combat theater, it took me a while to get used to normal living again. I had lived like the English the past few months, often in their homes, and had shared their restrictions and regulations. By comparison, the business-as-usual attitude in Washington seemed out of place. There were lots of cars on the streets despite gasoline rationing and everybody seemed to have plenty of money to spend, and I felt a little resentful that we weren't sharing the sacrifices of others. It seemed strange to be back in my own country and find things sort of twisted.

After a few days in Washington, Ward and I proceeded to Dayton, where we wrapped up our business with the Air Corps and continued to Burbank, arriving June 1. After being away so long, I looked forward to having at least a week off to see my family, and I can't forget Hall Hibbard telling me to take a couple of days. It struck me funny at first, but when I found out the reason I didn't mind.

The prototype XP-80A, the first jet airplane to go into production in the United States, was ready to make its first flight, and I had been chosen to fly it.

11

Jet Pilot

The Army wanted one so Kelly Johnson designed one, and that is how the jet airplane came to America. The year was 1943. In the decade since that fateful decision, jets have revolutionized military aviation in this country and throughout the world and made airpower mankind's major weapon. Combined with the atom bomb it is probably irresistible.

America's first airplane to fly on jet power was the Bell P-59 Airacomet, a conventional airframe with a pair of Frank Whittle's de Havilland Halford engines mounted in the wings. It flew late in 1942. This tardy American effort to get in the jet race after it had started was really just a flying test bed for a borrowed engine, and though it carried the hopes of our War Department on its tired shoulders, it was a compromise and was foredoomed to failure.

The fighter planes of World War II were not designed for jet speeds, as we learned with the P-38 in our battles against compressibility. The experimental Bell Airacomet, far from living up to its name, was actually no faster than the P-38, which was already in service. There was no chance of matching it against German jets like the Messerschmitt 262, with speeds up to 540 miles an hour. What was needed was a brand-new plane with brand-new performance, and it turned out the P-80 was the answer.

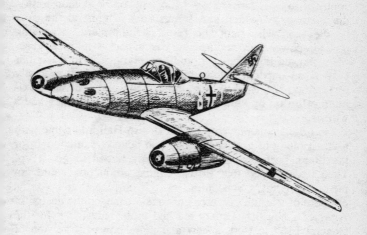

Me-262

In June, 1943, the Army Air Corps assigned Lockheed the task of building a jet-propelled fighter. We had been trying since 1939 to sell them a jet plane of our own design, the L-133, powered by our own jet engine, the L-1000, so it was perhaps natural that they came to us. But the L-133 was a radical design by 1943 standards, and because time was so short we decided to play it safe with a more conventional type of airframe, using an existing British engine. The prototype XP-80, known to her associates as *Lulu-Belle*, was the result. Designed from scratch by Kelly Johnson, Lockheed's chief research engineer, the XP-80 was built and flown in 143 days—a job that normally takes a year and a half.

Johnson and his engineers, huddled in the bitter cold of a January morning at the secret Army test base at Muroc, listened to *Lulu-Belle* scream as Milo Burcham lifted her off the desert floor. It was hard to explain the damp eyes, because there wasn't any wind. More than blueprints had gone into that airplane.

We were amply rewarded by what we saw. After testing the controls to his satisfaction Milo put on a demonstration the memory of which still brings back a glint to the eyes of the men who built the historic little plane. Shrieking down in power dives and flashing past in deck-level speed runs, Milo showed his wide-eyed audience the quality of their fair lady. Army experts, watching in pleased amazement, promptly reclassified the P-59 as a training plane and ordered maximum effort on building the new P-80. They knew they had a winner.

Lulu-Belle was powered by the British Halford engine with a thrust rating of twenty-five hundred pounds, not enough for maximum performance, but the Army hoped to get it up. Then it developed that British engine production could not meet the Army's schedules for this airplane, and so the pressure of wartime requirements again changed the design of America's new jet. Orders reached us to redesign it for the General Electric I-40, a new and more powerful version of the British engine, which was already in production in the United States. Time again was all-important, and Kelly Johnson beat his own record. The XP-80A, a bigger and heavier airplane with a new engine, was designed and built in 138 days. When I got home from England it was ready for me to take it up.

We called it the *Gray Ghost*—for that is what it looked like—with its sleek aluminum surface painted and waxed to a smooth, streamlined finish of gray lacquer. It could climb more than 45,000 feet high and had a top speed over 550 miles an hour. This was America's secret weapon to combat the German jets—the fastest and highest-performing airplane in the world.

When I returned to Burbank, Milo and Jim White had both flown *Lulu-Belle* several times. Milo was now Lockheed's chief pilot, succeeding the late Marshall Headle, and his successor as chief engineering pilot had not yet been appointed. Joe Towle, who had been Milo's assistant in engineering, was now the senior pilot in our department, and one of the first things he did when I reported back to work was have me checked out in jets. Early in June, Jim and I flew up to Muroc in our twin-engine Cessna, the *Bamboo Bomber*, and I walked over to *Lulu-Belle* and climbed in.

I had always dreamed about the perfect airplane and how it would fly, but little did I realize I would ever see it. This was probably the closest thing to it in the entire world. I will never forget my first flight in this little airplane, any more than I would forget my solo flight back in 1930.

This was the most effortless flight I had ever known. Without propeller noise or vibration, the XP-80 accelerated smoothly down the runway, and as it reached flying speed it went into the air with no more than a slight pull back on the control stick. After the gear and flaps were up it seemed almost like something you would dream about—hoping someday you would have an opportunity to fly such an airplane, and then wake up and wonder why it couldn't be possible. Here I was actually in it.

After I had flown jets quite a while I often said that a pilot wasn't very good who couldn't have gotten used to *Lulu-Belle* in a very few minutes. It was the most simple airplane to fly that you could imagine, considering what we had been flying previously. You had a few engine instruments, the usual flight instruments, and that was it. To go faster all you had to do was move the throttle forward, or pull it back to slow down—no regulation of the propeller, no fuss about mixture control or cowl flaps, no worry about head temperatures or whether the oil would run too hot—there wasn't such a thing. It was all very simple. This airplane even had an automatic starting system. All you did was get in, buckle yourself into the seat and hit the switch. Its only disadvantage was the engine, which was low on thrust. To make the XP-80 really good we needed at least four thousand pounds of thrust, and we got it on the next version of this airplane.

After I had flown *Lulu-Belle* several times, the *Gray Ghost* arrived at Muroc by truck early one morning after an all-night drive from Burbank, completely hidden by tarpaulin and with a police escort to make sure it didn't get held up in traffic. Jim White and I planned what we would do on the first flight, as this was to be my big chance as a test pilot. I was really graduating into big-time flying now and I wanted to do it up right. Jim was to fly *Lulu-Belle* and pace me, and if the tests were satisfactory he was to come alongside of me and we were going to put on a little race around the field.

Saturday, June 10, was the date set. We were having canopy trouble and the mechanics had been working overtime to get it fixed. In the meantime I had run a number of taxi tests up and down the lake bed, and although I hadn't done more than skip it off the ground a foot or so, I had become fairly familiar with the airplane already and had actually learned a lot about it.

Lulu-Belle was a great airplane because there was practically nothing wrong with it. But as is so often the case, the changes we made to stretch it out created problems. We had lengthened the fuselage, moved the cockpit forward, moved the engine to the rear and put a larger gas tank in the fuselage. These changes and others added up to a practically new airplane, and we had to test it to prove it would work.

Like the airplane, the I-40 engine had never flown either. It was the most powerful engine of its day, developing over 4,000 pounds of static thrust, but because it was new it still had limitations on it. Although it was designed for 11,500 revolutions per minute, it was restricted to 10,500 on take-off and I had instructions to reduce power to 10,000 rpm after take-off. The flight time on the engine was also held way down to prevent possible damage through excessive use; actually, we counted every minute it ran and conserved it every way we could. We were faced with a brand-new airplane and a brand-new engine, and it is a tough combination when you have to develop both at the same time.

The dry lake bed at Muroc gave me more room but it was pretty rough, so I chose to use the regular six-thousand-foot runway at the air base, taking off slightly downhill in case I needed the extra push. There was quite a crowd on hand, including top brass from the Army and top officials of Lockheed and General Electric, besides Kelly Johnson and his engineers. When everything appeared to be shipshape I taxied out, swung around and checked my instruments. Then I opened the engine up to 10,500 rpm and released the brakes. Acceleration seemed to be better than *Lulu-Belle*'s. However, it was a hot day, and as I was taking off at reduced power, I held it on the ground until past the halfway point, when I eased the stick back. At about four thousand feet the nose finally came up and I left the ground.

It didn't feel like it had too much steam. The weather was quite hot and the air was turbulent, and I immediately noticed the airplane was unstable. It wanted to pitch up and down and was very difficult to hold steady. I also became aware of a tremendous amount of heat coming into the cockpit from the left side around the throttle. I couldn't account for this and it was distracting to say the least.

I had my test card fastened to my knee on my left leg, which is normal procedure on a test flight, and was planning to check each point during my climb and note the various characteristics of stability and control. Then I would proceed to ten thousand feet to conduct landing gear and flap tests, stall the airplane, make a few maneuvers and speed runs, and finally pick up Jim White in *Lulu-Belle*.

However, I dismissed the test card from my mind almost immediately after leaving the ground, as I knew I had a real problem on my hands. As I reduced power to 10,000 rpm my speed dropped to 160 mph and I was just barely able to keep the plane airborne. It skimmed the ground for a considerable distance, and only after several minutes of circling around over the desert was I finally able to get up speed enough to start climbing, which was around 260 miles an hour.

After what seemed forever I reached ten thousand feet. Here I started to notice the longitudinal instability of the airplane, or its tendency to pitch and porpoise through the air. I decided it best to get right at the gear and flap tests and get them wrapped up, so in case anything happened I could be sure of landing the airplane. I tried the gear and it worked all right; then I made a clean stall and found the plane behaved very much like *Lulu-Belle*. Both planes showed a tendency to fall off to the right at the stall.

I then put my wing flaps down and checked their time, and when I raised them again I began having trouble with the flaps. The right flap failed to come up, and before I could check to find out the reason, the airplane began rolling violently to the left, and it took almost full stick to the right to keep it from rolling completely out of control.

I was just slightly east of the main base at Muroc, some six miles south of the north base which we were operating from, at an altitude of ten thousand feet. A tremendous amount of heat was still pouring into the cockpit, and this mental hazard, combined with the turbulent air over the hot desert and the instability of the airplane, didn't make me feel too good. I decided that things were piling up a little too much for me. There was only one place I wanted to be at that moment and that was on the ground.

I headed for the north base, meantime letting my gear down. I then tried to lower my left flap but the mechanism had jammed. My left flap was up and my right flap was down and that was where they had to stay. I didn't dare reduce speed further for fear of stalling the airplane, and it seemed the best thing to do was fly straight in at my present speed, which was about 180 miles an hour. Although it required full stick to the right to fly the airplane, I figured that so long as I held 180 miles I would be able to control it down close to the ground, where I could cut my power. If the wing did tend to drop at that point I would be almost on the ground and it wouldn't be too dangerous. This I did and it worked out fine.

I came in over the railroad tracks at about 180 miles an hour with four miles of dry lake bed in front of me, then leveled off and touched down at about 115 miles an hour. Actually I had control down to almost stall. The cockpit was extremely hot and I was soaking wet with perspiration, so I shut the engine off and let the airplane coast up to the hangar. No one saw me land, and it was several minutes before Kelly came out to meet me.

I told him what had happened and the many little things that were sort of catching up with me. "I'm sorry I couldn't give it a better test," I said, "but I thought it best to get down while the getting was good."

"Don't worry, Tony," he said. "You did the right thing. There is always another day. We can always fix it and fly it again. We are going to fix it, Tony, and don't you worry about that. We will make this the best airplane in the world.'' That was exactly what we did.

Whenever we fly a maiden voyage on a new fighter at Lockheed the boys who worked on the airplane always celebrate afterward with a picnic. Despite the disappointing results of this flight we didn't change the rules. After putting the *Gray Ghost* back in its hangar, we let our hair down. Kelly laid on the beer and sandwiches and he and I gave a talk about the airplane. Everybody had been working pretty hard, and it seemed to relax them and make them feel better.

We spent the next several days going over the airplane to fix the things that were wrong. The flap was no problem. The lack of engine power turned out to be a faulty tachometer that was running faster than the engine, giving me a false reading on engine thrust. With my power way down, it was a wonder I even got off the ground.

We corrected the longitudinal instability of the airplane with heavy bars of lead placed in the nose to move the center of gravity forward; later we learned this is a problem common to most jet fighters when flown without ammunition. They are designed to carry ammunition in the nose, and without this load they exhibit the same porpoising behavior.

With the help of our engine and accessory manufacturers we fixed most of the squawks and I took the XP-80A up for its second flight. With a new forward cg and a true engine reading it felt much better right from the start, and its general stability was greatly improved. But hot air was still coming into the cockpit, and that situation had not improved in the least.

Flight tests continued without a letup, however, as there was no time to lose in correcting any design defects and getting this airplane into production. As the engine got more time on it, its performance also improved. GE stepped up the allowable take-off rating by small increments, finally getting it up to 11,200 rpm. At this power setting I went up one day for a series of speed runs at 10,000 feet.

It was on this flight that the cockpit got so hot I decided to call it quits. After my second run it was absolutely impossible to touch anything in the cockpit, including the throttle and the stick; it was estimated later the temperature was over 180 degrees. My left forearm was so badly dehydrated that I had heat blisters for days. When I came down I said we would have to keep the hot air out or I was through. This got action, and it wasn't long before we found a faulty control valve was passing engine heat into the cockpit. When this was corrected it went a long way toward licking the heat problem in the cockpit, but it was still about 130 degrees. In those days we lacked air-conditioning for jet planes, and the speeds at which they fly and the heat created by the friction of the air make refrigeration an absolute necessity. As a direct result of my experience, Lockheed developed on the P-80 the first combined cockpit pressurization and cooling system for jet fighter planes.

Because of the heat I was forced to make many of my test flights in this airplane without a crash helmet. Lockheed pilots first wore them in the early days of the P-38, for protection at high speeds in turbulent air, when it was common to be thrown against the canopy every time you hit a bump. They were a makeshift sort of thing, built in England for motorcycle and auto racing, and they offered little of the protection afforded today by our modern aircraft crash helmets. I began flying the XP-80A wearing one but perspired so much I could hardly see to fly. Consequently I flew subsequent tests without a helmet until our engineers turned off the heat. It was probably unwise, but I went ahead and did it anyway.

It was on my second flight in this airplane that I noticed a peculiar grumbling sound, like rocks in the gear grinding up in the engine. It made a tremendous noise that caused the plane to vibrate and shake, and on the ground it sounded like an organ pipe that could be heard when the plane was a mile high.

This was our first experience with a new phenomenon which came to be known as "duct rumble." We flew the XP-80A many months, trying to find what caused this noise, before we discovered the reason for the trouble. The intake air ducts passing air to the engine lay at the wing roots in the

P-80, and uneven air flow at high speeds and low engine rpm created turbulent air inside the ducts at the fuselage wall. With wind-tunnel tests we developed a boundary layer "bleed" which bypassed this troublesome air above and below the wing, and both duct rumble and "snaking," which is a fast directional oscillation of the aircraft, were eliminated when this grillwork was installed in the ducts.

Another problem we encountered on early tests was starting a dead or partially flamed-out engine in flight. I first encountered it while running a test to determine the minimum trim speed with an idling engine.

Usually you start these tests up around ten thousand feet, which is high enough to give you ample time to stabilize your speed and hold it long enough to get the test point. This time, however, the burner cans began flaming out when I put the engine in idle position, and one by one the fire went out in half of my fourteen burners. When I opened the throttle again at about two thousand feet I found that my engine was stalled at about two thousand rpm and I could not get my power up; I had a hung engine. Not until I was a thousand feet from the ground was I able to ignite all the burners once more and increase engine power enough to fly the airplane home.

About this time we began flying the second prototype XP-80A, the No. 2 airplane in this series, which we named the *Silver Ghost* because of its distinctive color. This was a piggyback airplane, with an extra seat squeezed into the cockpit behind the pilot for a flight engineer. This permitted him to collect his data at the source firsthand and thus speed up our test program, which was under continual pressure from the military during the last year of the war.

The *Silver Ghost* was the first airplane in the world to fly with external fuel tanks on the wingtips, one of the many innovations designed and pioneered by Kelly Johnson on the P-80. Before this plane flew, all external fuel tanks were carried beneath the wing or the fuselage. Kelly moved them out to the end of the wings after demonstrating in our wind tunnel that tip tanks offered less drag, permitted higher speeds, improved both flight and glide characteristics and actually increased the structural strength of the wings in flight.

The first tanks on the P-80 had a capacity of 165 gallons each and were slung from the end of the wing by a bomb shackle which permitted the pilot to drop them in flight or bring them back for a refill as he desired. For a long-distance record flight across the United States in 1946, one airplane was fitted with 330-gallon tanks. In spite of this extra load of 1,200 pounds at the end of each wing the plane flew very well, and this ability of the P-80 to carry heavy loads was invaluable later in Korea, when it was used as a fighter-bomber against ground targets and carried bomb loads up to 6,000 pounds on the wings without damage to the plane.

It was on an altitude test of fuel flow from tip tanks that I lost my engine and had to make a deadstick landing. I was in the piggyback P-80, and Johnny Margwarth, the P-80 flight test engineer at that time, was in the back seat.

In those days very little was known about getting an air start with a jet engine, and although I tried everything I could think of I was unable to get it started again. When my engine quit I also lost my electrical power, which operated my hydraulic system, and without hydraulic pressure I had to pump my landing gear down by hand.

I started pumping and nothing happened. The hydraulic fluid had gotten very cold at high altitude, almost to the point of congealing, and using only hand pressure I was unable to draw the oil into my hand pump and lower my wheels. I pumped feverishly until we dropped within two thousand feet of the ground, at which point I was completely exhausted. I yelled to Johnny to give me a hand, and by leaning over me he was able to reach the pump handle and work it a few frantic inches at a time. Finally one main wheel indicated down and locked, and a few hundred feet from the ground the other main wheel and the nose wheel extended completely and locked in position—scant seconds from another belly landing.

In 1944 the Army proved to its complete satisfaction that it took a jet to beat a jet.

Toward the end of July tests began to determine how the first-line fighters then in service, the P-38, P-47 and P-51, stood up against the new P-80. Picked Army pilots flying the prop jobs converged secretly on Muroc, accompanied by specially-trained crews in America's newest and best bombers. With other Army pilots flying our two jets, *Lulu-Belle* and the *Gray Ghost* took to the air to play the role of Nazi fighter planes. The objective of this grim shadow-boxing was very simple: to find out what tactical formations, if any, could be employed successfully against the new German jets that were now appearing in the skies over Europe. The outcome was never in doubt—the P-80's were supreme. There were no formations or maneuvers that offered our best planes of 1944 any real defense against the greater speed and higher rate of climb of the jet.

These significant tests only served to increase the tempo of our test program on the P-80, if that was possible, as the Army drove with even greater urgency for early mass production of a plane to meet the German threat. Before long the YP-80, the first production airplane, rolled out of the factory at Burbank and I ferried it to Muroc for a thorough check.

As I took off that day I was suddenly aware of the tendency of the engine to surge and overspeed, and I reduced the

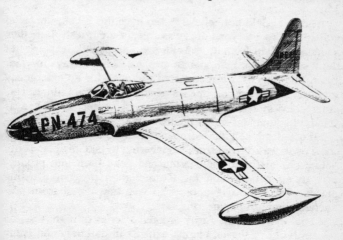

P-80 "Shooting Star"

rpm to prevent a possible engine failure. In those days we had a very simple fuel system, with a barometric control to compensate for change in air density when climbing or diving, and an overspeed governor to control the engine from overspeeding, which is extremely hazardous. It was a malfunction of this governor on the second YP-80 that killed Milo Burcham the following week.

He had just broken ground on his take-off when his engine quit at an altitude of less than fifty feet. The surrounding terrain was poor for a forced landing, so he tried to turn north into an open field. It was late in the day and there was a haze over the field, and apparently he failed to see a gravel pit lying directly across his flight path. Whatever the reason, his plane was sinking at a very high rate and he failed to clear the pit. He crashed into it a few feet from the top and the broken fuel tanks in his P-80 burst into flames.

I was flying a P-38 test when it happened. A few minutes later I landed and taxied up to the hangar, and when I saw the peculiar look on the faces around me I knew something was wrong. The mechanic who brought me my ladder told me Milo was dead.

At first I could not believe it—to have this great pilot, who was loved by everyone and was truly a great test pilot, thus suddenly drawn from us, was almost too much to expect. But the loss of a great man and an airplane is not always in vain. From this tragedy we recognized the need for an emergency fuel system to carry on in case of normal system failure. This emergency system was soon installed in the P-80 and is standard equipment on jet planes today.

Milo's death left the company without a chief pilot, and Joe Towle was moved from engineering to take his place. Jim White had also left engineering and gone back into production flying to work on the Constellation program, trading places with Ernie Claypool, who was transferred from production flying to engineering.

About this time the Army ordered a series of night tests on the visibility of the jet engine exhaust in darkness and Ernie was flying the airplane. He was at Muroc on this test program when he was killed. Joe Towle called me at home just before midnight to tell me Ernie's P-80 had crashed. He and the Army B-25 which was observing his flight had collided in the darkness and both pilots were lost.

This left me as Lockheed's only engineering test pilot. I guess Kelly Johnson didn't have any choice when he approached me a few days later and asked me to head the department. I was still junior in service to most of the company's pilots, and at first I thought he was kidding. When I finally realized he was serious I turned it down, explaining that I had my hands full taking care of my own problems without assuming those of others.

However, Kelly apparently had his mind pretty well set on it, because a week later he approached me again, this time with more firm reasons why I should accept, but again I declined the offer, much as I had done before. This still did not deter him, because a few days later he approached me a third time, and now I thought perhaps I had better take stock of myself and think it over.

After much deliberation I decided there would be no harm in giving it a try. Up to this time I had no experience whatsoever in managing people, especially for a large company, but I decided to give it a whirl. My selection was approved by the company, and in January, 1945, I became Lockheed's chief engineering test pilot, a job I have held ever since.

One of the first things I had to do was get a completely new staff of pilots. Kelly and Hall Hibbard gave me a free hand to pick my own men, and I looked over our production flight staff, interviewing the people I thought were best qualified for test flying. I preferred younger pilots, feeling that any lack of experience they might have would be offset by their aptitude and interest in test work. I felt that first of all a pilot has to be eager to do experimental flying, and secondly he must be qualified; without these two things you do not have the right man.

On this basis I selected Herman Salmon, who already had testing experience with an experimental commercial plane; Stanley Beltz, a former Lockheed mechanic who had learned to fly through difficult means; and Roy Wimmer, whom I had known years before while operating my instrument flying school. The fourth man I chose was Harold Johnson, the famous stunt pilot. He was older than the others, but I felt his wisdom and experience would be useful to our department. It was with this group that I started our new experimental test pilot division of the engineering flight test section, under the capable leadership of Rudy Thoren.

As I was now the only jet pilot left in the engineering department, my first job was to check out my new group in the art of jet flying, as this was to be the most urgent and important test work for many months to come. On March 20 Herman, Stan and I flew to Muroc for jet training. This was to be Stan's checkout day, and I was going to let him fly the *Gray Ghost*. First, however, I decided to make one short flight in this airplane myself on a duct rumble test.

It was on this flight that I had my first serious accident—a turbine wheel failure in the engine that cut the tail off the airplane and nearly cost me my life.

I had climbed to 15,000 feet and was on my descent in a high-speed letdown, intending to reach maximum level flight speed for this test at 10,000 feet. It was to be in the neighborhood of 480 miles an hour indicated, which would have put me well up around 575 miles an hour true air speed and at top rpm of the engine, which at that time was around 11,500.

At 11,000 feet the airplane began to shake slightly, and then suddenly without any warning whatsoever the nose of the plane dropped downward. Then it swung violently to the left with such force that I was hurled against the side of the cockpit. From there on the plane tumbled crazily through space, violently pitching over and about. It was this behavior, this terrible thing that was happening, that made me realize I had lost the tail of my plane. Then I realized that I was going to be killed.

At the rate of speed I had been flying I knew I must be falling toward the ground very fast. There was no way to judge it, as I could not distinguish between the sky and the ground. My head was becoming flushed from being repeatedly subjected to negative acceleration. At one moment I was thrown against the canopy and the next moment I would be bashed back down into my seat. With this going on, I was unable to gather my wits about me to release the canopy of the plane and try to get out.

The emergency canopy release was within a few inches of my left hand, where I had placed it just the day before in case something like this ever happened. But now I could not even think enough to act, and if I had I doubt I could have commanded myself to do anything about it. Then I realized this was the end, and I thought of my wife and children and my family. As these things flashed through my mind the airplane slowed up and the violent tumbling lessened, and I pulled myself together and went to work on the canopy release.

I grasped it in my right hand and gave it a violent jerk. In my excitement I pulled so hard it slipped from my grasp and dangled loosely on the end of its cable. Now I reached back with my left hand and seized the cable itself and brought it forward over my left shoulder. Taking another firm grip with my right hand I lunged forward with all my might, and this time the canopy came off the airplane.

Now the full force of the slipstream tore at me in the open cockpit as I strove to release myself from my seat. I was buckled in by my safety belt, and it took two slices at the belt buckle to get it free. As the belt released the plane was upside down and I literally catapulted out of the cockpit. There were no ejection seats in those days, but luck was with me, as I was thrown free of the airplane, still conscious and apparently unharmed.

A quick look at the ground showed me I was still at a safe altitude, so I did not open my parachute right away. I feared I might be falling too fast, and I did not want to take any chances of ripping my 'chute by opening it at a high speed. Instead I chose to huddle up in a ball and fall free at first to slow up and get away from the plane.

I had fallen like this several seconds when I stretched out to look around, and over to my right I saw the airplane exactly even with me, falling at the same speed I was. It was perhaps a hundred feet away, tumbling through space in crazy fashion, and sure enough, it didn't have any tail.

It was at this point that I realized it was best to open my parachute, which I did. It opened up fine, although this was only the second jump I had ever made, and I started to think about myself and take stock of my injuries. I had a bad cut on my chin, apparently caused by the buckles on my shoulder straps when I left the airplane, but otherwise I seemed all right. I was about to throw my oxygen mask away, along with the parachute rip cord which I still held in my hand, but it was a perfectly good mask so I tucked it inside my leather flying jacket.

As I neared the ground I started swinging, but I pulled one set of risers and spilled air on one side and it stopped. Then I started swinging close to the ground again, but this time I was too low to check it. I was afraid of dumping the 'chute. I hoped to hit on the upswing but I didn't. It was just like a high swing on a tree. I swung right into the ground, and it felt like somebody hit me with a sledge hammer. That's when I really damaged myself. There was an excruciating pain in my back and I fell forward and lay on my stomach for a minute or two until I was sure I was still in one piece. Then I tried to ease the pain by rolling over on my side and then on my back but it didn't help.

After a few minutes a highway worker came up and asked if he could put the 'chute under my head to make me more comfortable. "Sure," I said. "I would appreciate it very much." I was in a state of shock and with no control over myself I began to cry like a baby. Some women and children arrived and spoke to me. In about half an hour I was placed in a jeep and driven over the desert toward Muroc. Part way we were met by an Army ambulance and they put me in it and drove me to the base hospital some thirty miles away.

One of the things that still plagued me in my hours of agony was continually wondering what made the tail of the airplane come off. In about an hour our flight test group from North Base reached the hospital and that was the first thing they asked me. I explained everything I knew and with this information they left to find the wreckage. It was discovered the next morning near the spot where I had landed, and the turbine wheel was missing from the jet engine.

I was X-rayed in the Army hospital but they could not find anything wrong with me. I stayed overnight and was released the next morning, although the pain in my back was killing me. We drove to North Base in a company car and I was made comfortable in one of our rooms at the Desert Rat Hotel. There I waited for the arrival of the Lockheed transport plane and Dr. Poole, our company doctor. Many of the fighter pilots of the time who were running accelerated service tests on the P-80 came in to see me, including Chuck Yaeger, who became the first man to fly faster than sound, and the late Captain Fitzgerald and Don Gentili, who were killed later flying jet airplanes.

When we landed at Lockheed Air Terminal my wife was waiting for me. I was taken in an ambulance to the Good Samaritan Hospital, where a noted orthopedic surgeon was called in to examine me. The first thing he did was have me X-rayed again, and this time they found I had two crushed vertebrae.

I spent five weeks in the hospital, lying in bed while my injured spine healed. When I was ready to leave they wanted to put me in a cast. I felt this was going too far, as I would probably cut myself out of it before I had it on very long, and I told the doctor I much preferred to wear a steel brace. He finally consented, on my promise to wear it religiously at all times, which I did most of the time.

Six long months after my accident, after what seemed to me to be forever, he told me I could throw away my brace and fly again. It was too late in the afternoon to get a flight in that day, but bright and early the next morning I took a P-80 up and wrung it out until I had proved to my own satisfaction that I was finally well and strong again and could continue my flying career.

This accident left a mark on me that was different from any of the other accidents I had before. This was the first time I was ever really injured, and each time for many, many months afterward when I would fly a jet airplane I would think of what happened. On many occasions when I was demonstrating the airplane and wringing it out at maximum performance down close to the ground, I would think of the turbine wheel that broke and, O God! how awful it would be if it happened again. The turbine wheel was actually faulty and broke in two pieces while revolving at high speed. Both pieces flew out through the fuselage, tearing gaping holes in the side of the airplane, and at the speed I was flying the tail loads were too great for this amount of damage to the fuselage, and the weakened tail broke off. We still didn't know why the wheel split; all we knew was that General Electric had experienced several similar failures on the test stand at the factory.

This mystery about the cause of the accident inevitably slowed up our flight test work. It was because the testing on the P-80 was so important that our pilots consented to go ahead and fly the plane, although they knew the turbine wheels might be faulty. To minimize the danger as much as possible, they took off at reduced power and climbed to safe altitudes before increasing engine power, so if anything happened they would have a chance to get out as I did.

This went on for several weeks without anything happening, until finally we decided the faulty wheels had all been eliminated. We had no sooner relaxed, however, than we had another turbine failure—fortunately without injury to the pilot, an Army officer.

He was taking delivery on a P-80 at Van Nuys and had circled the field at low speed for a landing gear check when suddenly his engine quit. Unable to get back to the field, he made a successful belly landing in a bean patch south of the airport. Upon leaving the airplane he discovered two large holes in the fuselage and his turbine wheel missing—the same thing that happened to me the year before.

This was the last straw. At the request of the Lockheed pilots the Army called a meeting and I stood up and demanded to know of both the Army and General Electric if they knew how to test a wheel to find out if it would stay together. It developed they did not know—they thought they did, but apparently the methods they used were not foolproof.

It was some time later, after carefully going through their records, that General Electric found the cause of all our trouble. The turbine wheels were cut from large ingots of steel alloy. In the process of pouring the molten metal to form the ingots, impurities settled to the bottom, and the records revealed that all wheel failures up to that time had occurred with turbine wheels made from the lower portion of the ingots. Until they could devise some way to remove impurities from the metal General Electric stopped using the lower half of the ingots.

Engine failures continued to plague us in one way or another until after the war. Major Richard Bong, the nation's leading ace flying P-38's, who came home from the Pacific to be the Army acceptance pilot for P-80's at Burbank, was killed when he had an engine failure on take-off. It was because of his death and the resulting criticism of jet airplanes that we were forced to move all our jet flying from Burbank to the San Fernando Valley airport at nearby Van Nuys.

I did not read the official report of Major Bong's accident, but I flew many tests in an effort to determine what might have caused it, and I think I know the answer. It was the same kind of accident that killed Milo Burcham, and I am sure the same thing caused it—governor failure. Bong had an emergency fuel system, which Milo did not, but apparently he failed to turn it on prior to take-off. When his regular system failed he crashed.

On August 1, just before the war ended, the Army took the wraps off the P-80 for the first time and the taxpayers got their first look at the world's fastest airplane on the thirty-eighth birthday of the Army Air Forces. The new jet fighter was shown to the press and public at simultaneous exhibitions in New York and Washington. General Arnold, disclosing that the Allies now held supremacy in the field of jet-propelled aircraft, told the nation that both Lockheed and North American were building the P-80 in one of the most intensive production programs of the war. A total of five factories were concentrating on turning out this new fighter, and their target was thirty-five planes a day.

The war ended a few days later and many military planes were cut back or canceled completely, but not the P-80. Taking up where the P-38 left off, it continued in uninterrupted production at Lockheed, going into postwar service as the first plane in the new U. S. Air Force's all-jet fighter force. Performance continued to improve as G.E. and then Allison Division of General Motors built engines with increasingly more power.

Colonel William Councill flew a P-80 from Los Angeles to New York City in four hours thirteen minutes to establish a new transcontinental speed record. Colonel Alfred Boyd flew another P-80 623 miles an hour over a measured course at Muroc in 1947 to return the official world speed record to the United States after an absence of twenty-three years. In 1948 sixteen P-80's became the first American jet planes to fly the Atlantic Ocean and the first jets of any nation to make the round trip back home again. Starting in 1948 the P-80 was the first American jet assigned overseas, with units in Panama, Germany, Alaska and Japan.

It's just as well they were. In June, 1950, barely two

MiG-15

weeks after the last of nearly two thousand redesignated F-80's rolled off the assembly line to make room for newer Lockheed jets, history's first jet war started in far-off Korea. Five groups of F-80's in Japan and Okinawa, aided by a handful of P-51's, were the only planes we had on hand when the shooting started.

For many anxious months they were still all we had. If they had failed, I'm told we would have been driven out of Korea. Equally important, I think, if they had failed the jet airplane would have been set back years in its development, and our whole jet air force perhaps scrapped and built over at a fantastic cost in time and money.

All the world knows the F-80 did not fail. History tells how it proved the jet airplane is a better airplane. It did every job they gave it, in the air and on the ground, and came back for more. And when a newer, faster jet, the Russian-built MiG-15, came over the Yalu in November, 1950, it was an F-80 that shot it down in the world's first all-jet air battle.

That was a great day for *Lulu-Belle*.

12

Postwar Air Racing

Like so may other dirt-track pilots who gave up air racing for the duration, when the war ended and the heat was off I took advantage of the unaccustomed luxury of spare time to get back into speed flying. For the first time in four years my weekends were my own, and I could even miss work if I had to. The urgency of wartime testing was over, and now I could think seriously about the kind of flying I did before Pearl Harbor. I had never forgotten the thrill of being a winner, and with my job back on a peacetime footing I used this opportunity to race again.

Although nearly seven years had passed, I still remembered the Thompson Trophy Race at Cleveland in 1939 when I won second place. That was the last race before the war, but I had never lost my ambition to try again if the national air races were resumed. All through the war years I thought constantly of what kind of airplane I would use to win the Thompson Trophy when I started racing again, and I actually made plans as early as 1942 to get a P-38 if I could.

One night in January, 1946, while attending the weekly lodge meeting, as we call the QB's or Quiet Birdmen, I got my chance. We were sitting around swapping stories after dinner when something I heard made me prick up my ears. More than seventy-five hundred war-surplus airplanes had been flown into nearby Kingman, Arizona, Air Base to be sold at a fraction of their original cost, and new P-38's were on the block for $1,250. This was just what I had been waiting for.

Early the next morning I telephoned Kingman for the details, which were very simple: all I needed was a cashier's check made out to the U. S. Treasury and I could take my pick of the lot and fly away with it. It seemed too good to be true, and I felt like a kid about to get that new toy he wanted. I drew the money out of the bank, asked Rudy Thoren for the day off and started for Kingman, accompanied by my old friend Sammy Mason, a wartime instructor at one of the civilian flying schools and now the operator of a small but flourishing flying circus. I didn't know what I was going to do with a P-38 right at that moment, but for $1,250 I figured I couldn't go wrong.

We were at the air base when it opened the following morning and I was escorted over to one corner of the field where about five hundred P-38's were lined up waiting for somebody to take them home. Most of them had been flown less than twenty hours. As far as the eye could see there was nothing but airplanes. I spent almost all day climbing in and out of cockpits, and finally satisfied myself I had found a winner.

After handing over my money I took my new plaything up for a test flight around the field. Everything checked okay, so without further delay I said good-bye to Sammy, who stayed behind to drive my car home, and took off for Burbank, where I landed at the Lockheed airport and parked outside the flight test hangar. When I went in Rudy was in his office and I asked him to take a look out the window. He acted like he had never seen a P-38 before. After the excitement died down I told him I planned to strip the airplane to its essentials and convert it for acrobatics.

As the days passed and word of my new project got around the engineering department I found myself collecting a large and very enthusiastic ground crew. Glenn Fulkerson, who had been my P-38 crew chief in England, took his old job "on the cuff," as did the others. Most of the mechanics were men from the experimental department who loved the P-38 and shared my desire to show the public it was a great airplane.

We got our chance in May at Mines Field in Los Angeles, when the Hearst newspapers sponsored one of the first air shows to be held after the war. It was also my first opportunity to do in public many of the maneuvers I had performed in Army P-38's during the war. Deciding I needed a special insurance policy just in case, I applied for coverage to a Los Angeles broker in the following letter, which gives a good idea of my act:

Gentlemen:

Regarding my negotiations to purchase insurance coverage for my airplane and myself, I am furnishing you with an outline of my flight routine. This demonstration is identical to the ones I have put on for the past four years for the Army Air Corps. They are well within the limits of the airplane, and at no time is the pilot or plane in a dangerous attitude—speed, of course, being the criterion. My P-38 in particular is specially designed for this work, being even better than the standard P-38 pursuit plane, which I have demonstrated in the past. Following is an approximate list of maneuvers that I perform, going from one to the other:

1. Take off, climb to approximately 15,000 feet and make a dive down to and level off at a safe altitude. No dangerous speeds are attained—will be well within critical allowed.

2. A vertical climb with possible aileron roll on the way up.

3. Aileron rolls coming down.

4. Leveling off and doing a square loop with rolls on the straight sides.

5. A cuban eight.

6. An aileron roll in straight flight.

7. A circle doing aileron rolls.

8. A speed climb to altitude.

9. A dive with one engine stopped and propeller feathered.

10. An aileron roll in level flight.

11. Inverted reversements, straight flight.

12. Unfeathering demonstration.

13. Climb and dive, feathering one engine.

14. A chandelle.

15. Gear and flap extension and land with one engine dead.

Trusting that this doesn't make you shudder and raise the price of my premiums, I sincerely hope that we do business.

They must have thought it was safe because I got the insurance.

After Army and Navy pilots had thrilled the crowd with mass formation flights and precision stunt flying, it was my turn to perform. I held my P-38 down close to the runway all the way to the end of the field, where I pulled up and over on my back, followed with a half-roll to normal flight attitude, at which point I was going in the opposite direction from take-off.

I proceeded to execute my next maneuvers, first with both engines operating and then with one engine dead. This always got the crowd on their feet, and when I began my climb to altitude for the grand finale they were following me closely.

Down I came, picking up speed, and when it seemed I would fly into the ground I pulled up and over in a half roll. Back up I went again. Then both propellers stopped turning and down I came once more in a nearly vertical dive. At the last moment the nose came up and at three hundred feet I pulled out of the dive and went around and landed. I could see by the look on the faces around me that the act went over well, and I felt really proud, especially of the P-38.

The following week I got a telegram from Ben Franklin, general manager of the national air races, asking me to fly back to Cleveland to help set up the race program, and when I came home I had a contract in my pocket to put on my show. This was good news to the gang in Burbank, who immediately went to work to improve the airplane. It was the next month, as a result of these improvements, that we realized it was exceptionally fast, even for a P-38, and I decided to enter it in the 1946 air races.

We were looking for any new way to increase its performance, no matter how little, and with this thought in mind, Herman Salmon came up with a suggestion that was different and really helpful. It was his idea to contact the Minnesota Mining and Manufacturing Company, who made Scotch tape, and get enough tape to seal up the whole airplane. The resulting smooth surface would reduce wind resistance to a minimum and make the plane fly faster.

My crew had shaken down to about fifteen regular workers by this time, ten of whom agreed to take their vacations in September and go to Cleveland with me. Glenn and I went ahead in the airplane. We rented a big house near the airport to be handy to everything, and the gang made it their home when they arrived. Four drove my car back pulling a trailer loaded with spare parts and the others made their own way east from California.

Glenn and I had a few days to spare, so we took a day off and flew to Minneapolis to see the Scotch tape people. We really hoped they would sponsor us in return for the free advertising, which they turned down, but they were glad to give us all the Scotch tape we wanted. We gladly accepted this generous offer and returned to Cleveland with two boxes of tape.

A few days before the qualifying flights got under way I flew the course to give it a final check. This was an opportunity to time myself, and I averaged almost 380 miles an hour around the thirty-mile rectangle. It was pretty fast for a closed course in this airplane and as a result we were all extremely optimistic about our chances.

However, I knew I would be up against faster planes, and I left it to the gang to decide what we should shoot for. The Thompson Trophy Race, with first prize of $16,000, was the big money, but I wasn't sure I could qualify for it, and I was ready to settle for less. The boys replied that they were in Cleveland for all we could get, win, lose or draw, and they voted unanimously to enter the Thompson. The next day I filed my papers and qualified at 376 mph.

When the races started I was ready with my acrobatic act, flying two shows a day. The first show consisted of the usual stunts on one and two engines, with my deadstick dive in reserve for the final performance. Climbing to fifteen thousand feet, I feathered both propellers, shut off both engines and came screaming down in front of the grandstand, followed by deadstick maneuvers and landing. This went on for three days, with the Thompson race scheduled for the fourth and final day.

That morning Ben Franklin told me it was too much for any man to stunt and race the same day. Knowing my heart was in the Thompson, he generously offered to waive my acrobatic contract that day so I could race instead. It was a lucky break for us, as there was a lot of work to be done on the airplane, including the installation of two extra gas tanks to give me enough fuel for the three-hundred-mile grind.

We had kept the box well hidden, for fear of giving someone else an idea, but now we broke out the Scotch tape. Sure enough, it drew immediate attention. Several other planes were in the same hangar and the word quickly got around. Bruce Raymond, flying a P-51 in the Thompson Trophy Race, was the first to come over and ask if he could have some of our tape.

I didn't care, but I felt I had my crew to consider, and I thought they should decide. I told Bruce to ask Glenn and I was agreeable to anything they decided. Glenn turned him down. "If it was a part you needed or something else necessary to keep you in the race, we would be glad to help you," Glenn said, "but we kind of figured the Scotch tape was a speed secret, and the answer is 'no.' "

There wasn't much the other boys could say after that, but I understand there was quite a rushing business at the local drugstores that morning in Scotch tape. There weren't many places open on Labor Day, and a number of crew chiefs had their scouts out trying to buy tape. But it didn't do any good; we had tape up to five inches wide, and the little ¾-inch rolls in the stores couldn't begin to compete. When the P-38 came out of its hangar that afternoon it was literally a flying roll of Scotch tape.

Half an hour before starting time Glenn taxied the airplane to my take-off spot and the crew made their last-minute checks. With about ten minutes to go I climbed in the cockpit and made my final checks. When the five-minute flag went up I started my engines, and at the one-minute flag I was all buckled in, with my canopy down and both engines running. As the seconds ticked off I gradually opened my throttles, and when the starting flag dropped I was practically wide open. I released my brakes and shot forward, one of a dozen planes gunning toward the scatter pylon at the end of the field.

Out of the corner of my eye I could see Tex Johnston in the lead in his powerful P-39 *Cobra 2*. He was in the air with his wheels up before the rest of us left the ground. I was off in second place about even with George Welch in a P-51, and Tex, George and I were leading at the scatter pylon, with the rest of the field well behind. About two miles down the No. 1 straightaway I saw George pull up with white smoke streaming from his engine, and I knew that was the end of the race for him.

The No. 2 pylon was in something of a hollow on the back stretch, making it difficult to find, but I spotted it by the large number of cars parked below. I knew the course very well by that time, having flown it several times to familiarize myself with landmarks, and from then on I was able to stay on course exactly as I had planned. I had the throttles wide open and now was trailing Johnston in second place.

Charlie Tucker's P-63 went out of the race in the second lap with landing-gear trouble as I concentrated on catching Tex. The race was ten laps around a thirty-mile course, and up to the halfway point I was gaining on him. Then he put on more power and started to pull away. As I entered the sixth lap I knew that I couldn't catch him, barring accidents, as he just had too much speed for me, and I concentrated on holding my own. I finished second with an average speed of 370 miles an hour, only three miles slower than the winner, and I won a total of $8,600 in prize money, including three lap prizes of $600. We were satisfied; our P-38 was up against the fastest piston-engine planes in the world, and second place was just as good as first to us.

My flaps were still taped in closed position. In the excitement of winning second place I forgot about them when I entered the traffic pattern and landed, and the next day we found the left outboard flap had been completely locked up by the Scotch tape. In failing to come down it had torn its cables out by the roots and practically ruined the flap system. We disconnected the right outboard flap to balance the trim and that was the way I flew back to California. It was the last time I ever raced an airplane covered with Scotch tape.

A new event for midget planes was a feature of the Cleveland air races the following year. Conceived as an event that would bring the race closer to the spectator, it was limited to stock engines of not more than 190 cubic inches displacement. The Goodyear Tire & Rubber Company agreed to sponsor the race for three years and put up prize money, and the Race Pilots Association voted to endorse it. I had never lost my early interest in midget planes, starting with the Pobjoy Special back in 1937, and I was no sooner back in Burbank than I began making plans to build and race a new midget plane of my own design at Cleveland the following year.

With my friends who worked with me on the P-38 I formed LeVier & Associates, a group of aviation enthusiasts to design and build midget racing planes. We pledged ourselves to build five metal monoplanes, and with five expert engineers from Lockheed's experimental department in charge and a total work force of nearly forty men, we set up a spare-time, back-yard organization and got started.

The job was spread among five groups, each directed by an engineer. Irving Culver headed the fuselage group, with Julius Jaeger on wings, Dave Hill on wheels and landing gear, Harold Bojens on power plant and Phil McLane on tail assembly. Actual fabrication didn't begin until after Christmas, leaving us only eight months to build five complete airplanes. We continually underestimated our time requirements, and as we fell progressively farther behind schedule I kept chopping the project until finally we were down to two airplanes. Looking back now I can see we would have been smarter to build only one plane and make it tops.

We eventually built and flew both airplanes, named the Cosmic Wind Specials. I called my plane *Little Toni* after my eldest daughter, and Fish Salmon had the *Minnow*. They were the smallest all-metal man-carrying airplanes ever built—having a wingspan of only 19½ feet and 16 feet long. Each powered by an 85-horsepower Continental engine, they had a design top speed of 200 miles an hour and cost about $15,000. As the prize money in the midget races at Cleveland that year totaled $25,000, if we won we figured to get some of our money back.

Working every night and weekends to get them finished in time, the midgets wore us all out but we made it. Glenn Fulkerson and I flew east again in the P-38, while John Clark, another Lockheed mechanic, drove *Little Toni* back on a specially-built trailer behind Glenn's Buick convertible. Fish Salmon was last finishing his plane and it was flown to Cleveland in a cargo plane.

We reached Cleveland to find some stiff competition waiting for us in the midget class. Billy Robinson, also a Lockheed mechanic, had entered the old Brown racer I bought but never flew back in 1936, using a Continental eighty-five-horsepower engine. Steve Wittman, one of the world's oldest racing pilots, was there with *Buster*, a midget racer of his own design, with Bill Brennan as pilot, and Art Chester's *Swee' Pea*, flown by Paul Penrose, was another new design.

The 1947 Cleveland air races were probably the greatest ever held anywhere. This was the year of races supreme. In addition to the Thompson and Bendix races, each with two divisions, and the Goodyear race, they had the Kendall Trophy Race for P-51's, the Tinnerman Trophy Race for P-63's, the Allison Trophy Race for F-80's and the Sohio Trophy Race for P-38's. With the Halle Trophy Race for women, practically everyone with a desire to race had a chance to do so.

I found myself entered in three races, and counting two heat races and two semifinal races in the midget class, I flew a total of seven races in two days, including five on one day.

This was the hardest day of flying I have ever experienced. In the last race that day I won the Sohio trophy and $3,000 prize money in my red P-38 with an average speed of 360 miles an hour, including $500 for the fastest lap. That night I slept like a baby.

It was in the first heat of the midget class that I almost met my maker on two different occasions. Going around the scatter pylon as the race began I narrowly averted a mid-air collision, and later in the same heat I flew into turbulent air and turned upside down only seventy-five feet off the ground. If it had not been for the excellent design of my airplane and its very responsive controls I would certainly have crashed.

It was this experience that made me realize midget racing was far from the safe kind of air racing it was supposed to be. I had run into prop wash before but never like this. These small, light airplanes were like a feather in the breeze, and I began wondering if maybe air racing might be getting a little out of hand.

Six planes took off in the finals of the midget race, including Fish Salmon and myself. The course was a nightmare of high wires, buildings and trees. Bill Brennan in *Buster* won the event and $7,000 first prize money at an average speed of 165 miles an hour. Fish and I placed third and fourth respectively, winning $3,000 between us, but Fish came back the following year to win this race at an average speed of nearly 170 mph.

The last race of the show and the main event was the Thompson Trophy Race, and twelve planes started out of thirty-one entered, including my P-38. The course was smaller and tighter this year, with the laps cut from thirty to fifteen miles around, which cut the speed considerably. I had qualified at 366 miles an hour, or ten miles an hour under my qualifying speed the year before.

The Thompson Trophy Race of 1947 turned out to be the bloodiest air race ever staged, and the day of the race is still known as "Bloody Monday." It wasn't the fault of anyone in particular. The trouble was the souped-up engines in the big wartime fighters in this race, and the pilots trying to get every ounce of power out of them. My P-38 was the only plane in the race that wasn't having its heart pulled right out of it. I flew without turbo-superchargers, having removed them to lighten my plane for low-altitude acrobatics, and the best I could get was seventeen hundred horsepower per engine, but many of the others were pulling as much as twenty-two hundred and twenty-four hundred horsepower from the same engines.

I got off to a slow start, but luck was with me, as the scatter pylon lay directly in front of me. With twelve planes all converging on that one point I stayed down low, just brushing the treetops, and as I made my first quick snap turn onto the straightaway I broke out in front and in the clear. But my advantage was shortlived. Tony Janazzo and Cook Cleland, both flying Goodyear F2G's with Pratt & Whitney R-4360 engines, soon passed me, followed by several others.

The first crash came when the race had hardly begun. Jack Hardwick's Merlin engine blew up as he rounded the scatter pylon. He did a superb job of flying on borrowed time, finally getting down in a small clearing east of the airport. As he came in for a deadstick landing his P-51 hit a tree and the right wing ripped off. The plane caught fire and burned but Jack got out unharmed.

Going into the second lap, Charlie Walling dropped out with engine trouble. Two laps later my aileron boost went out and I realized I was in for a tough time the rest of the way, as this race was all ailerons and elevators. I tried to minimize the extra burden this threw on me by starting my turns about a mile from the pylons, and with that much time to roll into my banks the job was somewhat easier.

Coming up No. 3 straightaway and starting into my turn at the No. 4 pylon I sensed another plane close at hand. Looking to the right I was startled to see Skip Ziegler's P-40 flying not twenty feet away. I thought this was strange, as I didn't know he had qualified for the Thompson. He decided to fly anyway.

Skip was pressing me too closely and I didn't like it one bit. With my aileron boost not working, my pylon turns were extremely difficult under the best circumstances, and he certainly wasn't helping matters by crowding me like that.

I steepened my bank still more and tightened my turn until I thought my "G" suit would burst, and this time I got ahead of him. As I rolled out of my turn on the home straightaway I looked back and he was at least a third of a mile behind me.

My lead didn't last long, as he had more speed than I did, and although I could take him on the turns he caught up with me at the next pylon. I put on a little more speed now by increasing my engine rpm to thirty-three hundred. This was pretty high for continuous operation such as the race I was now flying, but I wanted to get Ziegler out of my hair. I settled down to flying a tighter race and the next time I looked back he was gone.

I had just completed the seventh lap and was rounding the No. 1 pylon when off in the distance I saw a bright flash of fire and a large cloud of black smoke and I knew that one of the boys had crashed. Later I learned that Tony Janazzo had augered in. It almost seemed that madmen were flying this race and each was trying to outdo the other regardless of the cost.

Next to go was Woody Edmundson, whose Merlin engine exploded and almost blew him from the cockpit as he rounded the third pylon in the eleventh lap. He crashed in an open field and was pulled from the burning wreckage dazed and badly cut about the head, but he lived to race again.

Entering the last half of the race, five of the thirteen planes had already pulled out or crashed. Next to go was Skip Ziegler, No. 13 to start. As I rounded the No. 4 pylon I saw his P-40 crash in the railroad yards off to the right of the home straightaway, setting a freight car on fire. Skip escaped with a broken leg.

Probably the hardest-luck guy who ever entered an air race was Ron Puckett. Ron couldn't start his engine and failed to get off with the rest of us. When he finally got in the air we had finished the first lap. Ron threw caution out the window and by flying with everything wide open was in fourth place when his engine quit again and forced him down.

With six planes left in the race, Cook Cleland went on to win, followed by Dick Becker in second place. I was glad when the race was over. I finished next to last and my average speed of 357 miles an hour was nearly 40 miles an hour slower than the winner.

As I got the checkered flag I pulled up to seven thousand feet and throttled back to minimum horsepower to conserve my fuel. With my hydraulic system out, I knew it was going to be a long, hard job to pump my landing gear down by hand. I went to the emergency system and started pumping, only to find I was able to move the pump handle just a couple of inches because the extra gas tank behind my seat was in the way.

This didn't have much effect on the gear, so I unhooked my safety belt and squatted down in the seat in order to get the maximum stroke possible on the pump. After five minutes my engines began cutting out, so I turned on a new set of tanks and returned to the pump. I kept up this process until all my wing tanks were dry and I was feeding gas from my last remaining fuel tank in the nose of the airplane.

I continued pumping until I had spots before my eyes and my head was aching, and after what seemed an eternity my wheels finally indicated down and locked and I got into the traffic pattern and landed. When my plane finally stopped I was so exhausted I had to be lifted out of the cockpit.

This was the last race I ever flew. My family and the company wanted me to give it up, and the next summer, just before the 1948 air races, I chose to quit professional racing. I made the decision of my own accord. Although I had a great love for racing, I began to see we had reached the point where there wasn't much to be gained from it. To tell the truth, it was getting out of hand. With the growth of cities, emergency landing fields had mostly disappeared, and the percentages were against you. Measured against the risks involved, it seemed the rewards were very small. And in the last analysis I could see that competition was getting too fast for my wartime airplane, and as I never had a sponsor I couldn't afford the cost of making it faster. I kept my hand in midget racing for a while, but not as a pilot. Billy Robinson flew *Little Toni* for me the next two years, until two fatal accidents made me call it quits altogether.

In 1949 I organized Pacific Air Race, Inc., to sponsor

midget races in southern California. Herman Salmon, Glenn Fulkerson, Charlie Tucker and Art Chester were my partners in this venture, with Herman and Art also flying. It was jinxed from the start. Two pilots were killed at our first meet at San Diego, one of them Art Chester, and the concluding meets at Newhall and Ontario were financial failures.

After the first fatal accident at San Diego I paid particular attention to the planes in the next race, hoping and praying that there wouldn't be any more. I had my eyes on Chester as he rounded the home pylon behind Steve Wittman, and the way he was flying I could tell he was out to win.

As he flew through Steve's prop wash his plane wavered to the left in the turbulent air, then right, followed by a half-snap roll into the ground. It was hard to believe that he was gone. Billy Robinson flying *Little Toni* behind Art was so saddened by what he had seen that he dropped from the race and landed.

With the main event still to be run off, we called a meeting of the surviving pilots and again warned them to avoid flying directly behind one another. Benny Howard had some very stern words to say on this subject, and his talk apparently made an impression, as the main event went off without further accidents, Herman Salmon winning the race.

We took the Cosmic Winds back to Cleveland in September, where they placed fourth and fifth in the Goodyear trophy race. That was Herman's last professional air race. He was being pressured to give it up as I did and Cleveland was his swan song. The $2,000 we won in the national air races that year helped pay off the debts we still owed on our midget planes, and when I returned to Burbank, LeVier & Associates and Pacific Air Race, Inc., went out of business forever.

It was just as well, because there were new jets ready to fly at Lockheed and I've had my hands full with test work ever since.

13

Jet Training

I had been flying jets only a few months when I saw the necessity of a jet training plane for student pilots.

Jet flying is easy but it is different too, and even experienced pilots had trouble making the change from propeller-driven planes. Except for take-off and landing, the jet does everything just about twice as fast as the conventional aircraft. In addition, the poor acceleration of early jet engines, the different take-off characteristics and higher landing speeds made it difficult and even dangerous to go directly from piston-engine planes into jets without transition training at the hands of an experienced teacher.

The Air Force met this problem at first by ground instruction in F-80's, but the student was still alone when he made his first jet flight and he had to solo without jet experience in the air. It was obvious to us that he could solo better and more safely if he did some jet flying with an instructor first. From 1945 to 1947 I saw many accidents and close calls in Air Force jets, all because the students lacked the safety factor present when they are checked out by someone with them in the airplane. Here are just two examples out of many that illustrate what I am talking about:

It is essential to reach a ground speed of at least 125 miles an hour before trying to take the F-80 off the ground, and I always tried to impress that on pilots. Let the airplane roll, I told them, it won't hurt anything, but get that speed, that's the important thing. I always explained in great detail the tendency of the jet plane to become airborne and then stall and settle back on the ground if the take-off is attempted at insufficient speed. One day I saw the result of a fairly intelligent pilot not heeding my warning.

He started down a six-thousand-foot runway at Muroc, which would normally be more than ample for an F-80, but in a matter of a few seconds I saw him attempt to raise the nose of the airplane. He got the nose wheel off the ground with the nose of his plane up high and the whole airplane at an extreme angle, and I crossed my fingers because I knew if he continued in this manner a crash would surely take place.

As he left the ground the nose went up still further, and sure enough the airplane stalled and fell back to the ground. Instead of heeding this warning, he continued to pull the nose up, and every time he left the ground the plane stalled and fell back again. Finally he realized the mistake he was making and he left the nose on the ground long enough to gather sufficient speed for take-off. By this time, however, he had used up most of the runway, and being unable to stop at that point he had to continue off the end of the strip. Luckily for him, the overrun was reasonably smooth, and he actually went through the weeds about a thousand feet beyond the runway before he became fully airborne.

The next pilot who made this mistake wasn't so lucky. He ran the full length of the field too, mushing off the ground and then falling back again, and at the last moment cut his power and tried to stop. At the end of the runway he ran into an A-26 bomber parked on the field, knocking off its landing gear, and the bomber fell on top of the F-80 cockpit, crushing the pilot to death. The investigating officer reported that the F-80 couldn't get off the ground because its center of gravity was shifting! That's how much they knew about jets in those days.

It was accidents such as this that brought our decision to build a jet training plane, although the Air Force didn't want one and we built it with our own money. Kelly Johnson called me into his office in March, 1947, and told me of the company's decision to construct a prototype trainer and try to sell it to the Air Force.

I immediately pictured a modified single-seat airplane like the piggyback version of the early F-80, but Kelly said the trainer would be a brand-new plane. It was going to be a real honest-to-goodness airplane, with two cockpits in tandem and dual controls and instruments. "The government needs a jet trainer," Kelly said. "Right now they don't want it but they're going to get it, and I think they will like it."

Although Lockheed had built over one thousand jet planes by that time, they all belonged to the Air Force. To proceed with our new project we got one of these jet fighters on loan, and it was this airplane that became America's first jet trainer. Using the experimental shop next door to the flight test division, a crew of fourteen men began work in August to build the prototype model. They took a standard F-80 off the production line, cut the fuselage apart and stretched it thirty-eight inches. In this extra space they installed a seat for a passenger behind the pilot. Air intake ducts on each side of the fuselage were lengthened and the airplane's electrical and hydraulic systems were extended. The biggest problem was designing a new seven-foot-long canopy to cover both cockpits.

Because the curvature of the canopy created severe suction loads during high-speed flight, new fittings were needed to withstand very strong pressures. Eight hardened steel hooks, four on each side, were designed to keep the canopy locked in place, each tested to withstand a pull of ten thousand pounds, which was more than the weight of the airplane. The whole canopy could be jettisoned or blown free by an explosive charge in flight if trouble developed and it became necessary for the occupants to leave the airplane.

On March 22, 1948, seven months after work began, I took the nation's first jet trainer up for its first flight at Lockheed's jet base at Van Nuys. It flew like an F-80, only faster. From that day forward we immediately launched upon a program of test flying designed to prove every feature of this new plane. The distinction of being the first man to ride as a passenger in the nation's first two-seat jet went to Woody Gaiser, the flight test engineer on the trainer project, who flew with me constantly. Sometimes Fish Salmon and I flew together to rotate the work and speed up the testing program.

It was on my third test flight that I had an accident that nearly cost me my life.

We were demonstrating the airplane to the Air Force for the first time, and there were a number of military guests at Van Nuys airport that day, headed by Lieutenant General George Stratemeyer. While waiting for the plane to be serviced I asked the general if he cared to ride with me. He chose not to, so when the plane was ready I got in and took off.

My plan was to gain altitude and dive on the airstrip directly in front of the spectators. These demonstrations always include dragging or buzzing the field at high speed, and the whistle of the approaching plane at low altitude, the knifing effect through the air and the rapid rate of closing which accompany this maneuver show the jet off in a thrilling manner. I then would follow my high-speed pass with a pullup, ending with a series of aileron rolls to give the show a little flash.

I came down across the field about fifty feet off the ground, going about 500 miles an hour, and at a distance of one hundred yards beyond the audience I started my pullup. I pulled up quite abruptly, reaching approximataly six G's, when suddenly there was a loud explosion and I was suddenly aware of tremendous gusts of wind and dirt hitting me in the face.

For a split second I thought the airplane had disintegrated and I had been thrown out into space. My natural instinct was to duck my head and hold on to the stick. As I did this I realized the airplane was still flying, and as it was now pointed upward quite steeply, I let it continue to climb. Then I gathered my wits and looked around to see what had happened, and much to my surprise I found the canopy had torn off the airplane and I was sitting out in the open. I must admit that it gave me a very uncomfortable feeling.

I looked back to see if the canopy had struck the tail and damaged it when it came off, but no damage was visible, and when I moved my controls they seemed to be working okay.

By this time I had climbed to around ten thousand feet, and I decided to fly around at this altitude to test the plane for any other possible damage before coming down again and landing.

It was soon apparent there was no need for further alarm, as the airplane was flying satisfactorily. The hooks that held the canopy in place were wide open and the whole thing was gone. My next thought was to establish radio contact with the ground. I called the tower without getting any answer, and it was not until then that I realized my crash helmet was missing, together with the earphones attached to it. By some freak of nature my glasses were still on.

On the ground, meanwhile, there was utter horror, followed by a feeling of anxious relief. Through the billowing dust and dirt at the moment of my accident the group of dumbstruck onlookers saw the canopy hurtle to the ground, and then out of the billowing cloud they saw a round object resembling a human head tumble to earth. For one awful moment they thought it was mine. Then as the silver airplane climbed steadily upward they knew it was being guided by human hands and I was still alive.

By this time I had let down again and came in and made a normal landing. As I taxied to a stop in front of the crowd there was a rush to the airplane to see if I was injured, but I waved reassuringly from the cockpit to show I was all right. For a minute I just sat there looking down at them, too exhausted to move.

A quick cockpit examination by our engineers showed what was wrong. My high G pullout, resulting in a negative load, released the tension on the canopy hooks enough to spring them, and at that point the canopy handle dropped of its own weight and the canopy jettisoned itself. The vertical stabilizer was wrinkled by the violent shock to the airplane when the canopy detached itself but otherwise the plane escaped damage.

The Air Force liked what they saw of our new plane in California, but to really sell it and get a production order we took it on tour to the East Coast. Our plan was very simple: visit as many Air Force installations as possible, give jet rides to as many passengers as we could find, and by demonstrating the plane to the right people, hope to find a customer. This was an official company project, and we did it with Air Force approval, but basically it was just another barnstorming trip, and I was the pilot.

With Elly Hawkes as my flight engineer and a handpicked group of our best mechanics as ground crew to service and maintain the airplane, we left Burbank late in June. After stops en route to fly military passengers at several Air Force bases, we reached Washington, D.C., early in July to begin a series of jet rides for civilians.

Our passengers this time were leading newspaper and magazine aviation writers and editors from New York and Washington. Except for a handful who had flown piggyback in the early Bell P-59 Airacomet during the war, they were all strangers to jet flying, and none had ever experienced the full thrill of a jet. If they liked the ride we gave them we felt they might write stories that would interest others in jets.

Flying out of Andrews Air Force Base near Washington, nearly fifty newspapermen and military passengers rode with me that week in our jet trainer. July is hot in Washington but we had good weather, and for six days I flew a regular schedule of passenger rides every day. We were aiming at three rides every two hours, with refueling between every flight, and some days we did even better. Lockheed and the Air Force had the boys lined up and ready for me, and there was always another passenger waiting to get on board when I came down. Elly Hawkes briefed each man on emergency ejection procedures as he was strapped in the cockpit and John Guenther stuck a $25,000 life insurance policy in his hand and we were off.

The routine I used in demonstrating the airplane at Andrews was pretty much of a constant pattern. I had it figured out that the best way to show the airplane off was to give the passenger a maximum-performance take-off and climb at a steep angle for the first few hundred feet, followed by a maximum-performance climb to about ten thousand feet. After that I would go through a few simple maneuvers, starting out with stalls, and actually allow the passenger to follow through on the control stick if he desired. This was generally followed by a high-speed run at ten thousand feet, concluding with a zoom over the field and a series of aileron rolls. A jet airplane rolls very easily and all the passengers made at least one aileron roll to get the feel of it. Everyone who flew with me at Andrews was anxious for the full demonstration, including fellows who had never flown before.

When it came to demonstrating the airplane to military passengers, many of them from the Pentagon, I offered to show them the excellent glide characteristics of the jet airplane. Due to its clean design and low drag, it was possible to glide our jet trainer great distances with a dead engine, and I demonstrated this on many occasions by actually shutting off the engine in flight.

I also demonstrated the go-around characteristics of this plane, sometimes referred to as wave-offs, if necessary in making a landing. Although it was quite common with the conventional propeller-driven plane, this maneuver was considered difficult for a jet plane at that time due to the poor acceleration of its engine. In fact, however, it was extremely easy to perform, and in many cases the jet did just as well as the reciprocating engine.

Word of our jet rides got around town, and before the week was out several Navy officers showed up to see what was going on. This was an Air Force show and they were buying the gas, but our Navy friends had come a long way to ride with us, and the Air Force graciously offered to let them fly. Two or three officers went up with me, and were so impressed with the airplane that they asked me to bring it down to the naval test center at Patuxent River, Maryland, for further demonstrations. I said I would be happy to do so and suggested they get in touch with Lockheed to arrange it.

The next stop on our barnstorming trip was the big Air Force test center at Wright Field, Ohio, where I spent another week flying military passengers and newspapermen. It was here I think we reached the people who later bought the airplane. By the end of this week I had made over eighty flights without any mechanical trouble, but the airplane was getting fairly tired and needed overhaul. I was ready to fly it back to Burbank when I received orders from the factory to return to Patuxent for demonstration flights for the Navy.

Several top Navy people rode with me there, including John Brown, Assistant Secretary for Air, and Admiral Pride, chief of the Bureau of Aeronautics. They all asked for the complete demonstration, so I took the opportunity to show them the many advantages of the jet airplane over earlier types. The only disagreeable flight of the entire trip occurred at Patuxent when I was flying a young naval lieutenant. We were at twelve thousand feet when for some reason or other he suddenly jammed the stick forward and the airplane nearly pitched out of control. As I wrestled the stick out of his hands I asked him what he was trying to do, and he said he just wanted to see if a jet would be a good dive bomber. I reminded him it was no way to treat an airplane, and I told him if he had any more maneuvers in mind I would appreciate it if he would notify me in advance.

When I got home I learned from Rudy Thoren and Kelly Johnson that our trip had paid off. The Air Force and Navy both recognized the advantages of our airplane as a transition trainer between primary instruction and the student's solo flight in jets, and we soon had orders to build it for both services. The Air Force version was designated the T-33 and the Navy version became the TV-2. The Navy trainer was also ordered for the Marine Corps, and today this airplane is used by all three services to train their jet pilots. It is also built in Canada under license from Lockheed as a jet training plane for the Royal Canadian Air Force, and Lockheed-built planes are furnished to ten other foreign countries by the U.S. government under the Military Defense Assistance Program.

Like the F-80 jet fighter from which it was developed, the T-33 is a low-wing, all-metal monoplane with tip tanks and tricycle landing gear. Its Allison-built J-33 jet engine is capable of driving it through the air at speeds in excess of six hundred miles an hour. It is small as jet planes go, weighing only eight thousand pounds, but it is one of the most versatile aircraft ever built.

In addition to its primary duty of teaching pilots to fly jet fighters and bombers, it is used for air-to-air and air-to-ground gunnery instruction, high-speed navigation training, tow-target flying and automatic rocket launching. With the same performance as the F-80, it can be fitted with additional guns and used for combat if required. By the installation of aerial cameras it can also be adapted for high-speed photo-reconnaissance.

It has been widely used as a general utility airplane in the Air Force, doing everything from carrying passengers on high-priority emergency flights to flying combat correspondents and photographers against the enemy in Korea. The first published pictures of the air war in Korea were taken from the back seat of a T-33 by a reporter for *Life* Magazine. So successful that later planes had nothing more to offer, today after six years it is still the only jet trainer in production in the western hemisphere.

We began building T-33's in 1948, but the first order called for only a few airplanes, and for almost two years we produced only one plane per week. In June, 1950, the outbreak of the Korean war and the resulting buildup in the Air Force and Navy increased the need for training planes, and we soon received more orders which pushed the production rate considerably higher. Today we are building this airplane at the highest rate in its history.

Besides helping students learn to fly jets faster and better, the jet trainer was also intended to help them learn more safely. Everybody is interested in safety, especially pilots. It is a fact, however, that people who fly airplanes will have accidents, and that applies to military as well as civilian aviators. The Air Force and Navy are constantly trying to reduce the number of training accidents and we work with them all we can. For instance, I spend a lot of my time demonstrating the jet trainer and lecturing on it at air bases and flight schools. We have found this lecturing is one of the best ways of helping the people who use our product.

This work is getting heavier as jet pilot training increases in the armed forces. Last year I visited every base in the Air Force's Flying Training Command to lecture on flying techniques in the T-33. The students were air cadets, waiting to graduate and get their commissions, and they were eager to learn. They were especially interested in the stall and spin characteristics of the T-33, which had been a particular problem in their training, and it was one of my jobs to explain why they got into spins and how to prevent them.

This lecture work wasn't new to me, as I did a lot of it on the P-38 in World War II. But when the jet came along after the war the Air Force wasn't particularly interested in having the manufacturer tell it how to fly this new airplane, and it was not until we got our jet trainer that this attitude changed and we were able to get back on the bases and help answer their questions. I am glad to say that now the armed services call on us for information and advice whenever they need it. Proof of this is the fact that I spent most of last year out on the road lecturing to military students and pilots.

The armed forces needed our help after the Korean war started because the rapid expansion of pilot training in both the Air Force and Navy got beyond the ability of the military to handle it. Many of their instructors were excellent pilots but often they were green, and there were not enough of them. Compounding this problem was the constant turnover in teaching personnel that is inherent in the military system.

It's a changing thing, a rotational system that has existed since the year 1. As a result you never have real stability in your organization. Unlike industry, where people may stay in the same spot thirty and forty years, military personnel are automatically transferred to a new location in a year or two. The same turnover applies equally to instructors and maintenance people. A rapid expansion in the flying program under such conditions makes accidents inevitable.

The airplane or the pilot is usually the first to get blamed but it's not always their fault. The planes aren't perfect but they're about as safe as we can make them, and the pilot is doing the best he can. If something goes wrong he may get frightened, but it's nothing he can help. How can you control his behavior when he gets scared?

The average flying cadet today is a young kid, in a big group with a hundred others just like him, and they are being trained and pressured all the time. They may get through that pressuring, but it doesn't make them seasoned pilots, and if something happens later they never figured on they may panic. It's nothing you can train them for, because you never know how they are going to act until it happens.

Despite the rapid expansion in pilot training and the shortage of good instructors, I think the Air Force cadet is getting the best training today that has ever been given. It will improve still further and the Air Force will get better students as younger men are accepted as air cadets. The decision to drop two years of college as a requirement for pilot training and open the flying schools to high school graduates was a big step forward.

The younger a boy is when he learns to fly, the better his chances are to become a good pilot. He actually ought to start about sixteen years old. In the case of flying it is important to begin young, when you still have that youthful eagerness and courage, and your mind isn't set. The average boy who is interested in flying can become a good pilot.

If he wants to fly and has reasonably good health and an aptitude for the art, there is no reason he can't be a success at it. It is important to meet certain physical requirements, but that doesn't mean you need X-ray eyes and a perfect physique. For example, a man who doesn't have perfect vision makes his own corrections. I've been wearing glasses almost twenty years and I'm still able to fly an airplane.

I think we have made a mistake in this country by demanding physical perfection of young men who want to be pilots. If we spend $100,000 training a boy and give him a $1,000,000 airplane to fly we want him to be perfect. It would be nice if everyone was perfect, but today the demand is too great, and there are no longer enough of that kind to go around.

14

Penetration Fighter

Combat experience in World War II convinced the Air Force of the need for a long-range or so-called "penetration" fighter plane like the Lockheed F-90.

Our bombers operating out of England and Italy against European targets were vulnerable to German fighters, and as we penetrated deeper into enemy territory we had to develop fighter escorts that could stay with them. By modifying the Lockheed P-38 and later the North American P-51 with extra fuel tanks for long-range flights, we licked this problem and our bomber offensive went ahead with its job of destroying the German Air Force.

To give the offensive maximum effectiveness, however, and get the greatest utilization from our bomber escort, we also wanted fighter planes that could go down to low levels and carry the fight to the enemy in the air or on the ground at his home bases. Such targets of opportunity, as they were known, included enemy air fields, troop concentrations, transportation systems and industrial installations.

This kind of job obviously called for a fighter plane that excelled at everything—a plane that was rough enough to inflict heavy damage on ground targets, tough enough to take punishment from ground fire, fast enough to stand up to enemy fighters, yet big enough to carry the fuel for long flights and come home. This kind of plane, which had never been built, was named a penetration fighter. One of the first things the Air Force did when the war ended was ask U.S. aircraft manufacturers to submit design proposals for such an airplane, capable of doing everything well, and powered by the revolutionary new jet engine.

Lockheed spent about two years in preliminary design work, studying many different configurations and building and testing scale models in our high-speed wind tunnel. We developed and tested sixty-five major designs, including one delta-wing, before the final needle-nose, swept-wing shape was settled on in the spring of 1947.

It was a big airplane, twice the size of Lockheed's first jet, the F-80, and its forty-foot wings were sharply swept back at an angle of thirty-five degrees to help it fly faster than combat planes had ever gone before. Despite its size, it carried only one man, the pilot, who sat in an air-conditioned, pressurized cockpit well ahead of the wings for extra visibility. Behind him side-by-side in the fuselage were two Westinghouse J-34 jet engines, each designed to develop four thousand pounds of thrust. They were able to deliver even more power by use of a revolutionary new device called an afterburner. Although I had flown tests on such a device mounted experimentally in an early F-80 during the war, this was the first airplane ever designed for it as standard equipment. With these engines the F-90 was the fastest combat plane yet built.

We did not plan to fly the 90 at Burbank. Security was not a problem, as the taxi tests were enough to reveal it to public view, but we wanted the extra room afforded by the Air Force test center at Muroc Dry Lake in the Mojave Desert to make the first flight on any airplane as new as this. I ran the airplane on the ground at Burbank, however, for if anything was wrong it could be fixed much more easily at the factory where the plane was built. The taxi tests didn't show much except that everything looked all right. With that assurance to go on, we loaded the airplane on a trailer and drove it by road to Muroc in May, 1949, where I got ready to take it up.

I ran more ground tests at high speeds on the dry lake bed, checking various things like the brakes, and I skipped the plane off the ground to get the feel of it. It felt all right, so the next morning I made my first flight. The 90 had no sooner become airborne than it developed a very serious problem with the ailerons. I was unable to keep it from rolling rapidly from side to side. I was always behind it with the control stick, and I had to use both hands on the stick to maintain any form of equilibrium.

I flew for several hundred feet just above the ground, trying to control the airplane, but I was unable to settle down. It was an extreme case of overcontrolling on my part, and yet I couldn't keep from doing so. Now this sort of thing doesn't normally bother me. I have never been a pilot who tends to overcontrol, but this was something I couldn't keep from being rough. Finally I decided this was a ball of snakes and I was going to get back on the ground. I chopped the power and landed and taxied back to the hangar, where our engineers were waiting for my first report.

When I told him what had happened Kelly Johnson immediately recognized that we had a major problem. Our control experts flew up from the factory and we talked many hours trying to figure out what was wrong. I explained that it was impossible for me to keep up with the controls. The airplane would tend to roll one way or the other and I would resist it, and in my resistance the plane would react by rolling in the opposite direction, repeating the whole cycle all over again. The controls had no natural tendency to settle down.

In the next week I made eleven skipoff flights before we finally found the trouble. A special spring mechanism incorporated in the boost system to give the pilot a good feel over a wide speed range was coming in too suddenly, and was actually too strong and causing overcontrol.

The engineers could take it out, but it would raise my booster ratio to 118 to 1, which would be the highest ever flown on any airplane; I would be able to control it without any trouble but the controls would be exceedingly sensitive.

They asked me what I felt and I said by all means go ahead and fix it—118 to 1 or 200 to 1, I didn't care, make it anything but take out what you have now. When you get it fixed I'll be able to tell you whether I can fly it or not.

They went to work and fixed it and the following morning

I made another flight; it was a short flight but the controls now handled normally, and the next day, June 4, I made the official first flight of this new airplane.

I took off normally and climbed to ten thousand feet. The airplane was heavy but climbed fairly well. As is customary on first flights at Lockheed, my only assignment this trip was to take off and land. As soon as we get a new plane in the air we start figuring out how to get it back down again, and for that reason we don't perform many maneuvers. On a first flight it is considered wise to do the bare minimum necessary to assure yourself that the plane is safe to fly.

We knew it would fly, of course. As a matter of fact, we knew beforehand almost exactly what its performance would be. Before I took off Kelly told me what my take-off speed, stall speed and other performance would be, and they turned out to meet his predictions within one mile an hour. That's how far we have advanced today in the art of designing airplanes. But predicting how the plane will behave is another thing, and that's what the pilot has to find out.

At ten thousand feet I began a run at military power, and as my speed increased the plane started to shake from nose to tail like a dog shaking water off its back. Not knowing the reason for this behavior, and fearing it might be of serious nature, I immediately throttled back and the shaking stopped. After testing the wing flaps and landing gear to my satisfaction, I came down and landed. Despite its size, the plane handled as easily as an F-80. Everything considered it was a successful flight and I was satisfied we had a winner. There were problems to be ironed out, but the important thing was that the 90 liked to fly, and that is always the mark of a good airplane.

The next thing we had to do was choose an aileron boost ratio where the airplane could be flown with a reasonable amount of ease. We were trying to reach a balance where the controls would be neither too sensitive nor too sluggish, and we arrived at a ratio of 60 to 1 which turned out to be quite satisfactory. After this problem was licked we turned our attention to the shaking at high speed, which we corrected by a minor redesign in the contour of the airplane at the junction of the vertical stabilizer and the fuselage.

Whenever you fly a new model during its development stage you run into problems of stability and control, and the 90 was no exception. Very early in the flight tests I found the glide speed of the airplane was much higher than it should have been, and in power-off glides I had to maintain a speed of at least 190 miles an hour to be sure of making a smooth landing. On investigation it was discovered the leading edge of the wing at the fuselage was actually stalled out. This was affecting the flow of air over the fuselage and tail and causing the poor glide characteristics. We changed the shape of the leading edge of the wing and it made an entirely different airplane out of the 90. It is things like this that often don't show up in wind-tunnel tests, and remain unknown until you build the airplane and fly it. Wind-tunnel models are sometimes too small to test everything, and when the airplane flies it doesn't always behave according to expectations. That is why we have test pilots and a test program.

The 90 was the first airplane to use afterburning as standard equipment. This method of increasing the power of a jet engine is extremely simple yet highly effective. By injecting extra fuel into the tailpipe of the engine and igniting it, the engine thrust is increased appreciably, with a corresponding increase in power. It's just like a kick in the pants. This extra power enables the plane to climb and fly faster, with no penalty except higher fuel consumption.

Only afterburning makes it possible for present-day airplanes to exceed the speed of sound in level flight, as jet engines have not yet attained sufficient power to drive them through the sound barrier using only the basic thrust. Despite its noise, complexity and fuel appetite, the afterburner is here to stay because it will be the most practical engine for supersonic flight in the foreseeable future. For example, at twice the speed of sound it is twice as efficient as the nonafterburning engine, despite the fact it is smaller and lighter and takes up less room in the airplane.

Like anything new, the early afterburner had its problems,

and I had my share of them. The first time I flew with one I couldn't get it lighted.

I exhausted all the known methods at that time, plus a few new ones dreamed up by the engineers on the ground, and then got permission to try some of my own. In about thirty seconds I had both afterburners going and this is how I did it.

Accelerating the engines close to maximum rpm, I pushed forward on the throttle abruptly, injecting excessive fuel into the engine. Part of the flame went downstream to the afterburner fuel nozzles in the rear of the engine, causing them to ignite, and I got a start right off the bat. Later we developed this idea into the present method of lighting afterburners, known today as hot-streak ignition. It's just like a pilot light on a gas stove. A small fuel jet installed in the engine burner cans squirts a streak of burning fuel downstream through the turbine wheels to ignite the fuel in the afterburner. It has turned out to be a sure-fire system.

After completing flight tests on the 90 I began the gunnery tests, using the No. 2 airplane, which was now finished and flying. The 90 was armed with six 20-mm cannon, located in the belly of the airplane ahead of the wing, and was the only one of three planes in the penetration fighter competition that was completely equipped tactically per specification. While flying at Muroc I made my first belly landing in this airplane.

I had completed my firing and was returning to base when I found to my dismay that my nose wheel would not extend for a landing. The main gear moved up and down, but the doors covering the nose wheel wouldn't even open. After exhausting all normal means of getting the wheel down, such as diving and shaking the airplane, I called the field on my radio and told them I planned to make a belly landing. I suggested they call Kelly on the land line in Burbank and tell him so he wouldn't be too excited when he found out about it, and in the meantime I flew around the field waiting for his answer.

In a few minutes they called me back on the radio, with Kelly hanging on the other end of the telephone, and said he wanted to know if I had tried everything. I said everything normal, and he asked why not pull the emergency extension lever. I replied that I wouldn't be able to get my main wheels back up if I pulled it, and if the nose wheel didn't come down after all I would have to land that way. That wouldn't be too smart because the airplane would nose over, and sitting up in the nose the way I was I might burn my feet.

Kelly agreed this was right and I told him I had a belly landing all figured out. I was going to make a fast, gradual approach, keeping my speed well up so the plane would touch down in a very flat attitude, and as the belly of the fuselage was quite flat anyway due to the twin-engine design, the 90 had quite a nice belly for that sort of landing.

This I did, letting down on course, with Chuck Yaeger, who was flying at the same time in another airplane, coming alongside and pacing me. When I got down close to the lake bed he called me on his radio.

"It looks good from here, Tony," he said. "You've got it made. Chop her." The lake bed is so smooth I couldn't tell if I was five inches or five feet in the air, and unknown to me the tail of my airplane was already on the ground. I dragged along this way for nearly two thousand feet, my tail on the ground and my nose high in the air, and when I chopped the power I crashed down with such tremendous force I thought my back was broken. X-rays showed I injured my coccyx. It still becomes very painful if I sit in one position longer than an hour or so, and that is the reason I seldom make long flights in airplanes.

I made about one hundred flights in the 90 and flew it faster than sound about fifteen times. It behaved almost identically every time I took it through the speed of sound. I have also flown other planes supersonically, and I have found very little difference in their behavior once they are past the sound barrier. The 90 and the F-86 for all practical purposes handle almost identically. The same thing is true of the 90 and the F-94C, although the 94C is a straight-wing airplane. Once the plane is supersonic, the shape of the wing doesn't really matter.

As a man who has flown faster than sound in both swept-wing and straight-wing airplanes, I think the straight wing is best for all-around performance in all speed ranges. It behaves just as well at supersonic speeds, and it is better than

F-86 "Sabre"

the swept wing at lower speeds because it provides better lift. For instance, the straight-wing airplane can take off in a shorter distance and land at lower speeds, which means it can use smaller airports. It is also more maneuverable.

At very high speeds between 750 and 1,500 miles an hour the choice lies between the straight wing and the delta wing, with the swept wing running a poor third. At these speeds, up to Mach 2 or twice the speed of sound, our engineers believe the thin straight wing again promises the best performance. It offers less drag and therefore is capable of greater speeds, while showing superior stability and lift over both its competitors. I have not yet flown a truly supersonic straight wing, but that comes next, and in a year or two I think we will all know a great deal more about it.

After evaluating all three planes submitted in the competition for a penetration fighter, the Air Force decided against putting any of them into production. All offered about the same performance, but none met the requirement sufficiently to warrant a production order. Actually, the World War II concept of an all-purpose airplane was already obsolete when the F-90 flew.

It was obsolete because the requirement was unrealistic. With the engines available at the time, it was impossible to build an airplane that would do everything well. With the engines available now, we might design a new penetration fighter that would more nearly approach the requirement, but sometimes it is better to chalk an airplane off as experience and go on to something else. It may also be that the requirement itself is obsolete.

By that I mean there may no longer be a need for the kind of all-purpose fighter plane the Air Force wanted in 1945. That is nearly ten years ago, and since that time the concept of airpower has changed radically. The trend now is toward specialization. Instead of one plane that can do all things well, today the Air Force is looking at several different planes, each of which can do only one thing well, but do it better than any other plane in the world.

The outbreak of the Korean war in June, 1950, midway in the Air Force evaluation program of the new penetration fighters, also affected its final decision against buying such an airplane. The need for combat planes in a hurry, with the emphasis on planes like the F-86 that was already in production, undoubtedly took money away from newer types that could wait. It is possible that the Korean war also convinced the Air Force it needed different types than those previously planned for. Lockheed certainly came out of the Korean experience convinced of the need for a highly-specialized air superiority fighter like our new XF-104.

The Korean war also pointed up the need for a stronger air defense, built around new jet planes with all-weather capabilities, and the 90 was not an all-weather fighter. As a result of the war and its threat of an even greater conflict, the concept of the daytime F-90 inevitably gave way to the reality of the all-weather F-94, which was in production and immediately available to meet the new requirement for an airplane to defend the United States against attack from the air.

Our struggle to bring the F-94 into being is the next chapter in my story.

15

All-Weather Fighter

Air Force interest in a twenty-four-hour, all-weather jet fighter for air defense of the United States began in early 1948 with a design competition for a new kind of airplane. Such a plane is commonly known as an interceptor, which is something of a misnomer, as day fighters can also be used to intercept enemy bombers; the new plane is more correctly referred to as an interceptor with all-weather capabilities—that is, it is equipped with radar and other electronics which enable it to take off and return to base on instruments and also locate and attack enemy targets automatically. In a program to get this kind of airplane in service, the Air Force invited several aircraft manufacturers to submit designs, with the intention of selecting the best and awarding contracts for their construction. Lockheed did not participate at first; we were building the F-80, testing the T-33 and designing the F-90, and I guess the Air Force had other plans for us.

Late that year they came to us. Other planes designed for the new requirement did not measure up and time was running out: could we build an all-weather fighter and how soon could we deliver it? This was like old times again—the kind of work we always thrived on at Lockheed, when somebody was in trouble and came to us for help.

Hall Hibbard and Kelly Johnson didn't have any blueprints for an all-weather jet stored away in the file cabinet, but they will try anything once, and this was no exception. Their answer to the first question was an immediate "yes." As to how long it would take, they needed a couple of days to answer. First they had to decide whether to start from scratch or try to adapt an existing airplane to the new job.

The prototype T-33 jet trainer was already flying and the airplane was going into production, and if it could be modified to carry radar, it undoubtedly offered the quickest solution to the problem; by comparison, the minimum time required to design and develop a completely new airplane would be eighteen months to two years. The T-33 airframe was fully qualified for combat duty, as the trainer itself was just a stretched-out F-80. It then remained for us to find out if the airborne radar available at that time could be carried in the airframe of the T-33.

Investigation disclosed that it not only could be, it had to be used in a two-seat airplane, under the full-time control of a radar operator. Radar had not yet been perfected that could be operated entirely by the pilot. As the T-33 was the only two-seat jet fighter-type airplane in the nation, not only was it adaptable to the existing airborne radar in this country, it was the only jet that could accommodate the installation without building an entirely new plane.

By putting radar in the nose, replacing the student flyer with a radar operator and installing afterburner in the jet engine for better performance, we decided the T-33 could be converted to a satisfactory all-weather fighter, and we so advised the Air Force. As to when they could have it, we wanted a few days to build a prototype, and if it flew without serious stability and control problems which would require major redesign work, why, in six months we could start delivering airplanes.

Because we planned to use the same wing, tail, engine and fuselage, our prototype all-weather fighter turned out to look like a T-33 with a greatly-elongated nose section. In fact, it was the original trainer prototype, which I had flown a few months earlier and which was still available for test purposes. Working in our experimental shop, we designed and installed the wooden mockup of a radar nose in two days and I took the plane up on a test flight. Performance was quite good, as it flew just like a T-33, which flies like an F-80, only faster. The results were so encouraging that engineering went immediately into design work on the production airplane.

Because we could build F-80 fighters, T-33 trainers and the new F-94 on parallel assembly lines, using the same major sub-assemblies for all three types, we were able to get in production in record time. In fact, we moved so fast there was no time to build afterburner units for the Allison J-33 jet engine, which was not yet equipped with the new auxiliary power system, and the first production airplane flew without an afterburner. A trailer truck hauled the new plane from the Burbank factory to our jet base at nearby Van Nuys and on April 16, 1949, I took it up for its first flight. Glenn Fulkerson, later our flight test project engineer on the new airplane, rode behind me as observer in the rear seat, which was fitted out with new instruments for a radar operator. Without afterburner the performance of the airplane offered nothing new in the way of speed and climb, but we were satisfied. We knew it could do the job assigned to it.

The first model was the 94A, a small airplane by present jet standards, with a take-off weight of fifteen thousand pounds. However, it could fly more than six hundred miles an hour and its service ceiling was over forty thousand feet. It had the straight wing of the T-33 and the F-80 and the same basic fuselage, but the nose and tail were stretched out to accommodate the electronic equipment and the larger tail pipe required for an afterburner. The big changes were inside the airplane where they could not be seen. As this model is still in service, details of its radar are secret, but with this equipment it has shot down many targets which the pilot never saw.

The 94A was so successful that the Air Force soon placed additional orders for a new and improved version, which became the B model. Incorporating new instruments that had been perfected since the original design was laid down, and benefiting from the lessons we learned in building and flying the first airplanes, the 94B had more range and improved all-weather capabilities, including wing and tail de-icing. Its improved performance came largely from the new Sperry Zero Reader, which gave it a near-perfect homing system. In previous instrument flying the pilot had to observe and co-ordinate several different instruments, but with the new Zero Reader all of the required data was graphically presented on a single indicator that showed him nearly everything he needed to know for safe flight and approach for landing.

It was through the changes in the 94A to the B model that Lockheed engineering, under Hall Hibbard and Kelly Johnson, decided we needed even higher performance, an airplane with greater top speed and greater altitude capabilities. If we were really going to have an airplane that could intercept an enemy who might approach our shores it should be able to reach at least fifty thousand feet, as the bombers would certainly come in high if they flew at any altitude except on the deck. It was through this feeling and desire for a more modern and better airplane that Lockheed decided to build the third model of this series, the F-94C.

The Air Force turned us down. They felt they didn't need another 94, as they had brand-new all-weather fighters coming along by this time, and in their opinion the 94 was an old airplane and could not keep pace. But our engineering department was confident that the new model would hold its own in any league and our management backed them up, and the upshot was that we built the 94C with our own money.

It costs several million dollars to develop a new plane like this, so we could afford to build only one prototype airplane for testing. We began work in 1949 and the first plane was ready in January, 1950. Because of its many new features and much higher performance, we felt it wise not to test it at our own jet base at Van Nuys until we knew more about it, and we got Air Force permission to fly it at Edwards Air Force Base, formerly Muroc, in the Mojave Desert. The plane was trucked to Edwards from Burbank and on January 18 I took it up.

I soon realized that our major problems with this airplane were going to be stability and control, both of which were marginal in certain respects. The first thing I noticed was the Dutch roll, or the tendency of the airplane to wallow through the air, resulting from too much dyhedral without enough directional stability. Dyhedral is the upswept angle of the wings in relation to the fuselage. In this plane we had swept the wings upward to provide gravity feed from the wing-tanks and simplify the fuel system, and this sweep-up had actually given the plane too much dyhedral. I did not carry tip tanks on the first flight and the plane rolled violently. We found that tip tanks dampened the roll considerably, but we didn't really lick it until we redesigned the vertical fin to increase the directional stability of the airplane.

Control was the thing that gave us the fits. At lower speeds control was quite adequate, but as we started to push the speed up toward the sound barrier we ran into a condition of inadequate control at high speeds. Like every Lockheed plane since the P-38, the 94C had a hydraulic booster system for the ailerons, but the new plane was getting up into higher speeds than ever, and now we found the boost was out-of-date. Like the F-90, the 94C required a new boost that would handle correctly over a wide speed range. Once more we had too much control, a system so sensitive that the plane was touchy to handle, and Air Force pilots who flew the C model were quick to complain about this behavior. We finally had to put in a whole new booster system for the ailerons.

We also had trouble with the elevators. They were not hydraulically-boosted in the beginning, but at the speeds the plane was now attaining we realized the pilot could no longer operate them unaided. To give him maximum control at high speeds we developed hydraulic boosters for the elevators and installed them for the first time on this airplane. They provided an adjustable ratio which permitted the pilot to select any amount of elevator control he desired. If he was light-handed he might prefer a high ratio of boost which would make the elevators very sensitive, while a heavy-handed pilot who didn't like things too touchy could screw the ratio down. We tried a long time to find a happy medium, one condition that would take care of all speeds and all pilots, but finally concluded that it could not be done.

Among the many new features pioneered on the 94C, undoubtedly the most important from an aerodynamic point of view was its new thin straight wing. This was the first time a tactical airplane capable of very high speeds had been built with a straight wing, and the 94C was the first plane other than purely experimental research aircraft like the Bell X-1 to exceed the speed of sound with a straight wing. The design philosophy behind this development was not new, as Kelly Johnson had argued for many years that planes could fly just as fast with straight as with swept wings; the problem was to build straight wings thin enough to go fast and still strong enough to stand the load, and that was what we were able to do for the first time in this airplane.

Actually we had no choice. To go faster we had to make the wing thinner. The only alternative was a swept wing, a major design change that was so costly it would have defeated us before we got started. We were not trying to build a supersonic wing, but in our efforts to make the old wing

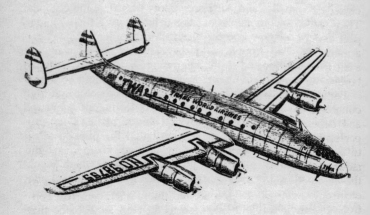

Bell X-1

faster the airplane ended up capable of exceeding the speed of sound in a dive.

From a combat point of view the outstanding feature of the 94C was its new armament. Except for an experimental German model in World War II it was the first fighter plane ever built without guns. Instead of machine guns or cannon used in fighters previously, this plane was armed only with rockets—the new "Mighty Mouse" developed by the U. S. Navy as an air-to-air missile, and each one packing the punch of a big gun.

The installation we developed for these rockets was also new. Rockets had been carried by aircraft previously, but only as auxiliary armament, and always in external pods or mounted free outside the airplane under the wings. But we were using them instead of guns, so we put them where the guns would go—inside the airplane. In a brilliant and highly-effective installation our engineers designed the 94C to carry twenty-four of these new rockets in a ring around the airplane's radar nose. Hidden behind rocket doors that opened inward when they fired, they were housed in newly-designed rocket tubes closed at the rear to increase their accuracy and firepower. They were mounted in direct line-of-flight for maximum impact on the target and were without doubt the most lethal armament yet installed in any fighter plane. Tests showed that a hit from just one rocket would literally explode the biggest bomber in midair.

Perhaps the most difficult and vexing problem we encountered on the 94C was the development of an adequate and dependable automatic pilot. In addition to its improved performance and armament, this airplane was also designed to have better all-weather capabilities, including completely automatic tracking and firing, and the heart of our system was the automatic pilot. By taking advantage of the latest type of electronic equipment, built around the new Hughes fire control system, it was our intention to develop an airplane that would fly and fire itself.

Unlike the earlier models, in this plane the radar operator would no longer have to guide it to the target and the pilot would no longer have to pull the trigger. By tying in the airborne radar to an automatic pilot and the fire-control system, we believed it was now possible to build an airplane that would automatically home on any target, and when the proper position was reached, automatically fire its rockets. This was about the closest thing to a sure hit short of a guided missile.

The first automatic pilot in the 94C was a new instrument built by Westinghouse. It was good but it had been designed for an older and slower airplane and it didn't work out for us. It was so jittery it was hard to keep up with the stick, and on the first flight I made with the autopilot it practically beat me to death in the cockpit. We fought with it for a month and finally the experts decided a complete redesign was necessary. After that we worked with it almost two years before it did what we wanted.

Despite its many good features and the faith we all had in the airplane, the 94C was still not acceptable to the testing agencies. We ran into considerable opposition from the very beginning. They claimed performance wasn't enough better than the 94B to warrant the change, and they said stability and control were inferior and it would be a dangerous airplane to fly. For these and many other reasons they continually recommended the airplane be dropped from consideration for a production contract.

When the bugs were out and the instruments were in we finally sold it and got a production order, but it took a long time. Two years elapsed from my first flight in the prototype airplane to the day the first production plane came off the assembly line. We were still working out problems as late as a year ago, but they are all behind us and today the 94C is on the first team. It is the only Air Force plane in service that has no flight restrictions on it and it is the best-equipped plane of its type ready on the line for intercepting enemy bombers.

The 94C was not designed as a Mach 1 airplane, and only after improvements in the controls and the tail did we arrive at a configuration we believed we could dive past the speed of sound. Then we built up to sonic speed by gradual stages.

I made my first supersonic dive in the 94C over Muroc from an altitude of forty-five thousand feet near the end of 1950. I broke through the sonic barrier about thirty-three thousand feet and actually went about as fast as I did in the F-90 a few months before. My true air speed at that altitude was over seven hundred miles an hour. However, the 90 was underpowered and we couldn't climb as high with it. If we had gotten the 90 up higher we would have gone faster because it was basically a faster airplane.

We wanted to dive the 94C faster than sound to show its capabilities. We were building a new airplane in an era of high-speed flight and we had to meet the competition. Supersonic flight was on everyone's lips—would it exceed the speed of sound?—that was all they ever asked you. We felt if we didn't push the airplane up there with the rest of them we didn't stand on good, solid ground to argue about it. Actually the airplane didn't have to go that fast. Its primary mission will probably be flown at speeds that are under the speed of sound.

Once we took the 94C through the sonic barrier it was easy, and the airplane has done it many times since. I have often flown it faster than sound, and other Lockheed and Air Force pilots have done it many times more. As it was the first multiseat airplane to exceed the speed of sound, the 94C was also the first that could carry passengers supersonically. It was regular procedure for our engineers to ride as observers during flight tests on this airplane, and on one such test Glenn Fulkerson became the first passenger in the world to fly faster than sound.

We had climbed to forty-five thousand feet and were headed east above the San Fernando Valley. Glenn had been going along on most of my flights to help get more test data, but he had never been with me on a dive test before. I had reached my level flight speed with the afterburner on and was ready to push over into my dive. I told Glenn over the intercom to lock his shoulder harness and cinch up on the buckles because we were going to be hanging from the straps.

He acknowledged being ready and I pushed forward on the control stick until the G meter indicated zero, making us weightless. This is always an uncomfortable maneuver unless you are used to it. I had been making this kind of dive entry for many months and didn't mind it any more, but I heard a slight gasp from Glenn as the bottom dropped out from under him like a fast-dropping elevator.

I held the stick forward until we attained a sixty-degree dive angle, which I considered to be about best to reach the greatest speed. At forty thousand feet the angle had increased to sixty-five degrees and now my controls were about neutral. The 94 was accelerating so fast that all the little trim changes normally experienced at these speeds hardly had time to take place.

Every plane that can reach the sound barrier has to go through a troublesome zone called the transonic region. This region has a speed band that varies depending on the type of aircraft, and the beginning of the zone is the critical mach number of the airplane. It is in this region that the effects of piercing the sound barrier or so-called "wall" play tricks on the pilot by suddenly causing a wing to drop off to the left or right—the rudder to kick over one way or the other and maybe shake and vibrate at the same time—even the elevators may jump around and make the control stick move back and forth. The pilot attempts to fight this condition, but suddenly finds he can hardly move the controls, for now he is flying at the speed of sound.

Today I skipped right through this zone and didn't feel a thing. My plane being weightless during the early stages of the dive, there was very little load on my wings, and the powerful shock waves dancing over the airplane were being fooled as we slid by. I could tell when I went through the sound barrier. My mach needle paused at almost Mach 1 and then jumped up to 10 per cent above the speed of sound. I looked at my altimeter and it was unwinding rapidly as it did on my first supersonic dive in the F-90.

The plane was smooth and now I became aware of the sudden quietness that is always there, when you are flying faster than sound and the noise of the airplane is all behind you. It never fails to be a thrill—even if I did it ten times a day, seven days a week. We were plunging earthward at one thousand feet a second. As we passed twenty-seven thousand feet it became time for me to pull out of the dive.

I pulled back on the stick sharply, but there was no response, and the elevators seemed to be moving in a vacuum. Watching the nose of the plane I pulled harder, but it did not move. For several seconds I sat looking at the same spot on the ground rushing up to meet me.

I grabbed the stick with both hands and pulled with all my might. If the nose didn't start coming up in a second or two I would have to cut my power and put my dive brakes out. I counted silently—"and one"—"and two." As I strained every muscle against the tremendous air loads pressing on the elevators I could hear myself breathing hard through the intercom. Glenn was silent, taking down the comments I had been grunting into the microphone, and there was no other sound except the hissing of the air over the plexiglas canopy of the falling airplane.

Then the nose started to respond almost imperceptibly, but I was very low now, much lower than ever before except one time in the P-38. There is never an easy way out—there is always a decision to make. I wanted to use the dive flaps, but at the same time I was curious to find out if the elevators could do it alone. Should I try it? As I considered the alternatives my right wing started to drop and our earthward rush slackened. I held the stick hard over to the left, just barely able to counteract the roll of the airplane. Slowly the nose moved upward toward the distant horizon.

At nineteen thousand feet we were still diving at a forty-five-degree angle—pretty steep for that altitude at the speed we were flying. My breath came even faster and beads of perspiration formed and ran down my face. Now the mach number had dropped to the point where my controls began to take hold again, and slowly the G's built up as the plunging airplane entered the long arc that led skyward. It would take one G to pull you out of a dive if you were flying to infinity.

At sixteen thousand feet two G's indicated on the accelerometer needle and the plane began to roughen. By the time the needle touched 5 the plane was bucking and pitching, but I had it made. Suddenly I was in level flight and then zooming upward. As I relaxed and eased the pressure on my controls, I asked Glenn over the intercom how he felt. "How do *you* feel?'' he replied. ''I thought you were dying up there in front.''

''No, just working hard,'' I said. ''Incidentally, you have just flown faster than any passenger has ever flown in an airplane, and you are the first passenger to penetrate the sonic barrier and exceed the speed of sound. Do you feel different?''

''Well,'' he said, ''maybe I got a few more gray hairs.''

Like the 94A and the 94B before it, the 94C Starfire is now on duty at continental bases of the Air Defense Command. Its assignment, like that of its predecessors, which are still in service, is the air defense of the United States. Last summer Lockheed delivered its twenty-five thousandth airplane, a 94C, to the Air Force, and dispatched it for duty with the Western Air Defense Force at Hamilton Air Base, California. Many more have joined it since throughout the country.

With other all-weather fighters on twenty-four-hour alert, they wait in the darkness for the signals that always come. So far they have been only signals—a private flyer who failed to file a flight plan, a commercial airliner late or off course. That is what the 94's have to find out.

They take off, flying a heading received by radio from the ground radar observer who is following the unknown aircraft on his radar screen. Brief minutes later, at the predetermined altitude and position, the radar operator in the 94 switches on his own radar scope and picks up the target. Then the 94 closes in, its guns or rockets ready, and flies alongside of the strange plane close enough to see it and identify it.

This is bad in a way, because the first guy who intercepts an enemy plane will probably get blasted out of the sky. Meanwhile the black watch goes on.

16

Present And Future

It would not be appropriate to end this story without describing the men with whom I work in test flying, nor would this book be complete without them. The other test pilots in the flight test division, together with the engineers and technicians who guide our test program, are the important people in my job because I would be unable to perform my duties successfully without them. Most of them have come up in aviation much the same way I have, so it might be said that this story is a story of many pilots.

As these words are written the work load in our department is at the highest point in its history, and the number of test pilots has increased correspondingly. We have more experimental airplanes flying today than we have ever had at one time, even during World War II, and to handle them we have ten test pilots now, compared to the one-man department I took over when I became chief test pilot in 1945. They are in addition to an even larger number of pilots who fly production airplanes at Lockheed, some of whom I borrow from time to time as the need for extra help arises.

Herman Salmon, a specialist on structural integrity tests on fighter-type aircraft, is my No. 1 man on jets. This type of work is very exacting and requires great skill and intestinal fortitude, as it involves wringing an airplane out to see how much it can take in the way of punishment. Herman has always had a flair for extra-hazardous flying, starting with spin tests he did on the P-38 during the war, and he is good at it.

Roy Wimmer's specialty is very exacting flying, involving performance tests on all our aircraft. This means getting the exact performance out of an airplane for a given condition, whether it be take-off, climb, speed runs, engine-out performance or whatever. Roy is a very quiet individual, but he has turned out some of the best performance testing of any pilot in the world. He has had extremely wide experience in many kinds of airplanes, including wartime testing in England for the RAF, and the record will show that no one has ever excelled his test work in performance flying. When we have a very important test come up where we are hunting for a mile or two miles an hour, the engineers will always insist on Roy doing it.

Stanley Beltz is our specialist on instrument flying, and his record speaks for itself. I have always given him a free hand to work out his own program, and as a result of his research I feel we probably know more about instrument flying, especially in icing conditions, than any company in the business. Stan is also our specialist on the P2V series, and he is known all over the world in Navy circles for his work with this aircraft.

Jim White is one of our veteran test pilots and is exceptionally good on large planes. Jim is all business. When he is up there on the flight deck of a Constellation he is just like a big executive running his job in the front office. Jim is a meticulous person and well suited for his present assignment on special aircraft. It is very arduous and exacting work and he handles it completely by himself. That's his baby and I don't bother him. When it comes to flying it's got to be perfect with Jim or it won't be done at all.

Bob Matye is one of our youngest men and a former Air Force pilot. He flew during World War II and was one of the first Air Force officers to fly jets. Bob started in the production department and transferred to engineering flying, where his specialty is aerial gunnery and radar search flying in our all-weather fighters. He is young and ambitious and an excellent pilot.

Sammy Mason also came to us from production flying. He is world-renowned for his skill as an acrobatic flyer and made an outstanding record as a civilian flying instructor for the Army in World War II. His specialty is spin-testing fighter-type aircraft, in which his great experience in the field of aerobatics is paying off. Had it not been for Sammy's ability as a pilot we both would have crashed last year when a light plane he was flying got caught in the propwash of a DC-4 and turned upside down fifty feet off the ground. Sammy got it back under control but I doubt that I could have done so.

Red Mulvihill flew with the Navy and like Bob Matye he has great ability and is young and eager to learn. He should become an outstanding experimental test pilot. Robert Massey is our youngest pilot, being twenty-eight years old.

He and Matye were classmates during their cadet days. Massey is an excellent instrument pilot and will undoubtedly aid Stan Beltz in our all-weather operations. Ray Meskimen, who completes our team, has been flying longer than any of us. Ray became an aviator in 1919 and has picked up over fourteen thousand hours in the air. He is fifty-five years old but he is as hard at it today as he was when I first met him, and he can fly just as hard as the rest of them.

As for myself, I like to fly fighter-type aircraft. My specialty is stability and control, that is, analyzing an airplane qualitatively speaking. How well does it fly? What are the controls like? I take keen interest in analyzing the behavior of an airplane and in trying to determine how it can be improved. I have often said an airplane could have the greatest performance in the world, but if it had poor stability and control it would be worthless, because pilots would not want to fly it.

With very little guidance on my part all these men took hold and to this day I still believe my method of picking pilots and letting them run their own jobs is basically correct. It has always been my theory that if a man is capable of flying an airplane and he has common sense, he should be capable of running his own tests. Only when there's something unforeseen does he have to ask for advice, and then we take the problem in to the engineers and talk it over. In other words, it is expected of the pilots that they carry on their own test program and make it their business. I do very little meddling. I have never meddled in another fellow's work so long as he was carrying it out to everyone's satisfaction, and I make it a point never to needle a pilot or put the thumb on him. Every man is an individual and I have allowed it to work that way.

A test pilot may be anywhere from twenty to fifty-five years old. Starting young is fine in this business. I ought to know, I got into it early enough. Actually, that's the best time to get in, but a young man bears watching, because usually he is not seasoned. He has good reflexes and lots of nerve, and as he gains experience and learns the dangers and hazards involved in test flying, he becomes more useful to the company he is working for.

I would say that in the test pilot business a man is at his peak between thirty-five and forty-five years old. If he can keep his health and live moderately there is no reason he can't keep on flying after that, giving up the more hazardous work gradually as he goes into the later years past forty-five. When a pilot gets beyond that age he naturally tends to slow up. Only on rare occasions do you run across a man who is old in years but young in spirit, and that holds true for test pilots.

As I mentioned, our work load is at an all-time peak, and to keep from being glued to the desk I have had to assign my pilots some duties besides flying. When I'm not on hand, Roy Wimmer supervises the transport and patrol bomber work at Burbank and Herman Salmon takes care of the jet division at Van Nuys. This permits me to get out in the field and visit various military bases using our planes, especially jets.

Lockheed originally did all its test flying at Burbank, with maybe one or two airplanes at Muroc during the war, but now we're scattered out at four different places, and each test base has a number of planes. It is no longer possible for one man to fly all the planes, but we still maintain a high degree of proficiency among the older pilots, so we are never without someone to take care of any assignment that comes along.

When we have a special test of any kind requiring a large area such as the Muroc Dry Lake to operate from, we go up there to fly, even though it might be a Navy P2V or a commercial Constellation. The Air Force always makes us welcome. This large expanse of dry lake bed saves an enormous amount of money in safety, because when dealing with new or experimental airplanes it is very important to have a safe place to land in an emergency.

I have always said, and I suppose many people realize it but forget it, that when you are dealing with experimental airplanes you are dealing with something that can mean an awful lot to the security of our country, especially in time of war. If test pilots and the flight test crew in charge of an important new airplane don't take every precaution to keep it from being damaged it could be a serious loss to the country.

Lockheed "Constellation"

I've seen it happen through the years and it is happening today.

For example, in World War II, the Army grabbed our first P-38 to set a new transcontinental speed record. It was a grand idea, but the only thing a speed record would give them was some newspaper headlines for a day and that's about all. Instead of waiting a few weeks until we knew more about the airplane, they took it when it had hardly been tested. The engines failed going in for a landing at New York City and the airplane fell short of the field and crashed. What did that do? It set the P-38 back about two years, because we had to start from scratch and build another prototype airplane and run a whole new test program, and as it was the best fighter plane we had at that time, that incident may very well have lengthened the war.

I could fill pages with things like that I've actually seen. It has happened many times, and it all comes from the eagerness of the armed forces to get hold of a new airplane and exploit it as fast as they can. There's an awful tendency to pressure the manufacturer to deliver a plane before it has been thoroughly tested. Maybe that's necessary. All I know is I see what happens, and only too often the airplane crashes and gets a bad name because it wasn't ready, or the project may even be killed before the manufacturer has a chance to develop it. It's nice to have lots of guts and nerve and say you'll do something come hell or high water, but often high water comes and you are up to your neck in it.

In my department, a pilot is assigned to an airplane perhaps a year before it flies, even before the experimental shop starts making parts. He talks it over with our designers, perhaps calling on his own experience to make suggestions.

When it reaches the construction stage he watches the prototype airplane take shape. By reading the engineering reports and discussing the specifications he pretty well knows what it will do before it even flies.

When the day comes for the first flight, he has already taxied the airplane and even skipped it off the ground. The first flight is usually quick and dirty. He takes the plane up, runs a few simple tests on the flaps and landing gear and gets back down safely. That is the important thing the first time.

On the following flights he runs a complete series of performance tests laid down by the flight test engineer. If the airplane doesn't give too much trouble it will go right through and complete its tests in minimum time, but if something is wrong and additional development work is required, that is allowed for. The pilot works continuously with engineering, getting their advice and giving them the benefit of his experience. In a matter of one hundred hours of flying practically everything is known about the airplane that can be learned, and the only thing left to do is build it or bury it.

My job is to see that these airplanes are flight tested in accordance with the requirements set up by the flight test engineers. Before every test flight there is a preflight conference between the project engineer and the pilot, and the entire test in question is thoroughly discussed so that both parties understand the problem at hand. After the flight is completed there is a postflight conference, and in the case of transport planes the entire crew participate. Nothing is left to chance.

In many cases our pilots flying tests on transports face greater hazards than the fighter pilots, because it is harder to get out of a cabin-type airplane in the air if something goes wrong. Most fighters now have ejection seats to aid the crew in abandoning a disabled aircraft. In all planes large and small there is always constant performance testing, a tedious job that means flying many hours in a straight line, and this probably requires more adaptive skill on the part of the pilot, especially in transports, than any other kind of work.

Danger is the thing that makes test flying different. I don't say you can't be in danger on the ground. Lots of people are. You walk the streets and your neck is out a mile. However, it is an accepted fact that our profession is one of the most dangerous in the world, and for that reason there are only a handful of men in it. It's not a popular profession for the simple reason that it is dangerous, so usually there are only a few pilots available for it. It is so difficult to get test pilots in the armed forces that they have set up schools to train them, both in this country and in England.

I have always considered myself an average pilot, so I guess my life would be typical. I'm up at six in the morning and eat a hearty breakfast and get to work at 7:30. I don't ever remember a morning when I didn't wake up feeling anxious to get to work. Flying has always been that way and when it stops I suppose I might quit.

The first thing I do at the office is read the flight test board to find out the airplanes that are scheduled to fly that day and the expected hour of take-off. These schedules are made up the night before by the engineers. I assign the pilots to fly the planes but the engineers schedule the flights according to the requirements of the test program.

We have forty-five minutes for lunch and our day ends at 4:15. This is not a firm schedule, as we are always on call. Because of the nature of our work we may go on a trip or run an important test at night or early in the morning. The job is irregular because of its experimental nature. They try to make a production out of it, and every month we get a new plan called master scheduling which is supposed to schedule all our work thirty days in advance. I just look at it and smile to myself and think we'll be lucky if we can stick to this for a month. It's generally hard to do.

When test pilots are not working they are very much like other people. Far from spending all our free time drinking and chasing women, as some people seem to think, we live every bit as modestly as the average person. Of course a single man is a girl chaser—he's probably looking for a wife—but of those who are married I would say that my pilots are as happily married as any group, and that includes me. Because of the extreme tension under which he works, I consider a happy home life essential to a test pilot.

We all have our hobbies and other outside interests. I am fond of sports and like to ski and motorcycle. Stan Beltz and Jim White are great hunters, while Herman Salmon is interested in boys' clubs. Two of my pilots are very active in the church. Roy Wimmer is a Mormon and an assistant to his bishop, and Sammy Mason gave up training to be a flying missionary to come to work for us. Needless to say, these two men seem to have a better control of the human emotions than all the others put together. Only Herman Salmon owns his own airplane and flies as a hobby after work.

My wife has done some flying but she is not particularly keen for it. Consequently I have not coaxed her to fly because I see no point in doing so and I let a sleeping dog lie. On the other hand, she has never objected to my flying or hampered me the way many wives have hampered their husbands; I know men who probably would have been wonderful pilots had their wives encouraged them instead of holding them back. I am sure my wife worries to some extent, just as my mother did when I was a boy; it's natural for a woman to worry, and I suppose wives and mothers are very much the same. However, I have never bothered her or told her of my flying experiences and she has never really made a point to find out exactly what I do, although I am sure she realizes what the type of work is. When I go to work in the morning her last words are "Please be careful."

When I am asked to predict the future of the test pilot, I see no particular change. We are going to need him as long as we build airplanes for people to fly in, and I expect that will be for some time. Such an airplane will have a pilot and it is obvious that a test pilot will fly it first. The trend in certain phases of military aviation is toward guided missiles and pilotless aircraft, and when we have learned all the secrets of atomic power the day may come when we can put atomic engines into unmanned planes and carry passengers into outer space. Maybe we wouldn't need a test pilot for that. However, I don't think that space flying will come for some years, probably not in my lifetime. There are too many obstacles still beyond our grasp. It is theoretically possible, however, and I will go along with the gag.

As to the future of the airplane, I think we can expect some changes. The key to progress will continue to be the engine. Generally speaking, the airframe manufacturer is usually ahead of the engine manufacturer; the power plant never quite gives us what we need, and this of course affects the performance of the aircraft. But the turbojet engine is here to stay for a long time, and assuming it continues to develop more power and give better fuel consumption, I think we will have good jet transports in service in this country within five years.

I am not overenthusiastic about the turboprop engine, which is a jet engine turning a propeller, although I am aware of the greater efficiency and lower operating cost which is claimed for it. The pure jet engine is such a wonderful way to fly an airplane I have lost my interest in anything with a propeller on it; I think it would be a backward step. I agree with our engineers that it is possible to go right to the pure jet for a commercial airplane.

Other types of power plants such as the ramjet and the rocket have a military application but they are still highly experimental and it is too early to say whether they can be used commercially. Twenty-five years from now we may have the problem licked. By 1980 Hall Hibbard believes that rocket-powered aircraft will be circling the earth at altitudes of 300,000 to 400,000 feet. This is not flight into space, which comes later. Air is the thing that has held our speeds down so far, and these planes will go very fast, because they will be outside of the earth's atmosphere. However, the heat rise due to these enormous speeds within our atmosphere is quite a problem and until high heat-resistant metals are developed our speeds will certainly be restricted.

Long before that, however, before 1960, I believe the public will be flying very high and very fast in jet transports that will offer the most comfortable form of travel yet experienced. They will cruise at six hundred miles an hour at altitudes over forty thousand feet where the pilot can have his choice of the smoothest ride. This ability to pick your flight path, coupled with the fact that a jet engine is basically smoother than a reciprocating engine, will combine to give the passenger almost complete freedom from noise and vibration. If the engines are placed in the rear of the airplane he will hear no engine noise whatsoever as the jet blast will be all behind him.

Jet transports will fly below the speed of sound at the start because they will be big airplanes, which at supersonic speeds present structural problems. The light, strong metals like titanium, capable of withstanding atmospheric heat generated at supersonic speeds, are not fully developed either, but they are on the way and I am confident they will be ready soon. Assuming the power plants are available to drive large airplanes that fast, supersonic jet transports should be flying within fifteen years. When that time comes the air traveler will literally enter a new world; flight is so easy beyond the sound barrier I think that is where we were meant to fly.

There has been a lot of talk about the future of the private airplane, or personal plane, powered by a small jet engine that will take off in the backyard and fly you to the office at five hundred miles an hour. If I really thought the sky was going to be filled with as many airplanes as the cars they are driving around the highways, I would take to the hills. It isn't practical today for the average man to fly from home to work, and even if he did, he couldn't afford to own an airplane. We don't need the personal plane today because there is little market for it. That may change in the future. My own feeling is it will not become practical until we get an airplane that can take off and land vertically with complete safety, and from what I know that is a long way down the road.

The military planes of the future will resemble our present fighters and bombers, but will of course have much higher performance. They will improve rapidly for the simple reason that this country realizes it must keep abreast of every new development in aeronautics to safeguard ourselves and the other free nations from aggression, and the cheapest way to do that is to have more research and development. Military planes of the future may include pilotless aircraft powered by rockets and supersonic ramjets, guided by their own airborne guidance systems, and flying at many times the speed of sound. It is conceivable that such vehicles could deliver target-seeking missiles in the air and return automatically to the ground.

Speed is the big accomplishment of the past twenty-five years. I have been flying more than a quarter of a century, and in that short period of time I have seen airplane speeds increase from one hundred to sixteen hundred miles an hour.

I would venture to say that aviation will advance almost in the same proportion in the twenty-five years that lie ahead.

It can be a wonderful blessing to the world or a terrible instrument of destruction. I think any intelligent person will agree that in a war of jet airplanes armed with atom bombs nobody would win. It is no longer a case of being "firstest with the mostest"; if another war starts we will be prepared to retaliate in a matter of minutes, and when that day comes it is going to be a terrible mess. Such being the case, I would think twice before I started anything.

I don't know what will happen. But I will be eligible for retirement in twenty-five years, and if I can hold my job that long and the Lord is willing, I expect to get my pension.

Here is a preview of the next volume
in the Air and Space series—

BARNSTORMING

by Martin Caidin

The Way It Was

The rules were simple enough—even if they were loosely applied and even more liberally interpreted. Landing fields were a gift of God and the sweat of a farmer's back, and part of the game was guessing about the low stumps or the ditches that you couldn't see. You played the wind by gosh and by guess, and you looked for cows with their rumps pretty much pointed in one general direction, for there's no better natural wind sock in the business than the tail end of a cow; the stronger the wind the more likely you were to see all those cow-rump wind indicators.

It was flying, said some of the old-timers, the way that God intended man to fly. He had to be a part of his machine, to wear his airplane instead of climbing into it. And the old-timers were hard to argue with. You came to know the sky by instinct and feel and smelling the weather almost as much as you did by studying the clouds and hunting for the signs splashed across the sky. You looked for the wispy signature of coming storms in mare's tails way up in the high blue, and you watched the way the anvils formed atop the looming cumulus. You looked for wind shifts and at night you stared, half out for beauty and the other half for knowledge, at the ring that might form around the moon, for there was a gentle wash of ice crystals in the night heavens that also told you of coming weather. Sometimes you smelled the air as much as you studied your altimeter to watch for pressure changes. And when you talked to the farmer who came warily from his barn to stare at your strange wood-and-fabric contraptions, you tried to draw him into personal conversations, for every farmer with his corns and aching shoulder and his intimacies with the habits of animals was, without knowing it, a superb meteorologist.

As to where you would go in your caravan with the humpbacked dromedaries that bore wings and coughed and snarled behind the big flashing wooden propellers—why, anywhere and any place close enough to roads and a center of population would do. If you could get the wheezing, staggering planes in and out of the field, and entice people to come out to watch you skid and career on the ground and through the air, and let them know that yes, you and a couple of the others were sure-enough likely to get killed right before their eyes, and if you were smart enough to collect your money *before* your death-defying aerial show—why, you were in the barnstorming business!

You were a member of the aerial circus troupe, a vagabond with wings. Your calling card was your profession itself; the kids were awed about and wild over the very fact that you were a live, real, sure-'nuff *aviator*. The girls, the young girls with wide eyes and long lashes and bodies that were something to see beneath their thin summer cotton dresses, etched clearly in the wind . . . well, they sort of took your mind off flying and led you to think about barns and hayfields beneath the summer moon. But that always had to be for later; for now there were the farmers and their wives and families, and the storekeepers and the local businessmen, and you had to look at them shrewdly and play your crowd smartly.

You learned how to act on the ground with cunning; no matter what you might personally believe, you made friends with the kids and you also made friends with every con-founded hound and mixed-breed dog that came loping up to the field. For the country folk would sometimes judge a man as much by the way their dogs reacted as they would through forming their own opinions. And even if you hated the curs, you never showed it. You were first, last and foremost a showman, and if you were good enough and you had the breaks with you—your engines didn't crack or the big props splinter, and you set up your show when there was a high pressure area and clear skies instead of low and scudding black masses directly overhead, and some other smart barn-storming sonofabitch who was a thief and a pirate hadn't come in here first and ruined everything—why, you'd eat well and sleep comfortably (maybe even in a bed instead of under a wing), and stash away an extra bottle or two of fine bourbon, and have enough money to pass around to the whole crew and also pay for gas and spare parts. Even the sheriff might not demand his little stipend on the sly before you ever did anything in his territory; once in a while you ran into a decent sort, with the star pinned carelessly to his shirt.

When the breaks went that way, then the whole world had never looked quite so good nor the sun shone so clearly, nor that body etched in the windblown cotton dress beckoned so enticingly.

You were a barnstormer and the sky belonged to you, and you came to earth to please the folks and make them laugh and gasp a little and even shriek when they thought someone was about to be splashed across the ground. You were a showman and you put on the grandest show ever seen any-where on *or above* the whole world. You had three rings for your performance like none that man could ever build.

Your high-wire act took place hundreds of feet in the sky, and your Big Top changed every day with the height of the fleecy clouds that sparkled in the high blue. You came to live with the problems of an old, many-times repaired engine that might quit at just the wrong moment. An engine failure was *always* at the wrong moment when you had a friend standing on the upper wing, because he might just be standing on his hands or was about to transfer to another plane, sans parachute, or performing some insane stunt that the crowd loved; any sudden acceleration could throw him wildly off balance and if that happened, at just that wrong moment, the crowd might be witness to what they secretly hoped to see—the blood of a man pulped out of his body as it smashed into the unyielding earth.

These facts of life, unpleasant as they were, went along with the good times. It was a kaleidoscopic mixture of both. Subject to the whims of weather, the perils of an empty wallet, the idiosyncrasies of mechanical devices and the unpredictable fancies of the audience, the barnstormer pursued a life of vicarious thrills not calculated to rest, comfort, or longevity.

John Moisant was one of the first airmen to realize that the threat to longevity came from sources other than the fragile and wicked contraptions of the year 1910 that he and his friends flew. It was in the summer of that year, Moisant's lips pressed tight and his anger fair to choking him, that he faced an angry Texas crowd. They were not only angry, but had the means to vent their emotions, as they demonstrated in thunderous fashion by drunkenly firing volleys into the air from ugly-looking Colt .44's.

It was at that moment that Moisant, who led what was probably the first real barnstorming troupe in the world, realized that those who flocked to the impromptu airfields to watch the show were not necessarily air-minded. Their lusty yells and roars, punctuated with a mixture of breaking beer bottles and booming shots into the air, seemed almost to be a response to their smelling the blood they had come to see splashed wetly across the grass.

With this stage setting there began the wild and often frantic era of barnstorming. It was an era ushered onto the American scene along a high-breaking wave of enthusiasm for flying and for things of the sky. It fired the imagination of the entire country, and immediately it was starred with its heroes and its favorites, and conceived of by the public as essentially a spectator sport staged and carried out by wealthy and eccentric daredevils.

Moisant, for example, was a practicing architect until the flying fever shot through his veins. The fascination for the air was to prove his end shortly afterward when, trying to please a screaming and threatening crowd, he lost his life in a crash. Moisant thus provided the ultimate thrill to his audience, the spectators witnessed the gore they had come to see, and Moisant unknowingly—and quite unwillingly—helped to create a precedent that would endure for decades.

Our story of the barnstormers of America is, essentially, that of the flying circus. For this is the other, and perhaps more fitting, name for the barnstormers. Theirs was a circus. Their purpose, their intent was to please, to entertain, to thrill and to excite their audiences, made up of men, women and children of all ages and the inevitable dogs. Their skill was not nearly so important as the manner in which they demonstrated risks and thrills with their aircraft; the drunk act that appeared dangerous, but was not, was far preferred to the superb, and perfect, demonstration of aerobatics which might quickly bore, and thus greatly annoy, the rowdy onlookers.

The greatest wellspring of barnstormer pilots and mechanics proved to be the aerial debris of World War I—debris in the form of dashing young men, trained only for combat flying and the knowledge of blazing death should they lose an aerial duel, filled with the morbid excitement that it engendered, who came with discharges fresh in their hands into the unsettling world of peace. These were the men who had to *keep* flying in order that they might live, for to live was to them to experience life to its utmost. And whatever were the hazards and the perils of barnstorming, it could not, of course, be equated with the finality carried in the twin Spandaus of a Fokker. There was also the matter, somewhat more prosaic but nevertheless demanding, of being able to eat—so the young warriors turned to the air and the promise it held for their living and their livelihood.

Barnstormers, flying mostly Jenny biplanes left over from the scrapheap of 1918, hopped and struggled across the face of America from one pea patch to another, in the process caroming from cloud to cloud, dashing down valleys, and much too often barely evading mountains obscured within cloud and fog. They thrilled millions of people at large fields and isolated pastures with such acts as wing-walking without parachutes, snatching handkerchiefs from the tops of waving weeds, low-level aerobatics that included deliberately scraping wing tips in the dust or "slapping" the ground in wing-tip-to-wing-tip maneuvers, smoke-writing in the sky, spectacular delayed parachute jumps while trailing behind them a white plume of flour from XXX sacks. They jumped from one plane to another, engaged in mock dogfights, made wild takeoffs and landings, clowned around, and affected World War I flying togs. They stood patiently for pictures with local boys and femmes and, whenever they could do so, took up the locals for quick rides, for whatever ready cash it might bring.

Often, these scratch air shows were barely one jump ahead of the sheriff, and only a stagger away from mechanical failure.

And while the barnstormers lived their precarious existence, they introduced aviation to the most distant corners of the country. It was this success in publicity—despite the rash of financial failures—that brought an unexpected respectability and a new meaning to the air circus. The United States Army, faced with the problems of "selling" aviation to the people and their elected representatives in Washington, D.C., turned to the ready-made audience that flocked to air shows. Whenever possible, decreed the brass, the military would utilize every advantage of the glitter and sparkle of the "open house" air show.

Robert S. Johnson remembers what it was like in the summer of 1928, just outside the town of Lawton, Oklahoma; he remembers what it was like to look up into the sky and—

There were three of them. Each with double wings and a whirling propeller flashing in the bright Oklahoma sun. I first saw them as they rolled on their backs, arcing over to inverted flight to begin a plunge to the earth. The ground seemed terrifyingly close to the descending trio. For a moment the sun gleaming off their whirling propellers made three simultaneous flashes of light in the sky. The beautiful winged machines increased rapidly in size, slicing downward from the blue as a single entity.

I did not know it then, and I would not appreciate for years to come the rare spectacle of precision piloting which

I observed. I could only stare, utterly fascinated, as the three little pursuits seemed to rush headlong to oblivion, about to dash themselves into the ground.

Then I heard their cry. A shrill and weird sound; the painful whine of the engines, whirling propellers faster and faster as they flung the little planes through the air.

The three pursuits were almost into the ground, when the planes were wrenched from their dives. Three hands, operating as one, gripping control sticks in three different cockpits, flawlessly timed, hauling back. The trio snapped up into the sky. I followed every motion, struck dumb, staring, as the pursuits zoomed up and over, twisted and turned intricately as as if a single hand were maneuvering them, then floated mysteriously in an invisible balance of their wings and of gravity.

In later years, I have been able to look back and recognize this scene as *the* moment: the very first time I had ever *seen* an airplane. The fascination of these three snappy pursuits, orange wings bright in the sun, alive, incredibly agile, held for the eight-year-old boy I was then the barest promise that would one day be fulfilled in a way not even the dreams of youth could imagine.

What was it like at one of these air spectaculars, at the circus to which one and all were invited? As Bob Johnson recalled:

I'd seen the airfield many times before, but it was only a big empty space with high and thick buffalo grass covering the field. There were plenty of those in Oklahoma, and Post Field was nothing special. But something was going on; hundreds of people milled around the field. And so many cars! They were parked, it seemed, by the hundreds.

Wagons and horses were also on the field, making the whole place look like a county fairground. Clouds of dust boiled up and . . .

There! In the sky! Three tiny airplanes . . .

That military air show with its spectacular three-ship formation flight was the first for Bob Johnson; it was not the last.
For the barnstormers were to come through Lawton, and with
the fire singing in his veins, the mention of an airplane was
enough to bring the youngster and his friends rushing to the
local fields. The magic words had been shouted: "The
barnstormers!"
Johnson recalled:

On several occasions, barnstormers came to town to put
on flying shows. They landed on large open fields near
Cameron College, bringing in all different kinds of two-
seat and three-seat open-cockpit biplanes. Our entire troop
would go out to the fields to help the barnstormer pilots. In
addition to their daredevil acts, the pilots took up passengers for rides. We helped people to and from the planes,
and aided the barnstorming group in controlling the crowds.

All this for the promise that we would each get a ride in
a plane before the day was over. The promise was worth
it; especially to me! Not even the hot, dusty, and crowded
fields dampened my enthusiasm, or passing the day without food, or carrying water buckets, or dashing about
madly to deliver messages. *Anything* was worth it—just so
long as I'd get my chance to fly.

But somehow whenever my turn came to fly, the day
would be over. The pilot would grin in a friendly way and
say, "Sorry, kid. Got a schedule to keep; I've gotta leave.
Maybe next time." And away he would go.

I was twelve years old when the Great Day arrived. I
should say the Great Night. It couldn't have come as a
bigger surprise.

A giant (it was a giant in those days) Ford Tri-Motor
transport—corrugated skin, three roaring engines, and blazing with all manner of lights—landed at the municipal
airport. That pilot sure knew his business.

The Tri-Motor was lit up like a county fairground.
Lights had been fastened to the wings and the fuselage
until it looked like a big carnival show floating through the
night skies.

Dad took the entire family down to watch the Ford taking off and landing at the airport with passengers, for short flights over Lawton, to let the townspeople see what the place looked like at night. It was an eerie sight, and I think perhaps that pilot had once worked at a circus. As the plane flew over the edge of town the pilot released a string of Roman candles. Immediately the sky blossomed forth with a procession of fireballs, brilliant and multicolored, illuminating the entire valley. This pyrotechnic display, of course, caught the interest of people in the town, who flocked by the hundreds to the airport just to see what was going on.

And then, out of the blue, Dad asked *the* question.

"Son, would you like to go up?"

Would I!

I climbed aboard. The interior of the Tri-Motor was dark. The smell of gasoline and oil came to me; I was aware of the feel of the metal. Wonderful sensations all; I drank in every moment.

I was tense and breathless as the pilot hit the switches. The engines ground over slowly and abruptly burst into a shattering roar. The airplane shook and vibrated as it rumbled over the ground, taxiing across the field and swinging into position for takeoff. From the window I could see the wing outlined dimly against the night sky, and an engine with blue exhaust flames ghosting out from it.

The moment arrived. The roar deepened, increased in volume as the pilot fed power to the engines. I felt a sensation of sudden and rapid movement . . . a rumbling as the airplane accelerated in its dash over the ground.

I expected—a sudden upward rush, I suppose, a feeling of soaring. There was none of this. Without prelude, the vibration and the bouncing just stopped. The engines roared sweetly, a new note, a throbbing, in their voice.

I could hardly believe it—I was flying! Nose glued to the window, eyes wide open and hungry, I stared out and down at the lights so far below us. I could see for miles and miles. Far off in the distance lights gleamed through the night. I had a feeling of enormous depth, of a vast and endless plain stretching before me.

All too soon, the motion of the airplane changed. We were returning to earth. Wind whistled past the wings and the engines descended in volume to a friendly sigh. A rumble, ever so slight a jar as the wheels touched. Then the vibration and bouncing on the grass as the pilot taxied back to the operations shack.

We had been aloft for fifteen minutes—the best quarter hour of my life!

Perhaps the reader has recognized the name of Robert S. Johnson. The young boy who saw his first airplanes in the sight of the diving Army pursuits, who made his first flight in the big Tri-Motor of a barnstormer, went on to earn his own wings. And then in World War II, behind the controls of a mighty Thunderbolt fighter, Bob Johnson in eleven months shot down twenty-eight German fighter planes in aerial combat to rank as one of America's greatest fighter aces.

Many of the men who flew the aerial circus troupes as barnstormers later became world famous. Men such as Frank Hawks and Charles Lindbergh began their aviation careers with the gypsy fliers. Others, who flew as much and often for many more hours and with a far wider range of aerial activity, are not so widely known. But their stories—such as that of Tommy Walker, whom we will meet in a full chapter devoted to this unusual cloudbuster—give us thrilling and intimate glimpses of what barnstorming really was like in terms of behind-the-scenes views and personal trials, tribulations, and wild fun—as well as constant brushes with death.

Men like Walker were barnstormers before and after World War II, and they were a very special breed who performed the full gamut of aerial circus antics. They added to the curriculum of the three rings by both flying and performing parachute jumps. They accepted immeasurable risks by deliberately smashing airplanes into houses, cars, trains and special obstructions. They leaped from cars to planes, from planes to cars, and jumped back and forth from planes to boats—to say nothing of switching planes in flight.

Out of World War II came a rash of new barnstorming

pilots, jumpers and stuntmen. For a while the sport, as now it had come to be considered, faltered and seemed committed to the musty pages of history. There were a few aerial shows that toured the nation, but they were bereft of finances, weary of overdue bills, and afflicted with the rash of a postwar America. The rash was suffered in a plague of high-density areas within which flying was strictly controlled and new regulations rushed in to being which were enough to snarl any pilot and his airplane in ground-chaining frustration. And what could the old circus troupe do with the people of a nation who were overwhelmed with supersonic jets, hydrogen bombs, rockets to the moon, and the other glittering paraphernalia of this new and frightening world?

And then, something seemed to happen. Despite the nuclear mushrooms that stalked into the high heavens, despite the fiery ignition of wars across the globe, despite even the dazzling impact of men rushing into space, there began anew the fascination for "things with wings that fly."

Barnstorming today is experiencing a tremendous, vital resurgence. The patched-pants jumpers have been replaced with flashy skydivers, the new planes are superb, the organization is getting smart. But the drunk act is still with us, and showmanship is more important than it ever was before. The pilots are sensational, their aerobatics flown with razor-sharp precision. But the crowd still demands the element of thrill, the smell of danger, the chance that death will spring, full-blooded and hot, into the rings of flight.

Every now and then the crowd is rewarded, and there is the ghostly background of the roar of the Roman Colosseum when the stretcher bearers carry away into a shiny new ambulance the lifeless form of one who didn't make it, who paid the crowd in the coin they had secretly coveted.

That's the way it was a long time ago. It's the way it is today and—fervently hope the barnstormers—the way it will always be.

To live . . . is to live life to its utmost. These men wouldn't change it for the world.

A NOTE ABOUT THE BANTAM AIR & SPACE SERIES

This is the era of flight—the century which has seen man soar, not only into the skies of earth but beyond the gravity of his home planet and out into the blank void of space. An incredible accomplishment achieved in an incredibly short time.

How did it happen?

The AIR & SPACE series is dedicated to the men and women who brought this fantastic accomplishment about, often at the cost of their lives—a library of books which will tell the grand story of man's indomitable determination to seek the new, to explore the farthest frontier.

The driving theme of the series is the skill of *piloting*, for without this, not even the first step would have been possible. Like the Wright Brothers and those who, for some 35 years, followed in their erratic flight path, the early flyers had to be designer, engineer and inventor. Of necessity, they were the pilots of the crazy machines they dreamt up and strung together.

Even when the technology became slightly more sophisticated, and piloting became a separate skill, the quality of a flyer's ability remained rooted in a sound working knowledge of his machine. World War I, with its spurt of development in aircraft, made little change in the role of the flyer who remained, basically, pilot-navigator-engineer.

Various individuals, like Charles Lindbergh, risked their lives and made high drama of the new dimension they were carving in the air. But still, until 1939, flying was a romantic, devil-may-care wonder, confined to a relative handful of hardy individuals. Commercial flight on a large scale was a mere gleam in the eye of men like Howard Hughes.

It took a second major conflict, World War II, from 1939 to 1945, to provoke the imperative that required new concepts from the designers—and created the arena where hundreds of young men and women would learn the expertise demanded by high-speed, high-tech aircraft.

From the start of flight, death has taken its toll. Flying has always been a high-risk adventure. Never, since men first launched themselves into the air, has the new element given up its sacrifice of stolen lives, just as men have never given up the driving urge to go farther, higher, faster. Despite only a fifty-fifty chance of any mission succeeding, *still* the dream draws many more men and women to spaceflight than any program can accommodate. And still, in 1969, when Mike Collins, Buzz Aldrin and Neil Armstrong first took man to the Moon, the skill of piloting, sheer flying ability, was what actually landed the "Eagle" on the Moon's surface. And still, despite technological sophistication undreamed of 30 or 40 years earlier, despite demands on any flyer for levels of performance and competence and the new understanding of computer science not necessary in early aircraft, it is piloting, *human* control of the aircraft—sometimes, indeed, inspired control—that remains the major factor in getting there and back safely.

From this rugged breed of individualists come the bush pilots of today, men who even now fly their little planes above the vast, icy expanse of the Arctic, landing in small open stretches, on wheels, skis, or pontoons, carrying with them all the spare parts they need to repair their own craft. The first of the AIR & SPACE series is about one such pilot—*The Last of the Bush Pilots,* by Harmon Helmericks.

The horrors of World War II bred and trained literally hundreds of pilots. Here the expertise of piloting in life and death situations began to teach the designers. *Fork-Tailed*

Devil: The P38, by Martin Caidin, is the story of a fighter plane whose deficiencies cost lives until its pilots used their combat experience to correct its faults. On the other hand there was the unbelievable strength of the War's greatest bomber, the Flying Fort. Pilots called it the airplane you could trust. It too, saw improvement both in design and effectiveness that was a direct result of battle, and the Fort brought its bomber crews home when the problem lay not so much in flying the monster as in landing an aircraft that was half shot away. . . . *Flying Forts: The B-17 In World War II,* by Martin Caidin, tells the magnificent, edge-of-the-seat story of this fantastic aircraft.

The War also saw the start of a new kind of flying machine— one without propellers—for jet propulsion was born at this time. And very secretly, right after the close of hostilities, Chuck Yeager was busy testing the X-1 and breaking the sound barrier. This was just the beginning. Even the early test pilots of the U.S. Air Force carried the speed of piloted jet aircraft to 1,900 miles an hour—nearly three times the speed of sound. Frank Everest flew his X-2 at these incredible speeds, and as high as 60-odd miles. John Guenther, noted aviation writer, tells the story of Frank Everest in *The Fastest Man Alive.*

After America first landed men on the Moon, the Russian space program pushed ahead with plans for eventually creating a permanent space station where men could live. And in 1982 they sent up two men—Valentin Lebedev and Anatoly Berezovoy—to live on Solyut-7 for seven months. This extraordinary feat has been recorded in the diaries of pilot Lebedev, *Diary of a Cosmonaut: 211 Days in Space* by Valentin Lebedev.

The Bantam AIR & SPACE series will include several titles by or about flyers from all over the world—and about the planes they flew, including World War II, the postwar era of barnstorming and into the jet age, plus the personal histories of many of the world's greatest pilots. Man is still the most important element in flying.

A NOTE ABOUT
THE AUTHOR

John Guenther

An author and former journalist, John Guenther has written extensively on aviation from his long experience as an Air Force officer in World War II and postwar aircraft executive. He has drawn on this intimate knowledge of military and commerical aviation in writing about the early days of flying in this country and the legendary pilots who tested our first jet and rocket planes. Their pioneering exploits helped pave the way to space flight, and Guenther coined the phrase, "the race for space," in telling their life stories. As a journalist, he wrote for Scripps-Howard newspapers, the United Press and *Newsweek* magazine, and following military service, has published some dozen books of biography, fiction, poetry, and drama here and abroad. A native of Ann Arbor, Michigan, he attended the University of Illinois and Harvard, and makes his home in New York City.